You are Greater than You Know

You are Greater than You Know

John H. Sewell

Copyright © 2010 by John H. Sewell.

Library of Congress Control Number: 2010904423
ISBN: Hardcover   978-1-4500-7228-1
               Softcover   978-1-4500-7227-4
               Ebook   978-1-4628-0125-1

All rights reserved. No part of this book may be reproduced or transmitted in any form or by any means, electronic or mechanical, including photocopying, recording, or by any information storage and retrieval system, without permission in writing from the copyright owner.

This book was printed in the United States of America.

To order additional copies of this book, contact:
Xlibris Corporation
1-888-795-4274
www.Xlibris.com
Orders@Xlibris.com
67389

CONTENTS

Acknowledgments 7

Introduction..9

Part I
I Am a Christian, But Just Who Am I?

Chapter 1:
  You Are in Union with Christ 15

Chapter 2:
  You Can Be Empowered by Christ 37

Part II
How to Experience God's Help
When You Are Hurting or Struggling

Chapter 3:
  Living in This World "in Christ" 73

Chapter 4:
  Rooting Your Marriage "in Christ" 99

Chapter 5:
  Handling Rejection "in Christ" 126

Chapter 6:
  Overcoming the Power of Sin 166

Chapter 7:
  "In Christ," Forgiveness Is to Be a Lifestyle 201

Chapter 8:
    Deliverance through Forgiveness 230

Chapter 9:
    What Every Church Member Needs to Know 269

References 301

ACKNOWLEDGMENTS

I WRITE THIS BOOK with much thanksgiving for my time with Victorious Christian Living International (VCLi). This ministry has been vital in my own spiritual growth as well as in the realization of my desire to help others find a vital faith that makes a real difference in troubled times. Most of what is written in this book has come through my reflection on VCLi's materials while I was ministering them to others. VCLi's model for discipleship is to (1) carefully and eagerly hear the Word, (2) gratefully apply the Word to your life, and (3) then share the truth you have learned with others. Disciples do all three. It has certainly worked for me. My life is rooted in that model of discipleship, and I will be eternally grateful for VCLi's ministry into my life.

I write with much gratitude to my staff. They have helped me present this material with far less grammatical errors and have challenged me to be more accurate in my presentation of concepts. They spent a lot of hours going over the material in this book. It's good that they spent a *lot* of hours, for if they had not been worn down by the length of the process, I don't think I would have ever finished making their suggested corrections. Thank you, Lou and Fran Guy, Elizabeth Jimmerson, Sophia Martin, and Lakeba Williams. My life is richer and this book is far better because of the many excellent suggestions and corrections you made in love.

I must also express my gratitude to my wonderful, encouraging wife, Sally. She could have complained bitterly at my preoccupation with this book and my absence from the home while I was writing it, but she did just the opposite. I am also glad I am through; I was afraid her patience would run out. I worked on the book, off and on, for a year. She says that the main reason she has encouraged me to write the book is so that our four children, Shelley, Trey, Stephen, and Michael, will know what I have been teaching the last twenty years. She thinks that this book will be a legacy they and their sixteen children will treasure. That would be nice. I hope she's right!

Many of you, with whom I have had the privilege of sharing discipleship ministry, have also encouraged me to put the things I taught you into writing; I am grateful for every affirmation, for it helped me start writing. Thank you, one and all. I've been stretched, but blessed, by doing this. It is a lot easier to teach than to write. When writing, your mistakes are being set in unfading ink for all to see for a long, long time; when teaching, your mistakes quickly disappear. Furthermore, when writing, you have to say it right the first time, for no one is present to ask questions for clarification. I'm hoping for the best!

INTRODUCTION

I WAS TWENTY-EIGHT BEFORE I experienced salvation in Christ even though I had been religious, a professing Christian, and active in a local church as far back as I could remember. As a preacher's "kid," at first I had no choice as to whether or not I would be active in the church. I'm sure there were times as a baby and a small child that I attended church crying in protest, but I was still there every time the doors opened. I do know for certain that there were later times I attended when it was not my first choice to be there but I didn't have a say in the matter. Thus early on, it was determined for me that I would be active in the church and that indoctrination *took*. When I became old enough to have a choice, being active in church was my choice. I liked the church. I liked its high moral ground and the way I was treated there. I liked the singing, the people, and the teaching. I was very comfortable there. But I was unsure of Jesus and the cross. I couldn't understand how something that happened two thousand years ago could have anything to do with me. In fact, I was a bit uncomfortable with all the attention Jesus got. I was a "God the Father" man. I honored Him and wanted Him honored, and sometimes I was jealous for Him. Nevertheless, my basic attitude was "even if some of the things taught about Jesus may not be true, the teachings of the Christian faith are still the way I will follow in expressing my life."

My salvation experience could be considered a bit unusual. I was a performer. I generally felt good-looking, athletic, and witty. In addition to that, I was a competitor and worked hard at everything. I had a driving desire to be the best at everything and enough ability to be deceived into thinking I could be. But in truth, I was only a bigger fish in a very small pond, deceived by my immaturity into thinking I was a bigger fish than I was. To my shame now, pride was my companion. I had a lot of ambition, but wisdom was not in place.

I was very religious. In high school, I was the church custodian. I remember that many times, when I was in the sanctuary for the purpose of cleaning it, I was drawn into long times of kneeling at the altar in prayer. I wanted to be a good kid. My parents loved me, and I loved them, and I didn't want to disappoint them. Unfortunately, I did much better on the outside than I did on the inside with my thought life. Furthermore, I did better in public than in private. My sense of personal goodness was a state of deception that came through comparison with select others. I performed well, but Jesus would have lumped me in with the Pharisees of whom He said, "**Hypocrites! For you are like whitewashed tombs—beautiful on the outside but filled on the inside with dead people's bones and all sorts of impurity**" (Matt. 13:27 NLT).

As an adult I continued to be active in the church, functioning as a teacher and leader and getting involved in small groups. *I was seriously religious, but lost.* I was deceived a long time. My salvation experience didn't come until I was twenty-eight. One night I was listening to a sermon on a cassette tape. The preacher was talking about the character of the Pharisees who placed Jesus on the cross. As I listened to the preacher describe the Pharisees involved in the crucifixion of Jesus, I realized that had I been there I would have joined with the Pharisees in shouting "Crucify Him!" I was like them—religious but in desperate need of being saved from my sins. For the first time in my life, I understood how something that happened two thousand years ago could have something to do with me. It was people like me (the Pharisees) who were most able to arouse righteous anger in Jesus. I repented and was born again. Since then, I have learned a lot more about Who Jesus is and of my great need for a Savior. My eyes are open, and my sins are no longer hidden from me, but instead stand out so that I can see clearly. I praise God for His mercy toward an arrogant, sinful, religious young man.

About a year after I was "born again," I experienced God's call into full-time ministry. I turned thirty my first month in seminary, and two years and three months later, I had graduated and was serving in a full-time appointment. I was saved. I was committed and Spirit-filled. In the eyes of my congregation, I was successful. But something was still missing.

My heart's desire was to preach and teach a faith that made a real difference in the way people experienced their Christian walk. I wanted to communicate a faith sufficient to empower believers to be victorious even when they were caught up in depressing and sometimes devastating circumstances. I wanted believers to know the joy of the Lord as their strength. Certainly an all-powerful God could grant that. That seemed to be happening in some churches. Yet I mostly experienced Christians as having the same struggles with sin and deception as non-Christians. I struggled too. I even went back to seminary to work on a doctorate in hopes that I would discover something that I was missing so that I might disciple others more effectively. I encountered failure there too.

After twelve years in pastoral ministry that almost everyone, except me, considered very successful, I left the security of the pastorate to begin a faith ministry in the area of Christian counseling. I believe God led me into this ministry so that the desire of my heart for victorious Christian living for all could be more fully realized "in Christ." God was granting me my heart's desire. In working to help Christians overcome their problems over the last twenty-one years, I have found the faith I was searching for. I am now sixty-seven years old. I have learned faith principles and have had time to watch and reflect on the effect of these faith principles in my own life and in the lives of the hurting who have come to me for help. Most who have come to me have found victory, but I have prospered far more. *The purpose of this book is to share with you the faith principles rooted in Christ that have, in all kinds of circumstances, blessed my life and the lives of those to whom I have ministered over the years.*

Scripture declares, "If anyone is in Christ, he is a new creation; the old has gone, the new has come!" (2 Cor. 5:17 NIV). But in what way is the old gone? What is new? The first two chapters of this book are rooted in this 2 Corinthians passage and are foundational. Everything else I share will be built on this foundation. If you are not quite clear in understanding after the first two chapters, hang in there. The foundational truths presented in these chapters will be applied in every succeeding chapter. I believe that before you are through reading this book, you will be rejoicing with me in our Lord's provisions for meeting our every need.

In chapter 3, you will discover God's plan for approaching the ordinary things of life in a new and transforming way that will inject them with new life. In chapter 4, you will rejoice in the simplicity of God's plan for building solid marriages. In chapter 5, you will discover how past rejection can trigger thought patterns in yourself that cause you to continue to experience rejection in your life, but also how to walk out of that rejection. In chapter 6, you will be given help in understanding the mystery of "walking by the Spirit" and a plan for experiencing the victory of that walk. In chapter 7, you will discover God's provision for dealing with the hurt that often comes to us through relationships—even those relationships that are most treasured. In chapter 8, you will be introduced to God's powerful provision for undoing the harm that has come to you through the hurtful relationships and experiences of your past. Finally, in chapter 9, you will be introduced to basic things I believe every church member needs to know but often doesn't—basic Christian principles that can transform the nature of our church experiences.

We often hear preaching about "faith," and well we should. The author of Hebrews declares, "Without faith it is impossible to please God" (Heb. 11:6 NIV). The emphasis is often on growing a strong faith, and our faith should be strong. But before faith becomes strong, it should first be accurate. We can have strong faith in an untruth that will affect us adversely and sometimes even cause us great harm. For example, when someone is experiencing the medical condition known as anorexia, they almost always believe they are fat. This false belief can cause premature death. Adolf Hitler believed strongly but wrongly, and many perished because of his beliefs. Today, many have become victims of a very few radical Muslim martyrs who have exhibited a strong faith that has brought death to many innocent people. They are victims of the faith of the martyrs. Christians too have historically propagated strong faith that has brought much harm. Slavery and racial prejudice are examples. Thus "the faith" as a body of *accurately* perceived truths will be an important emphasis of this book. Paul instructed his disciple, Timothy, to "hold on to the pattern of wholesome teaching you learned from me—a pattern shaped by the faith and love that you have in Christ Jesus. Through the power of the Holy Spirit who lives within us, carefully guard the precious truth that has been entrusted to you" (2 Tim. 1:13-14 NLB). Faith has content. *What we place our faith in is more important than a strong faith. What Christians believe can be harmful as well as helpful.* My prayer for you is that in reading this book and interacting with the Scriptures it presents, you will discover an accurate faith paradigm for viewing life on earth that will enable you to experience victory as you face the trials this fallen world will bring your way. *What* we believe is extremely important, for our lives reflect our belief systems, for good and for bad.

PART I

I Am a Christian, But Just Who Am I?

CHAPTER 1: YOU ARE IN UNION WITH CHRIST

THE ATTEMPT TO discover the truth as to who we are as Christians in a sin-plagued world can be very confusing. The Christian community is divided into denominations and even nondenominations. Though all tend to agree on the essentials, there are also differences. Who is right where there is disagreement? When we add our own personal problems with sin into the mix, discovering who we are as Christians becomes more challenging. What should we expect of ourselves? What should we expect of other Christians? What should we expect of God? *We are Christians, but just who are we?*

The Concept of "Christ in Me" Can Promote Performance Based Acceptance and Be Confusing

Most of us seem to be comfortable in thinking of ourselves as Christians in terms of "Christ in me, the hope of glory" (Col. 1:27). When we were born again, we received the Holy Spirit. The phrase *Christ in me* calls attention to the idea that the Spirit of Christ within us is God's power to make us different. While this is true, this way of looking at our faith causes us to focus on our performance—to constantly evaluate what we do, don't do, think, say, don't say, etc. We then tend to focus on *our performance* when trying to determine how good of a Christian we are. But how do we measure our performance as a Christian? What is to be our standard for measurement? When I was a pastor I struggled with comparing myself to ministers who were pastors of larger churches. Why was their church larger? What were they doing that I wasn't doing? What was deficient about the message I was preaching? The bottom line became "what is wrong with me?"

Many of us compare ourselves with our fellow church members. We may struggle with fitting in with them. What do we need to do to gain significance, to be well-thought-of by others in our churches? What are we to do when we don't feel accepted by others? What are we to do with the moral failures of our past? Do we dare reveal them? Even worse, now that we are a Christian, what are we to do when we continue to fail? Should we just expect to keep failing? Will there ever be victory in the areas in which we continue to experience failure? What would people think of us if they knew of our struggles? How do we control our tongues and our judgmental attitudes—our tendency to look down on others? Why do others look down on us? How do we truly love others? How can God really love me? How do we overcome our selfishness and our self-centeredness? Our performance creates real dilemmas for us in our Christian walks.

Some would say we should compare ourselves to Christ in order to determine how we measure up as a Christian. But when we compare ourselves to Christ, we look pitiful, and our Christian ego suffers substantially, so we don't tend to do that very often. More often, we will compare ourselves to others who we consider to be "good" Christians. Yet that also creates problems for us *because* we usually compare our entire person (secret thoughts and all) with their Sunday-in-church public person. We tend to do that because that public person is the one we have experienced. That comparison doesn't make us much more comfortable than comparing ourselves to Christ. It's not very comfortable—or even sensible. Even the best-behaved people who exhibit positive images while in church will have some things about themselves that would be quite embarrassing were they to become public knowledge. This is especially true in our thought lives. Does the preacher ever wish he were fishing instead of in church? Did, or do, the deacons and deaconesses wrestle with the same thoughts we wrestle with? Probably so! Everyone does better in their public lives than in their private lives. We would feel much better about ourselves if we could look only at our Sunday behavior (if it doesn't include our behavior on the way to church). But we know we can't do that. Yet the Sunday behavior of others is what we are observing and then comparing ourselves to. Because we compare *all* of our behavior with only the *partial* public behavior of others we look bad.

There is one other comparison we tend to make. The worst (but probably most common) comparison we make is to compare ourselves with obviously lost people. The reason this comparison is extra bad is because it causes us to look down our noses at the very people we should have compassion toward and offer Christ to. That comparison may feel good, but it is wrong. It is not of the Spirit of Jesus.

Comparing ourselves to others creates a problem for us. Then we need somebody to fail so that we can feel better about ourselves. Needing others to fail doesn't seem very Christian, and it isn't. We don't often stop to realize it, but *through this concept of comparing ourselves to others, we have been subtly taught to get our worth at somebody else's expense.* We must have uglier, more plain, or plain ugly girls to compare ourselves to if we are going to think of ourselves as pretty. Thus, prettiness comes at the expense of the less pretty. That doesn't sound very Christlike, does it? It takes less-intelligent people for some to be classified as smart. We must have klutzy people if some are to stand out as athletic. No one wants to be the worst of the crop or even mediocre. So we naturally want people to be below us, and the more the better. Perhaps that is why Christians are often so judgmental. Our own sin problems naturally cause us to accentuate the sin problems of others so that we will look better. Even though we know it is not right, we can take delight in the failure of others. That ought not to be, but it is.

Our Culture Can Distort Our Understanding of the Bible

All of our lives, we have been compared to someone else. So we tend to do the same and, in effect, get our worth at someone else's expense. Christians are not generally an exception to that rule. We bring what we have been taught in our culture right into our churches.

Our understanding of everything new to us begins by comparing "the new" to what we already know. Thus, the known tends to influence our understanding of the new. In the same way, our culture also influences the way we understand the Bible. Our worldview can create major problems for us when we read the Bible. Paul teaches in 1 Corinthians 2:14 that "the man without the Spirit does not accept the things that come from the Spirit of God, for they are foolishness to him, and he cannot understand them, because they are spiritually discerned" (NIV). When we approach the Bible from our worldview (which is our known), we are likely to misinterpret biblical truth that is new to us. For instance, consider 1 Corinthians 1:30:

> But by His doing
> you are in Christ Jesus,
> who became to us
> wisdom from God,
> and righteousness,
> and sanctification,
> and redemption. (NASB)

What does this passage mean? Because of our performance biases, it is easy for us to wrongly see this verse as meaning that if God has done a work in us so that we are "in Christ Jesus," then we should see these evidences of what He has done. We should be full of wisdom, righteous in our behavior, sanctified, and redeemed—and all in ever-increasing measure.

How do you "measure up" when we view 1 Corinthians 1:30 this way? If you were to give yourself a letter grade reflecting your "wisdom from God," would it be an A, B, C, D, or F? *Righteousness* means "rightness with God." If you were to give yourself a letter grade for your rightness with God, what would it be? *Sanctification* means "totally set apart to serve God." That's like being pregnant. You either are or you aren't. So we either pass this criterion or we fail. Most believers *want* to be totally set apart to serve God, but we still recognize a lot of selfishness in us that is in conflict with that desire. So, if honest, most of us would have to give ourselves a grade of W (for *Wish* we were) in the area of sanctification. Finally, there is redemption. *Redemption* means "to buy back; to recover as by paying a fee." We run into a problem with our evaluation of ourselves here. Redemption has absolutely nothing to do with what we do. It is 100 percent by God's doing. Thus, we can't give ourselves a letter grade as to how well we perform in this area.

We have gone off on a wild-goose chase in the paragraph above. Remember, the point I'm trying to make is that we often misunderstand the Bible because of the worldview that has shaped us in trying to understand the Bible. Our worldview can then distort the truth God's Word is presenting to us. Think about it: If we can't give ourselves a letter grade for redemption, then why should we give ourselves a letter grade for wisdom, righteousness, and sanctification? If redemption cannot come about through our doing, then why should we assume that the first three should be by our doing? Are we looking at this Scripture passage incorrectly through our "performance" worldview rather than through the context of this passage? We most certainly are, and the reason we are doing that is centered in the way we naturally picture "Christ in me."

Christianity Is Rooted in Christ's Performance, Not Ours

As believers, we know that "Christ is in us." But it is equally true that we are "in Christ." In fact, the Bible records us as being "in Christ" much more often than it records Christ as being in us. Yet, because of our culture's emphasis on our performance, many Christians, if not most, think that

Christ in me is the more common of the two phrases. But the truth is that *in Christ* is the more common by a ratio of ten to one. Furthermore, these two phrases create two totally different pictures, and understanding their difference is essential. *We must understand that Christianity is rooted in Christ's performance, not ours.* God votes to emphasize believers being "in Christ," ten to one, over "Christ in us."

Still, both phrases are true, and this can present a rational difficulty. Elementary geometry teaches us that if A is fully contained in B and B is fully contained in A, then A must be the same as B. So, how can it be true that both Christ is in us and we are in Christ, for we are not the same as Christ? Certainly "Christ in me" *and* "me in Christ" cannot be understood to be saying Christ is the same as "me." Every sane person understands that. Let's look at this problem graphically to try to gain clarity.

 Logically, these two Venn diagrams cannot both be true. Unless Christ and the believer are one and the same, these diagrams present opposites. Since the believer and Christ are not the same, can *both* claims even be true?

The Bible says they can! I want to show you how this can be, but first, let me ask another question that will help explain this truth. Who wants eternal life? Everyone, you say? Okay, next question: what is eternal life?

What Is Eternal Life?

If your answer is "living forever," then no one needs to worry because if the Bible is right—and it is—then we all would already have eternal life. It is just a question of where and how we will live eternally after our earthly bodies die, in heaven or hell. I used to think of eternal life in terms of God giving me a new body when I die so that I would live forever in heaven after my time on earth was over. But that would mean that eternal life doesn't begin until we die. That's not what the Bible teaches, so I was wrong. Could it be that we are looking at our world's definition of eternal life and the Bible has a different meaning when it uses that expression? Let me share what I have discovered. Let's look at what Scripture teaches through the eyes of John. He begins his epistle: "That which was from the beginning, which we have heard, which we have seen with our eyes, which we have looked upon, and our hands have handled, concerning the

Word of life" (1 John 1:1 NKJV). Who is this talking about? *That which was from the beginning* has to be either the Father, Son, or Holy Spirit, for they were the only ones present in the beginning (or before the beginning of our world as we know it). The only one of these three it could be is Jesus, for no man has seen or handled the Father or the Holy Spirit. Furthermore, John, the writer of this epistle, calls Jesus the Word in John 1:14: "And the Word became flesh and dwelt among us, and we beheld His glory, the glory as of the only begotten of the Father, full of grace and truth." Clearly this first verse of 1 John is speaking of Jesus.

Now let's look at verse 2 to see who John proclaims Jesus to be: "And the life was manifested, and we have seen and testify and *proclaim to you the eternal life*, which was with the Father and was manifested to us" (1 John 1:2 NASB; emphasis mine). John declares Jesus to be "the eternal life." With that understanding of eternal life, 1 John 5:11-12 makes sense: "And the testimony is this, that God has given us eternal life, and this life is in His Son. He who has the Son has the life; he who does not have the Son of God does not have the life" (NASB). *Jesus is the eternal life*. So if you have Him, then you have eternal life. If you don't have Him, then you cannot have eternal life, because He is eternal life. We should not be surprised at this. Jesus Himself claimed He was the eternal life. In John 14:6, Jesus declared, "I am the way and the truth and the life. No one comes to the Father except through me" (NKJV).

How Do We Obtain Eternal Life?

The next question then becomes "So, how does *Jesus's eternal life* become our eternal life?" John 17:1-3 answers this question through a prayer Jesus prayed. "Father, the time has come. Glorify Your Son, that Your Son may glorify You. For You granted Him authority over all people that He might give eternal life to all those You have given Him. Now this is eternal life: that they may know You, the only true God, and Jesus Christ, whom You have sent" (NIV). Jesus acknowledged that He would give eternal life to all the Father brought to Him, and then defined it. "This is eternal life: that they may know You, the only true God, and Jesus Christ, whom You have sent" (v.3).

Eternal life comes from *knowing* the Father through the Son. What does Jesus mean by *know*? Here is how the Septuagint (the Koine Greek version of the Bible) used the Greek word translated in English as *know*. "And Adam *knew* Eve his wife; and she conceived, and bare Cain"

(Gen. 4:1; emphasis mine). *Know* is the word for deep intimacy, a complete knowing. When two people live in a strong, healthy marriage, they deeply know one another. They know both the good and the bad, things their respective parents didn't even know. God knows us totally, and He desires that we also deeply know Him through Jesus Christ. *The eternal life God offers to believers is about relationship—a deep intimate relationship with the Father made possible through the work of the Son and the Holy Spirit—an intimate relationship that will last forever.* Everyone lives forever, but for some there will be no endearing relationship with God after their earthly body dies. When God moves one to seek eternal life "in Christ" He is offering an intimate heart to heart relationship for all eternity with man's personal Creator, not just an extension of life.

We want . . . But God Wants . . .

What man normally wants when he approaches the Heavenly Father through the Son in order to seek eternal life is quite trite when compared with what God wants to give the seeker.

- *The seeker wants* to escape the fires of hell, and God grants that wish, *but God wants* the seeker to be able to overcome the power of sin and live a holy life.
- *The seeker wants* to be granted entrance to the place called Heaven, and God grants that wish, *but God wants* to adopt the seeker and make him a member of His royal family.
- *The seeker wants* to be forgiven and God grants that wish, *but God wants* the seeker to be cleansed from the taint of sin (see I John 1:9).
- *The seeker wants* to share His concerns with God and gain His help, and God actively listens to those concerns, *but God wants* the seeker to care about His concerns also—for our sakes.
- *The seeker wants* to share his heart with God, and God tenderly holds his heart in His hands, *but God wants* the seeker to care about His heart also—for our sakes.
- *The seeker wants* protection from the hurts of the world, *but God wants* ever present fellowship, an intimate sharing of thoughts and desires, mutual listening, valuing, and respect—for our sakes.
- *The seeker wants* to be in God's presence when he dies, *but God* offers His presence *now* and with it love, joy, peace, patience,

kindness, goodness, faithfulness, gentleness, and self-control (see Gal. 5:22-23).

Eternal life is the eternal sharing in the life and heart of God. It is about relationship, not fire insurance or longevity. That being said, let us now look at God's provision for our experiencing of eternal life "in Christ" by drawing a picture that illustrates how both "Christ in us" and "we in Christ" can be true without implying that we are Christ.

The circle on the right represents Christ's eternal life. The circle on the left represents the life of the born-again believer. The joining of the two circles represents the relationship of the believer with Christ, a relationship Biblically described as "in Christ".

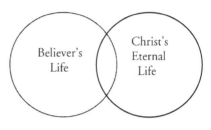

"In Christ"

We Are in Union with Christ

To be "in Christ" means to be in *union* with Christ. You may have recognized the figure above as a Venn diagram. If I asked you to show me the union of the two circles in that diagram, you would likely show me the intersection of the two circles, i.e., the area they both have in common. It is natural to think of our relationship with Christ as lying in the area that we have in common. However, you would not be right mathematically or biblically. The union of the two is all that is in one combined with all that is in the other. The union is all that is in each of the two circles combined.

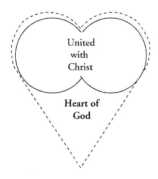

Incredibly, to be "in Christ" means that all that is of Him is joined with all that is of us. If we unite 10 cents with 20 cents, we have 30 cents. He takes all of our sin. In turn, we receive all of His righteousness. His life is combined with ours. It is a union, a uniting of His life with ours! Because of the magnificence of this truth, I have enclosed the united circles within the dotted heart to indicate that believers have been encompassed by the heart of God.

If this is true (and I aim to biblically convince you that it is), this is an incredible act of God. The thought of this truth alone should totally change our outlooks. It means that no matter what is happening to believers in this world, not only is Christ *with us* and *for us*, but also that He has totally redefined and revalued us. *Being conscious of this truth* should always have a profound effect on the way we experience our present circumstances or situations. A present tense awareness of this truth will change the impact of harsh words being expressed against us or even the impact of impending death. So let's explore this truth further.

Our Union with Christ Is Like the Marriage Covenant

The Bible refers to our relationship with Christ in terms of the *marriage union*. The most comprehensive teaching on marriage in the New Testament is found in Ephesians 5:22-33. However, verse 32 seems out of place. It reads, "This mystery is very great, but I speak concerning [the relation of] Christ and the church" (AMP). The context of this verse is marriage—how to be one with your spouse. Dr. David Seamands, my pastor while I was in seminary, sometimes quipped, "Men and women are barely the same species." I expect we all can relate to his statement. How do two persons who are so different become one? Those of you who are married know that sex alone doesn't bring about oneness, though sex is a part of oneness. It's a mystery. But look closely at this statement. Paul is saying the relation between Christ and the church is like the marriage relationship. Marriage is the *illustration* Paul is using to describe the relationship between Christ and believers. Both are covenant relationships. *Testament* means "covenant." The Old Covenant between God and man was through law. The New Covenant between God and man is through grace. Incredibly, Ephesians 5:32 teaches that *the New* Covenant *relationship between God and man is like unto the covenant relationship between a man and his wife.*

A rebellious young lady, age sixteen, tired of living at home under her parent's rules, ran away to New York. There she was able to obtain a credit card and lived pretty well for a time, though all the while she was running up a big debt. Soon letters began coming demanding repayment with interest on her debts, and then eventually phone calls started demanding the same. The credit card company wanted its money back, and she realized she had no hope for paying it back. She became depressed and worried. What was she to do? She was in a bad dilemma.

Fortunately for her, a young man entered the picture. He was attracted to her, and she was attracted to him. One day he proposed. She accepted, and they exchanged wedding vows, entering into a *marriage covenant.* She had become *Mrs. Billionaire,* and things were different. What happened to her debt? It was paid off! Through marriage, what was hers alone becomes his too, and what was his becomes hers. Her debt had been too much for her resources, but now she is the wife of a billionaire with new resources, and it's no longer a problem!

Do you realize that I just shared the Gospel with you? We too are like this girl. We have rebelled against God and have run up a big debt, a sin debt, which we could never pay off. In fact, we are adding more to it daily. And there is a consequence: "The wages of sin is death [eternal separation from God]" (Rom. 6:23 AMP). Furthermore, there will be no government bailout, for Jesus has proclaimed, "For truly I say to you, until heaven and earth pass away, not the smallest letter or stroke shall pass from the Law until all is accomplished" (Matt. 5:18 NASB).

We Go to Heaven as His Bride or We Don't Go at All!

Our situation is like unto that of a young lady who is an impoverished resident of Sudan and wishes to come to America to live—the land that she has heard is a wonderful land of plenty. But she discovers that she has a problem: the immigration quota is filled for Sudanese. America, the land she longs to live in, is thus a forbidden land to her. What is she to do? Why, marry a legitimate American citizen, of course, so that he might bring her to America as his bride.

Correspondingly, there is a place we all would like to live in one day. It is called heaven. The problem is that heaven (the habitation of our holy God, who cannot be in the presence of sin) is closed to persons with an unpaid sin debt. But there is one person, and only one, who never sinned, and thus is a legitimate citizen of heaven: Jesus. Jesus is able (and the only one able) to pay our sin debt. He offers to all of us sinners a covenant relationship like unto the marriage covenant so that He might bring us to heaven with Him to live as His bride forever.

We go to heaven as the bride of Christ, or we don't go at all. When we enter into this covenant relationship with Him (that is like unto the marriage covenant), all that is ours becomes His, and all that is His becomes ours. He pays our sin debt. "He himself bore our sins in his body on the tree, so that we might die to sins and live for righteousness; by his wounds you have been healed" (1 Pet. 2:24 NIV). In turn, we get all that is His. We become citizens of heaven with Him (see Phil. 3:20 NLT). We who believe, win! *Satan*, our archenemy, the thief who comes to kill and steal and destroy those who can be the brides of Jesus if they so choose, *loses* (see John 10:10)!

Let's now revisit 1 Corinthians 1:30 and reconsider this verse point by point:

> But by His doing
> you are in Christ Jesus,
> who became to us
> wisdom from God,
> and righteousness
> and sanctification,
> and redemption. (NASB)

"By His doing." Jesus is the only man who has ever earned the right to enter heaven by virtue of perfectly keeping the Law. All of the rest of us have sinned, fallen short of the glory of God, and earned death, eternal separation from God (see Rom. 3:23; 6:23). We all must be saved by the work Jesus has done on earth on our behalf, for we cannot save ourselves (see Eph. 2:8-9). The Law, by which so many would seek salvation, only condemns us, destroying our claim of being worthy of entry into heaven by virtue of our keeping of the Law better than most. "For no person will be justified [made righteous, acquitted, and judged acceptable] in His sight by observing the works prescribed by the Law. For [the real function of] the Law is to make men recognize and be conscious of sin [not mere perception, but an acquaintance with sin which works toward repentance, faith, and holy character]" (Rom. 3:20 AMP).

"You are in Christ Jesus." To be "in Christ" means to be in covenant relationship with Him, a covenant of grace like unto the marriage covenant. That covenant alone is our assurance of heaven.

By virtue of our covenant relationship with Jesus, all that is His becomes ours. We have the following:

1. *We have "wisdom from God."* Why is it that Christians, Muslims, and Jews all claim to worship the same God, the

God of Abraham, and yet we all see Him so differently? As the Amplified Bible states it: "But it is from Him that you have your life in Christ *Jesus, Whom God made our Wisdom from God,* [revealed to us a knowledge of the divine plan of salvation previously hidden, manifesting itself as]" (1 Cor. 1:30; emphasis mine). Jesus, the second Person of the Trinity, is our wisdom from God. As Jesus states it, "I and the Father are one" (John 10:30 NASB) and "He who has seen Me has seen the Father" (John 14:9 NASB). Christians see the Father so differently from Jews and Muslims because they look at the Son to know the Father. As Christians, we believe that the Father is revealed through the Son. Through Jesus, we have knowledge of God's divine plan for our salvation, which was a veiled mystery until the coming of the Christ.

2. *We are "righteous." Righteousness* is a big word that means "rightness with God." Let me share a personal story (as best I recollect—it was a long time ago). I am an only son. In 1960, my mom drove me 230 miles to college in the only car we had. The only way I could get home was to hitchhike, something you could do way back then. This was before interstates, so it took five and one-half hours to get home. Needless to say, I didn't go home often. We didn't talk on the phone much and hardly ever wrote letters. However, during my senior year, I finally had a car, and I went home to see Mom and Dad. I was accompanied by a special young lady, Sally Sanders. Upon arrival, I hugged Mom and Dad and then introduced them to Sally. "Mom, Dad, this is Sally, and she is going to be my bride." Before that introduction to Mom and Dad, Sally was only one of two billion girls in the world. Mom and Dad had no relationship with her, no knowledge of her. But with one quick introduction, Sally went from "no" relationship with Mom and Dad to a very "right" relationship. Why? It was 100 percent because of her relationship with their only son. In a like manner, we have a right standing with the Heavenly Father, a "rightness" with Him, 100 percent because of our relationship with His Son. Because we are His chosen bride, we *are* righteous. We get an A+ in righteousness.

3. *We are "sanctified."* Remember, *sanctification* is a big word to describe being totally set apart for service to God. As soon as we

made covenant with Jesus to join with Him in a life mission to honor God the Father, to honor His Father (and now ours) with our lives, we were set apart with Him, sanctified "in Christ."

4. *We are "redeemed."* Think of the word *redeemed* as it relates to transactions that occur every day in your local pawnshop. If you need fifty dollars, you can take your color TV down to the pawnshop, and they will buy it from you, but with the agreement that if you come back with seventy-five dollars in three months, you can buy it back from them. When you come back in three months and buy it back, you have *redeemed* it. In Adam's loins, we were created in the image of God. But Adam fell, and we, along with him, became *slaves* of sin. How do you free slaves? You must first buy them, own them. Then you can set them free. We are redeemed, bought back from sin. "For you know that it was not with perishable things such as silver or gold that you were redeemed from the empty way of life handed down to you from your forefathers, but with the precious blood of Christ, a lamb without blemish or defect" (1 Pet. 1:18-19). We are *redeemed*, purchased through Jesus's shed blood, rightly slaves of God, but set free and made sons of God.

We Are as Mrs. Christ

Believers are the covenant brides of Christ. He has declared our worth to the Father, saying, "I have given them the glory that you gave me, that they may be one as we are one" (John 17:22 NIV). We have been redefined, made one with Him. All that is ours is His; all that is His is ours. We have been made one with the Father through the Son (see John 17:20-23). We are possessors of eternal life through our covenant relationship with the Son. Whether we are male or female, we have become as Mrs. Christ. The role of the husband on earth is a picture of the role of Christ in heaven. Jesus is the provider, protector, and leader of His bride.

Faith Is the Marriage Covenant

Our covenant relationship with Christ is clearly taught by Paul in his letter to the Ephesians. "For it is by grace you have been saved, through faith—and this not from yourselves, it is the gift of God—not by works, so that no one can boast" (Eph. 2:8-9 NIV). It is clear from this verse that our works have nothing to do with our salvation. If they did, we could then say, "God, look at what I've done. You owe me!" Some do think that way. They get angry with God when bad things happen to them, but I would rather not receive from God that which He owes me. I prefer grace, because according to the Law, my sin (whether it is a little or a lot) merits eternal separation from God (see Rom. 6:23).

This passage becomes easy to understand when you think of faith and grace as *acrostics*. The *faith acrostic is* the marriage covenant. Think about the traditional marriage vow, the one you likely made when you married your spouse. It began with the man saying,

> Forsaking
> All other women
> I
> Take
> Her to be my wedded wife [my unique woman in all the world!]

He vows to love and to cherish her, to treat her as his *unique woman* among all the women in the world. He is to go out and work for her, come home to her alone, have children with her alone, trust her to nurture their children, and combine all of his resources with hers as they go out into the world together.

Then the woman returns the covenant vow:

> Forsaking
> All other men
> I
> Take
> Him to be my wedded husband [my unique man in all the world!]

She vows to make him her *unique man* among all the men in the entire world. She chooses to combine her resources with his, to have and nurture his children, and to keep herself pure.

Saving *faith* too is expressed with a covenant vow like unto the marriage covenant. We pray,

Forsaking
All others
I
Take
Him (Christ) as my Savior [my *unique hope* for eternal life!]

We acknowledge that He is the only One who can save us and express our trust in Him as the only One who can take us to heaven with Him as His covenant bride. He is the One to whom we must look to know truth. We are to believe He is who He says He is—the unique Son of God. All of our hope for eternal life is to be centered in our *relationship* with Him.

Gloriously, Christ initiated our covenant relationship with Himself. Jesus said, "No one can come to Me unless the Father who sent Me draws him" (John 6:44 NIV). Before we entered into this covenant relationship by expressing faith in Him through our words, He had already expressed faith in us by having drawn us to Himself. So just as the man begins the covenant exchange by first making covenant with the bride-to-be, so has Christ preceded believers in making covenant promise to all of us who will believe and enter into covenant relationship with Him.

Once we have made this faith covenant with Christ, we become participators in His grace. Grace too can be thought of as an acrostic:

God's
Riches
At
Christ's
Expense

Actually, saving grace preceded this sanctifying grace, for were it not for His mercy, we, because we are sinners, could never have come into His presence.

That's All Good, But the Gospel Is Even Better Than We've Seen So Far!

This is why the gospel is called *good news*. It is God's mind-boggling commitment to us through Christ's suffering. But it is even better than what we have seen so far. Let us examine Colossians:

> ¹⁹For it was the Father's good pleasure for all the fullness to dwell in Him, ²⁰and through Him to reconcile all things to Himself, having made peace through the blood of His cross; through Him, I say, whether things on earth or things in heaven. ²¹And although you were formerly alienated and hostile in mind, engaged in evil deeds, ²²yet He has now reconciled you in His fleshly body through death, *in order to* present you before Him holy and blameless and beyond reproach—²³if indeed you continue in the faith firmly established and steadfast, and not moved away from the hope of the gospel that you have heard, which was proclaimed in all creation under heaven, and of which I, Paul, was made a minister. (Col. 1:19-23 NASB; emphasis mine)

Verses 19 and 20 state God's intention to reconcile fallen man to Himself. Verse 21 reminds us that we are like the sixteen-year-old girl in the illustration above who defies her parents' rule and runs off to another place so she can do her own thing. We were alienated from God, independently doing our own thing, engaged in wrong behavior. But now He has reconciled us (restored us to fellowship with Himself) through our repentance and His agonizing cleansing of our sins through the cross. That is old information, but new information follows. The twenty-second verse tells us *why* Jesus endured the cross. He endured the cross "*in order to* present you before Him [the Father] holy and blameless and beyond reproach" (Col. 1:22; emphasis mine). He did it in order to purify us so that we might experience eternal fellowship with God.

How can that be? How could anyone who has sinned such as we have be called holy? Perhaps we could rationalize that by thinking only in terms of present tense behavior. But what about the words that are added to *holy*, "blameless and beyond reproach" (v. 23)? By no stretch of the imagination could we consider ourselves *blameless and beyond reproach*. That does not make sense to the natural mind. But it is true, or else it would not have been stated as true in God's Word.

We may have trouble understanding this truth because we no longer understand the marriage covenant the way God intended it to be perceived. We have been confused by the state of marriage in a fallen world. We must go to the second chapter of Genesis in order to be able to rightly understand this truth. There we find God describing His intentions for marriage between a man and a woman. It begins this way:

> And the LORD God formed man of the dust of the ground, and breathed into his nostrils the breath of life; and man became a living being. (Gen. 2:7 NIV)

God takes dust, shapes it as man, and breathes life (spirit, breath) into man, and he becomes a living being. Verse 18 then tells us something special about the man He formed.

> And the LORD God said, "It is not good that man should be alone; I will make him a helper comparable to him." (Gen. 2:18, NIV)

We have often heard pastors quote the fifteenth-century French mathematician and philosopher, Blaise Pascal, who said, "There is a God-shaped vacuum in the heart of every man that cannot be filled by any created thing, but only by God, the Creator." That is theology, not Word. But the Word declares that God has designed man's heart to live in a special marriage relationship with a woman, unless God gives him special grace to live by himself. Ecclesiastes confirms that man is created with special friendships in mind: "Two are better than one, because they have a good return for their work: If one falls down, his friend can help him up. But pity the man who falls and has no one to help him up! Also, if two lie down together, they will keep warm. But how can one keep warm alone? Though one may be overpowered, two can defend themselves. A cord of three strands is not quickly broken" (Eccles. 4:9-12 NIV). I know these verses speak of friendship, but in light of "lying down together and keeping warm," it is not much of a stretch to say these verses also apply to marriage. The "third strand" is the couple's common devotion to God.

Sociology confirms the Word's declaration that man needs a woman. On average, a single man does not live nearly as long as a married man. Man *needs* a woman. Judging from my own experience, I must conclude that most men will not take care of themselves nearly as well as their wives take care of them. If my wife isn't home, I don't care whether I am home or not. It's just a house without her presence, not a home. Alone, I will eat too much junk food. My eating is bad enough married, but that's because I eat more than what she puts before me. Without marriage, it would be far worse. I thank God for my wife's help! One plus one is better than two. I have read about studies of oxen. Through the studies,

I have learned that when the amounts of weight oxen can pull alone are added together, the combined total does not add up to as much as they can pull harnessed together. As it is with oxen, so it is with a man and his wife. The two pulling together in oneness can accomplish more together than what would be accomplished if each strove through life alone.

God has not intended marriage for everyone. First of all, there are not equal numbers of men and women. Second, citing spiritual reasons, the apostle Paul thought it was better not to marry. He wrote, "Now to the unmarried and the widows I say: It is good for them to stay unmarried, as I am. But if they cannot control themselves, they should marry, for it is better to marry than to burn with passion" (1 Cor. 7:8-9 NLB). Thus, choosing not to marry may very well be a shoe that fits you, but being single wasn't a good fit for me. I personally like the "two are better than one" option.

Thankfully, in the Genesis passage, God has declared that marriage is in order for most of us, for He states, "It is not good that man should be alone; I will make him a helper comparable to him" (Gen. 2:18). Now it is logical to expect that in the very next verse God would then introduce Eve into this picture. But that is not what happens. In the following verse man isn't given a wife, but instead is given a job.

> Out of the ground the LORD God formed every beast of the field and every bird of the air, and brought them to Adam to see what he would call them. And whatever Adam called each living creature, that was its name. So Adam gave names to all cattle, to the birds of the air, and to every beast of the field. But for Adam there was not found a helper comparable to him. (Gen. 2:19-20 NIV)

I am going to take license at this point and read between the lines. God had a job for Adam, i.e., to name all created beings. I am guessing He paraded the animals before Adam two by two, the way they came into the ark Noah built. Naming the animals would have been easy for Adam at first. He would have started with three-letter names like *pig*, *cow*, *dog*, and *cat*. Four-letter words like *bear* and *deer* would probably follow. But finally, he had to come up with names like *hippopotamus*. (That's spoofing, of course, since Adam didn't use English, but you get the point.) And though the Word doesn't declare such, I would suspect that at this point, he is wishing that he had someone to help him come up with all these names. The Word does declare, however, an observation from the whole process of giving names to the animals: "For Adam there was not found a helper comparable to him" (v. 20).

If they did indeed come two by two, then he would have noticed that every living thing except himself had a "helper comparable to him." If so, I think he would now be quite ready for Eve to come along. Evidently, God felt he was, for next we read,

> And the LORD God caused a deep sleep to fall on Adam, and he slept; and He took one of his ribs, and closed up the flesh in its place. Then the rib which the LORD God had taken from man He made into a woman, and He brought her to the man. (Gen. 2:21-22 NKJV)

Bone of His Bones and Flesh of His Flesh

There is something interesting here. Adam was formed from the dust of the ground. Every other living creature was formed from the dust of the ground. Why didn't God just form Eve from the dust of the ground since that is the way He had formed every other living creature? Do you think there is something important about this difference? I certainly think so. Adam received insight that has been overlooked by most men since the fall of man. Adam understood that this woman was an extension of himself, a part of himself, not a totally separate entity. He said, "This is now bone of my bones and flesh of my flesh; She shall be called Woman, because she was taken out of Man" (Gen. 2:23 NKJV). It was not God's plan that husbands and wives would act independently of one another, but instead, would be considerate of one another, value one another's help, and function together in oneness. This is a vital elementary understanding that women as a whole seem to understand better than men. Unless their wives have taught them better, most husbands, when late in returning home, will not be considerate enough to call their wives to let them know they will be late. On the other hand, most women would call if they were late, for they seem to have a better understanding that the things that affect them also affect their husbands. Wives are not to be thought of as the old lady, but rather as a part of us—and vice versa. A basic foundational principle of marriage is that husbands would see their wives as part of themselves. If that were to become a heart attitude, most marriages would improve.

A thought came to me one day while I was considering this basic idea concerning how God intended for mankind to see marriage. Could it be that God sees those of us who are the brides of Christ to be an extension of Christ, a part of Him, rather than a totally separate entity? Let's go back to Scripture and find out.

> So husbands ought to love their own wives as their own bodies; he who loves his wife loves himself. For no one ever hated his own flesh, but nourishes and cherishes it, just as the Lord does the church. *For we are members of His body, of His flesh and of His bones.* (Eph. 5:28-30 NKJV; emphasis mine)

"We are members of Christ's body, of His flesh and of His bones" or, as we saw earlier in this chapter, united with Him "in Christ," as Mrs. Christ by covenant relationship. Thus, as members of His body—bone of His bones, flesh of His flesh—if He is holy, so are we. If He is blameless, then "in Him," so are we. And if He is beyond reproach, then "in Him," so are we.

More Glorious Truth from God's Word about the Believer

The language of the Bible is celebratory concerning the birth of God's children. It speaks of great joy in Heaven when the lost are found (see Luke 15:7, 10). It uses strong emotional language to describe the preciousness of God's chosen like, ". . . kill the calf we have been fattening. We must celebrate with a feast, for this son of mine was dead and has now returned to life. He was lost, but now he is found.' So the party began." (Luke 15:24, NLT). It uses familial words like *adopted* to describe God's chosen children. God is passionate about His children. Do not be confused because there is sometimes a lack of emotion by the church on Earth when someone is saved. At its best the church on Earth is but a poor imitation of the church in Heaven. The heavenly church has opened eyes. They understand the issues and struggles against darkness, and the miracle of new birth. So there is great rejoicing in Heaven when someone is saved. I can picture heaven erupting in joy when you were saved; much like a stadium erupts with joy when the home team has just scored a touchdown. God and all the saints in Heaven are excited about you and for you.

Bride is also a word that connotes excitement. Seeing yourself as the treasured bride of Christ captures some of the emotion Heaven exults toward you as a believer. When you pray, you are not some insignificant person raising an unimportant voice to God. You are Christ's bride, one chosen by the Father for His Son; one for whom Christ freely offered His life so that you might spend eternity in Heaven with Him; and one whom Christ greatly rejoices in because He loves you and now His sacrifice for you is not in vain. When you sing spiritual songs and hymns that declare His majesty and your adoration, He rejoices. Your voice is music to His ears because you are His loved bride and He desires to delight in you. Open your mouth and declare His glory! Because of your importance to Him, your words have the power to bless Him—and to hurt Him.

And you are not just a bride, but the bride of the King of kings and Lord of lords. When you go into the world, you do not go only in your name any more that Michelle O'Bama would go into the world as Michelle. She is the first lady, and she represents not only herself, but also the President of the United States. In like manner, God has chosen that when you go about in the world, you *will* represent Him. Whether you like it or not, others are going to judge Jesus by your witness—and God wants it that way. He values you so much that He has chosen you to represent Him, for better or for worse. **"We are therefore Christ's ambassadors, as though God were making his appeal through us"** (II Cor. 5:20, NLT). Furthermore, so that you may represent Him well (as His ambassador), He wishes to empower you and direct your walk. He has made provisions for you to have the satisfaction of representing Him well—He wants that for you for your sake. That's the subject of the next chapter.

I pray that you are beginning to see yourself in a new light! I certainly needed to be defined by my relationship with Christ rather than by my actions and thoughts. If we are honest, focusing on ourselves to determine how we measure up as a Christian is quite discouraging. God has made us significant and acceptable far beyond anything we might deserve. As Jesus said in John 17:21, **"We share in His glory."** *If you are a believer, you are greater than you know.* What Jesus has done for us is far greater than any of us can fully comprehend. May we learn to see ourselves as being "in Christ," supremely revalued, redeemed! *Knowing this truth is the necessary foundation for all of our responses to God. All of our actions should flow out of this heightened personal identity that is a gift from our loving Heavenly Father to us.*

Things You May Ponder and Discuss with Others

1. On a scale from 0 to 10, where 0 represents zero significance, acceptance, and worth and 10 represents maximum significance, acceptance, and worth, what numerical value would you assign to yourself?
2. From early childhood on, who are the people and what are the events that have had the greatest influence on the value you assigned to yourself in question 1? You may list several persons, things, or events.
3. Who or what do you tend to compare yourself to in order to achieve a measure of worth? How are you doing at measuring up to your standards?
4. What is present in your thinking that makes it hard to believe that God wants to gloriously revalue you by placing you "in Christ"?
5. How would your life be different if you could believe that you have been revalued "in Christ"? In what ways would your actions be different if you believed?
6. In what specific ways would life be different for you if you viewed Christianity in terms of relationship, i.e., as seeing Christ as one who has loved you and totally offered His life to you so that you might spend the rest of your life responding to His love and thus be ever increasingly shaped by His absolute love for you?
7. Have you entered into a covenant love relationship with Christ? If not, then why not? Will you do it now?

CHAPTER 2: YOU CAN BE EMPOWERED BY CHRIST

NOW THAT WE have looked at Scripture to know who believers are "in Christ," let's move on to think about *why* God unites believers with Christ.

Why Has God Placed Believers "in Christ"?

I awakened at four o'clock in the morning, finding myself thinking about this marvelous thing God has done by placing believers "in Christ." My thoughts were focused on *why*. Being "in Christ" is far above anything I could ever dream up as a means of personal worth. Why does God offer such extremely high valuing to believers? The thought that came to me was that God did this for us in order to deliver us from our "self" centeredness. *He must loose us from looking at ourselves to know who we are because we cannot focus on ourselves and our agendas and still be "one" with God.*

The Father, Son, and Holy Spirit are completely "one" because they are not focused on themselves (seeking their own valuing and following their own agenda) but are totally focused on valuing one another. The Spirit is focused on the Son's agenda and glorifying Him (see John 15:26, 16:13). The Son is focused on the Father's agenda and glorifying Him (see John 14:10). The Father is focused on the "kingdom of God" where His perfect, totally unselfish will is done (see Matt. 6:10). Thus, the Spirit is caught up in the Son's agenda and the Son in the Father's agenda. The Father's agenda is preparing those of us who are His spiritual children for life in the kingdom of heaven.

God places us "in Christ" so that we can join with Him in accomplishing His agenda for this world. He is not an irresponsible father intent on granting His children's every want, but rather a responsible Father working to prepare His children for eternal life in His kingdom. Furthermore, the kingdom of God is a place whose entrance not only requires a state of being born again (see John 3:3) but also often the experience of many hardships in preparation (see Acts 14:22, 2 Thess. 1:5).

It Would Be Wrong for Almighty God to Be Caught Up in Mankind's Agendas

Why doesn't God just help us with our agendas on earth? After all, that is what mankind seems to want from Him and to ask of Him. But *it would be wrong for God to be focused on my agenda or on your agenda when what He has in store for us is incomparably greater than what we seek for ourselves.* If He is love, He must require that we be focused on His agenda for everyone's sake. If He were to focus on helping us with our agenda rather than require that we focus on His agenda, then He would be devaluing us individually and mankind as a whole. If He gave Himself to supplementing our agenda, we would then obtain less than His best. How could a perfect God strive for less than our best? He must be at work to lift us above our self-centered focuses. What is best for us is not "self" glorification. For everyone's sake, we need to be focused on the kingdom of God, not on ourselves. *We need to be caught up in something far greater than ourselves.* Contrary to our wants, our real need is that God would deliver us from our desires for "self" glorification. What is truly best for us is that we would be consumed with glorifying our Heavenly Father. But that focus does not come naturally for us. Therefore, if God would have us learn to focus on His kingdom and His glory, He must deal with our "self" centered focus, a focus that draws all of us toward a lesser state of existence than God desires and has planned for His children.

God's Plan for Loosing Us from Seeking "Self" Glorification

One of the things God does to change our focus from our "self" to His "self" is surprising. In order to empower us to live beyond ourselves, to get our eyes off what this world has to offer us, He grants us value that far exceeds the greatest valuing this fallen world could offer us—He places us "in Christ." When we understand that we have been so greatly valued that our value cannot be increased, then we no longer need to do anything to try to gain greater value, for greater value does not exist. Walking in the light of this truth delivers us from needing to continue seeking greater value for ourselves from the fallen world and frees us to focus on giving value to others out of our excessive abundance. It is as Jesus said, "The kingdom of heaven is like treasure hidden in a field. When a man found it, he hid it again, and then in his joy went and sold all he had and bought that field" (Matt. 13:44 NIV). Our union with Him is the ultimate treasure!

Jesus said, "The thief comes only in order to steal and kill and destroy. I came that they may have and enjoy life, and have it in abundance [to the full, till it overflows]" (John 10:10 AMP). When we try to find life in this fallen world's way as orchestrated by the thief (Satan), we lose. All of the worth the world gives is passing away; it is temporary. But when we find life in God's way, "in Christ," we find an abundance of life that will not pass away—ever. Furthermore, God desires to impart so much life to us that it cannot be contained. He wants His life in us to be so great that it overflows and spills out of us so that it will touch and bless others too. *True lasting happiness is the result of joining with Christ in His life mission to glorify the Father; it is the overflow of His life manifested in us and through us, touching and blessing the lives of others.*

It is as simple as this: (1) we have been ultimately valued "in Christ" so that no higher valuing could happen to us; (2) God grants this excessive abundance of worth to His children, worth so great that it cannot be added to, so that we can break out of our patterns of seeking worth from others and can instead grant worth to others out of the overflow of our abundance "in Christ" (think of abundance as far more than we need for ourselves); and (3) when we are freed from needing to place emphasis on gaining worth for ourselves, then the greater good for all can happen, for we are freed to be givers rather than takers. As a result, we can become one in purpose with Jesus. It is then that Jesus's prayer for us, as recorded in the Gospel of John, becomes reality for us:

> I am praying not only for these disciples but also for all who will ever believe in me through their message. I pray that they will all be one, just as you and I are one—as you are in me, Father, and I am in you. And may they be in us so that the world will believe you sent me. I have given them the glory you gave me, so they may be one as we are one. I am in them and you are in me. May they experience such perfect unity that the world will know that you sent me and that you love them as much as you love me (John 17:20-23 NLT).

Inadequate Human Pictures of God's Plan for Our Oneness with Him

Human love gives us a limited, imperfect picture of God's plan for "oneness" with Him. When we are first infatuated with a significant other of the opposite sex, the object of our infatuation receives our full attention. That infatuation messes with our thoughts all day. We can hardly get our minds off them. We eagerly look forward to being in their presence. They are exciting to us, and we want to give them our best. We humans call that being in love. But as that relationship matures and our thoughts slowly evolve back to ourselves and what that significant other is *not* doing for us *now*, the relationship begins to deteriorate. Instead of eagerly giving, we find ourselves selfishly demanding and sometimes even being demeaning in our demands. Our "me" focus can become deadly to relationships, including our relationship with God.

Moving higher, let's contrast this human experience of being "in love" with the love of a mother for her newborn child. That newborn baby has done nothing but bring hurt to the mom. The mother was nauseous the first trimester—a most uncomfortable kind of sickness. By the third trimester, her figure is out of proportion, her graceful walk has become a waddle, and her discomfort abounds. She has been kicked, awakened, and inconvenienced. Then the newborn is placed in the mother's arms, a baby that is somewhat bloody, wrinkled, and likely has a lopsided head because of the passage through the birth canal. This baby can't do anything but poop, pee, and cry. Newborns can't even smile. And yet the mother loves the child with all of her heart. Why? What has this baby done to deserve being loved? The love flows 100 percent from the mom to the child. She has participated in the creation of this child and longed for this child's arrival. She has great hopes for this little one. It is not about what the baby has done to deserve love. It is all about the mom's commitment to her baby. I think this is the closest human picture of our Heavenly Father's love for believers.

The Rest of the Story: We Must Grow Up!

This new baby arrives loved, accepted, and 100 percent dependent on the mom. This total dependence is certainly okay with the mom—for a season. But things are not to stay that way. Moms teach their little ones to grow beyond their self-centered focus. *Big baby* is a term with very negative connotations. The child must be taught to care for his or herself and encouraged to become considerate of others. Though being loved and accepted is critical to the child's development, it is not enough to just be loved and accepted. A child that is not nurtured and encouraged to develop in responsible ways is cheated; it is not truly a loved child. There is not much pretty about a spoiled brat, which is what undisciplined children tend to become.

God's love for His newly birthed ("born-again" [see John 3:3-4]) children is like a mother's love for her newborn child. God will never love us or accept us more than the moment when we were born again. The whole heavens rejoiced for each of us when we were birthed into God's family (see Luke 15:1-10). We must know that! But just as is the case with a mother's love, God's love must also push us on to maturity; it must strive with us to make us responsible members of His family. Because God greatly values His children, He wants us to be a part of something greater than ourselves. Because we are His loved children, He will involve us in His kingdom work for our sakes. That's what true love does.

Yet there is a real problem in us that hinders our involvement in God's work. Whereas we grow and mature by becoming more "independent" of our parents, we must grow spiritually in the opposite way. We must become more "dependent" on God. If we are to do effective kingdom work, we must work at taking our eyes off ourselves and our limited abilities and placing them on our Heavenly Father and the resources He makes available to us.

We Must Learn to Honor Our Heavenly Father above Ourselves

I love the biblical account of the boy, David, and the giant, Goliath (see 1 Sam. 17). David was a boy, but a boy focused on the greatness of His God rather than on his own personal weaknesses. One day his daddy, Jesse, sent David to take food to his brothers, who were camped with Saul's army. Upon arriving, he found Saul's army cowering before the taunts of the giant, Goliath. For forty days, every morning and evening, Goliath defiantly shouted at Saul's army: "'Choose a man and have him come down to me. If he is able to fight and kill me, we will become your subjects; but if I overcome him and kill him, you will become our subjects and serve us.' Then the Philistine said, 'This day I defy the ranks of Israel! Give me a man and let us fight each other.' On hearing the Philistine's words, Saul and all the Israelites were dismayed and terrified" (1 Sam. 17:8b-11 NIV).

David was infuriated at the arrogance of this giant of a man who would demean and defy the Living God. David's words were, "Who is this uncircumcised Philistine that he should defy the armies of the living God?" (1 Sam. 17:26 NIV). All of the older more able men were looking at themselves and their own abilities and, as a result, were cowering before this Philistine giant. David's eyes were focused on his Living God. "David said to the Philistine, 'You come against me with sword and spear and javelin, but I come against you in the name of the LORD Almighty, the God of the armies of Israel, whom you have defied'" (1 Sam. 17:45 NIV). David's focus on God's majesty and power rather than his own relative weakness enabled David to challenge the giant. Then, because David chose to go out and face the giant "in the name of the Lord Almighty," God empowered David's boldness by using David's puny, seemingly insufficient weapon to destroy Goliath.

David's Faith or God's Faithfulness?

Please don't miss the main point of this story. This story isn't just about David's faith. Every story about faith is really more about God's faithfulness. David's Living God was being defied. David was representing God, not himself. The issue was Goliath's affront to David's God and God's kingdom on earth. He was standing with his God against an enemy of his God. He did what God gave him the confidence to do, and he did it well. He carefully chose five smooth stones for his sling. He fought the way he knew best and trusted God for the rest. As the lyrics of a song state, "Little is much when God is in it!" The result is history.

This is a story about the boy David's "oneness" with God. David chose to join the Spirit and the Son in glorifying the Father. He laid aside his agenda and took up the Father's agenda. He thus became "one" with the Father. *That is what God wants for all of His children.* It was Jesus's prayer for all of us who would believe because of the witness of the apostles. Remember, Jesus prayed, "My prayer is not for them [the apostles] alone. I pray also for those who will believe in me through their message, *that all of them may be one, Father, just as you are in me and I am in you.* May they also be in us so that the world may believe that you have sent me. I have given them the glory that you gave me, that they may be one as we are one: I in them and you in me. May they be brought to complete unity to let the world know that you sent me and have loved them even as you have loved me" (John 17:20-23 NIV; emphasis mine).

God could have used any of the men gathered there to defeat Goliath, yet He chose to use a boy, but a special boy who was so focused on the power and majesty of the Living God that he was infuriated by this affront to his God. *David was so incensed that he was readily willing to make himself totally available to his God in order that his God might use him to right this wrong. That is God's desire for all of His children—for our sakes.*

Why Did God Choose David to Defeat Goliath?

I believe David had two things going for him that caused him to be God's choice for delivering His people. First, he was the person most unlikely to be able to defeat Goliath, and thus history would know that this victory was God's doing and to God's glory. Has this not repeatedly been God's way in selecting persons through whom He would do His work? Paul says clearly to each of us, "To those called by God to salvation, both Jews and Gentiles, Christ is the power of God and the wisdom of God. This foolish plan of God is wiser than the wisest of human plans, and God's weakness is stronger than the greatest of human strength. Remember, dear brothers and sisters, that few of you were wise in the world's eyes or powerful or wealthy when God called you. Instead, God chose things the world considers foolish in order to shame those who think they are wise. And he chose things that are powerless to shame those who are powerful. God chose things despised by the world, things counted as nothing at all, and used them to bring to nothing what the world considers important. As a result, no one can ever boast in the presence of God" (1 Cor. 1:24-29 NLT). The disciples were a motley crew; none had pedigree. God can and will use you and me if we will choose to honor Him above all others.

Second, as a boy, David was not confused with the mixed allegiances that come to us as we mature in the world and become victims of its deceiving charms. Life was simple for David. It was about His Heavenly Father, not about himself. His identity came from God. Because of his singular focus, a powerful enemy of God could not defeat the mere boy, David.

Unfortunately, it didn't stay that way for David. Later in life, David became caught up in the things of the world, became "self" and "world" focused, and was subsequently soiled by the wrong choices he made when tempted by the world. As a result, he lost his sense of "oneness" with the Father. The account of his affair with Bathsheba and the subsequent plotting for the death of Uriah are evidences of that (see 2 Sam. 11). The result of David's lost sense of "oneness" with God brought about tragic repercussions. Even though David's heart was still for God, as evidenced by his quickness to repent when confronted by Samuel, there were still heartbreaking consequences for his sin that followed him all the rest of his life. God is our Deliverer and can work good out of our failures, but nevertheless, our contamination by the world, which is God's enemy (see James 4:4), will often cause us temporary woe.

In the same sense as in this historic account from David's life, every believer has to face people and things that defy God and seek to allure us to participate in sinful, fallen behavior—to live beneath who we are "in Christ." However, it is not the Goliaths we should fear, but rather Satan's clever deceptions. Just as David, nearly all of us will stand up against most obvious evil. It is the subtle challenges (temptations) that often appear harmless that are more likely to do harm to our character. They lure us to turn from singleness of purpose toward pleasing God, to compromise, and to loss of pure devotion to God. That is why believers are warned in Hebrews that "we must listen very carefully to the truth we have heard, or we may drift away from it" (Heb. 2:1 NLT).

Little Is Much When God Is in It

We are beat-up followers of Christ. We have failed. We have sins and failures just like almost all of the heroes in the Bible. But just as with David, though our failures are many, God is bigger than our failures. We have many shortcomings, but because we are God's children, we are still called to represent God to our world, even though that task is gigantic and we all feel ever so limited in ability. How can we accomplish such a huge, seemingly impossible task? Obviously, God must be at work in helping us if this is to happen, and He is:

> For we are His workmanship, created in Christ Jesus for good works, which God prepared beforehand that we should walk in them. (Eph. 2:10).

We Begin Our Christian Walk as Sinners with Potential, But with No Personal Merit Before God

A problem for our egos is that the valuing we have "in Christ" is totally from outside ourselves. It is 100 percent a gift from Him that is in no way merited. It is sort of like being an admired person's child. That's nice, but we can only run so far on Dad's or Mom's reputations. At some point, we need to achieve confidence through our accomplishments. My friend, Paul Downing, tells of meeting with a young man who was told that he had a lot of *potential*. When the young man heard this, he was crestfallen. Paul, being surprised at his reaction, asked him if he knew what *potential* meant. The young man replied, "Yeah, it means you ain't worth a damn yet." Unrealized *potential* can be quite discouraging! Feeling that we are unable to measure up to others or the expectations of others can have a paralyzing effect on us.

God Designates Work for His Children to Do

One of the sad states in life is that *before* we come to Jesus, we are all without personal merit before God: "All our righteousness [our best deeds of rightness and justice] is like filthy rags or a polluted garment" (Isa. 64:6 AMP). But it is not God's plan that we stay that way. His desire is to redeem us from the contamination of our world. Part of His plan to accomplish our redemption from the world's corruption is work that He has established to us that will bless us and others and will glorify God: "For we are God's workmanship, created in Christ Jesus to do good works, which God prepared in advance for us to do" (Eph. 2:10 NIV).

The work God assigns to us will impact us spiritually. It will also make a difference in our world and cause the fruit of love, joy, peace, patience, kindness, goodness, faithfulness, and self-control to be manifest in our lives (see Gal. 5:16-17). It will bring us eternal reward from God (see 1 Cor. 3:11-14). Furthermore, the work God assigns to us will have a God focus, both in terms of what we do and how we do it (see Col. 3:23).

All work is not the same. We can have a strong work ethic and be admired for it. But *if our work is done without a God focus, i.e., not done in harmony with His teaching and for His glory, then we are, in effect, accumulating significance from the world independently of God.* The Pharisees were good at working, at doing things that appeared good and righteous, but they were not pleasing to God because their works were done with a "self" focus that resulted in "self" glorification. That "self" focus resulted in pride, which God hates (see James 4:6). The work we do should be done for God's glory rather than to earn the accolades our world (or even our church) gives to good, respectable people. We are to do our work for the glory of God and to let God assign our worth rather than looking to our world to grant us worth because of our good deeds. *We can develop some pretty stinky attitudes when we work for the world's or even our church's accolades but then don't get them.* Our work becomes so much simpler when we realize that we have only one to work for, our Lord Jesus, who always judges accurately and righteously and independently of what others may think.

To help us avoid misdirected work, God does a work in His children. As Paul says it, "God is working in you, giving you the desire and the power to do what pleases him" (Phil. 2:13 NLT). If we are born of God, we have a new desire to honor Him in all that we do. This new desire is accompanied by the power to do work that pleases Him and brings glory to His name. But be warned: we have no ability to do the work that pleases Him in our strength alone. Even though we may feel like we are the ones doing the work to accomplish good things, we must remember that our work is but our response to the initiative of His Spirit within us. Apart from Him, we can do nothing of spiritual and eternal significance (see John 15:5). In fact, when the Spirit of Christ is not in us, we do not even have the *potential* for doing the Father's work. *So what are we to do about our inability to truly do the Father's work?*

How Do We Accomplish the Work that Fortifies Our "Oneness" with God?

Jesus taught us this: "He who abides in Me, and I in him, bears much fruit; for without Me you can do nothing" (John 15:5 NKJV). We must focus our efforts on drawing close to Him, on abiding in Him, on making our union with Him vital (the source of life). *Our eternal potential lies totally within God's heart "for" us*: (1) *with His desire* that we would spend eternity in His presence, (2) *with His drawing* of us toward Himself, (3) *with His redeeming of us* from the curse of sin so that we might spend eternity in His Holy presence, and (4) *with His placing of His Holy Spirit within us* to empower us to share in God's kingdom work on earth so that we might join the Spirit and the Son in oneness with the Father. Remember, Jesus taught us to pray, "Thy kingdom come, Thy will be done in earth, as it is in heaven" (Matt. 6:10 KJV). Either Jesus was spoofing us by teaching us to pray in this way, or else we are able to do far more than we think, but don't, because we are deceived by the fallen world. Jesus doesn't spoof believers!

Before we are saved, we can do nothing of eternal significance. But once we are saved, we have tremendous potential for doing God-honoring and God-directed work, potential that is realized by spending the rest of our lives "loving Jesus back" and by "walking after the Spirit." It is of the utmost importance that we love Jesus back. It would be a sad and unnecessary state for our marriages on earth if our spouse loved us sacrificially, but we loved only selfishly in return. The same is true of us as the brides of Christ. I believe that God, in His grace, does not want any of us to be without personal merit when we go to be with Him after our earthly life ends. He desires for each of us to have the satisfaction of looking into the face of Jesus for all of eternity knowing not only the extent to which Jesus has loved us, but also the joy of having sacrificially loved Jesus back through doing works in His Name while we are His bride on earth. Thus, He prepares a way for us to achieve eternal satisfaction by fulfilling our potential. God's desire for us is not only that we ponder the greatness of His love for us, but also that we eternally know the joy that is potentially ours through "walking after the Spirit" and loving Him in return.

We are recreated in Christ Jesus for good works. "For we are God's [own] handiwork [His workmanship], recreated in Christ Jesus, [born anew] that we may do those good works which God predestined [planned beforehand] for us [taking paths which He prepared ahead of time], that we should walk in them [living the good life which He prearranged and made ready for us to live]" (Eph. 2:10 AMP). Because we have His Spirit within us to empower us, we who are believers can now do works that bring eternal honor to His name. Before we were united with Him, we could do nothing of eternal spiritual significance (see John 15:5).

The Word speaks often of crowns that believers can earn on earth through their work "in Christ" (see 1 Cor. 9:25, Phil. 4:1, 1 Thess. 2:19, 2 Tim. 4:8, James 1:12, Rev. 2:10). Revelation 4:10-11 suggests that we will one day be blessed by bowing at Jesus's feet and experiencing the eternal joy of laying before Him the crowns we have won. By so doing, we will be gratefully declaring to Him our love and His worthiness of all the work we have done to return His love. *We return His love by loving others in the ways He would have loved them were He still on earth in a human body.* I believe this is why Jesus teaches us of treasures in heaven. What greater treasure could there be than the eternal pleasure we will gain through honoring our Lord by the way we have loved Him back in the way we have represented Him to mankind? *To be able to look into His eyes with the knowledge that He has loved us and that we have also loved Him in return will be a priceless treasure to us.*

For our sakes, Jesus was encouraging us to love Him back when He said, "Do not store up for yourselves treasures on earth, where moth and rust destroy, and where thieves break in and steal. But store up for yourselves treasures in heaven, where moth and rust do not destroy, and where thieves do not break in and steal. For where your treasure is, there your heart will be also" (Matt. 6:19-21). We see through this verse that our work is to be a matter of the heart. *It is hard to have a heart for Christ if we spend little time returning love to Him, for then our affections will be elsewhere.*

Paul speaks to this idea of work that brings eternal reward (treasure in heaven) in his letter to the church at Corinth. There he declares,

> By the grace God has given me, I laid a foundation as an expert builder, and someone else is building on it. But each one should be careful how he builds. For no one can lay any foundation other than the one already laid, which is Jesus Christ. If any man builds on this foundation using gold, silver, costly stones, wood, hay or straw, his work will be shown for what it is, because the Day will bring it to light. It will be revealed with fire, and the fire will test the quality of each man's work. If what he has built survives, he will receive his reward. If it is burned up, *he will suffer loss;* he himself will *be saved, but only as one escaping through the flames.* (1 Cor. 3:10-15 NIV; emphasis mine)

I can't help but believe that the "loss suffered" in Paul's last sentence in this passage above will include the loss of the personal satisfaction we could have achieved by loving others as Jesus would have loved them. We have only this lifetime to be made ready to meet Him face-to-face. It would be awful if, when we finally see Him face-to-face, we would appear before Him as one who has "escaped the flames of hell" through Jesus's severe suffering on our behalf, and yet also know that we have done little work on earth to show Him our love in return. Perhaps that is what the apostle John was referring to when he wrote, "Now, little children, abide in Him, so that when He appears, we may have confidence and not shrink away from Him in *shame* at His coming" (1 John 2:28 NASB; emphasis mine). How selfish can we get? Clearly seeing the splendor and unselfishness of Christ's love for us along with only meager attempts on our part to love Him back would be totally humiliating—a tragic waste of the potential that is ours via the Holy Spirit. Our Lord deserves far better from us. May we learn to "walk after the Spirit" and fulfill the potential that is ours "in Christ" – for our sakes and to His glory!

God's Help in Meeting Our Need to Love Jesus Back

Because of His love for us and His desire that we have personal dignity before Him, God has provided a way for us to do work that will earn us eternal reward. There is a problem, though, in doing this work. Jesus said it this way: "I am the vine; you are the branches. If a man remains in me and I in him, he will bear much fruit; apart from Me you can do nothing" (John 15:5).

Since "apart from Him we can do nothing," Jesus provided a way for the believer to always be with Him. He sent the Holy Spirit as another comforter so that He (Jesus) might always be with the believer. In fact, it is in the verses *immediately preceding* Jesus's warning to His disciples that "apart from Me you can do nothing" that Jesus teaches of the promised Holy Spirit Who would take His place on earth:

> If you love me, you will obey what I command. And I will ask the Father, and he will give you another Counselor to be with you forever—the Spirit of truth. The world cannot accept him, because it neither sees him nor knows him. But you know him, for he lives with you and will be in you. I will not leave you as orphans; I will come to you . . . . If anyone loves me, he will obey my teaching. My Father will love him, and we will come to him and make our home with him . . . . All this I have spoken while still with you. But the Counselor, the Holy Spirit, whom the Father will send in my name, will teach you all things and will remind you of everything I have said to you.

Peace I leave with you; my peace I give you. I do not give to you as the world gives. Do not let your hearts be troubled and do not be afraid" (John 14:15-18, 23, 25-27 NIV).

Here is man's dilemma: if we are to be able to do the works that will bring eternal reward, then we must obey God's commands. But we can't obey with our own strength alone. How many times have you failed to live up to your own spiritual good intentions? Because of our weaknesses, Jesus sent us the Holy Spirit so that we might share in His strength by choosing to "walk according to the Spirit." "For what the Law could not do, weak as it was through the flesh, God did: sending His own Son in the likeness of sinful flesh and as an offering for sin, He condemned sin in the flesh, so that the requirement of the Law might be fulfilled in us, who do not walk according to the flesh but according to the Spirit" (Rom. 8:3-4 NASB).

Flesh: **The Enemy within Us that Opposes God's Spirit in Us**

God provided a means for us to keep the Law by giving us the ability to "walk by the Spirit." But there is a very real and severe problem we must deal with that contends against our choice to "walk by the Spirit." Paul identifies this problem in his letter to the Galatians.

But I say, walk by the Spirit, and you will not carry out the desire of the flesh. For the flesh sets its desire against the Spirit, and the Spirit against the flesh; for these are in opposition to one another, so that you may not do the things that you please (Gal. 5:16-17 NASB).

Our problem in being able to choose to "walk by the Spirit" is our *flesh*. Actually, *flesh* is an even worse problem than it is presented to be in this Galatians passage. In his letter to the Romans, Paul declares, "The mind set on the *flesh is death*, but the mind set on the Spirit is life and peace, because the mind set on the *flesh is hostile toward God*; for it *does not subject itself to the law of God*, for it *is not even able to do so*, and those who are in the *flesh cannot please God*" (Rom. 8:6-8 NASB; emphasis mine).

What is this thing called *flesh* that sets its desire against the Spirit, is hostile to God, brings death to us, and renders us utterly incapable of pleasing God? Obviously, flesh is the stuff hanging around our bones. But that couldn't be what Paul is speaking of. Think of *flesh* in terms of your physical brain. The physical brain, per se, is not the problem. The problem lies in the way our brains have been programmed by this fallen world. This fallen world has shaped our thinking. *Think of flesh as our state of mind that is the result of this fallen world's programming of our brains.*

Because of the way our *flesh* has been programmed, *mankind now tends to seek his identity, to discover who he is, in terms of this fallen world rather than through relationship with God.* Flesh naturally focuses on the fallen world in its search for life's meaning and purpose. *Flesh* wants to fit in, to be accepted by this world in which we live. Two very significant aspects of the *image of God in man* have been perverted by *flesh*: our sense of "self" and our ability to be independent of sin. First, God gave us a sense of self so that, knowing that God wishes to restore His image in us and knowing the wonderful way He has honored us by placing us "in Christ," we could choose to honor others as He has honored us. But fallen man's sense of "self" is perverted and now seeks to gain honor from others rather than to give honor to others. Second, man was created independent so that He might choose to honor God first and foremost over all other persons and things and thus be blessed. But now, this gift of independence is perverted. It has become world honoring, seeking independence from God. *Originally, man was made in God's image and was to find his primary identity in his relationship with God. But now, he naturally seeks his primary identity through his relationship with the world.* (This paragraph will be discussed in greater detail in the next chapter.)

A State Worse Than Spiritual Darkness

Our *fleshly* attempts to gain our identity through conforming to the fallen world and its deceptions are bad and an affront to our Creator, but the Bible speaks of an even worse state than our seeking of identity from the world. The "even worse state" is seeking our identity partly from this world and partly from God. Jesus spoke clearly of this through parable in the sixth chapter of Matthew. May we have ears to hear what Jesus is saying.

> The eye is the lamp of the body. If your eyes are good, your whole body will be full of light. But if your eyes are bad, your whole body will be full of darkness. If then the light within you is darkness, how great is that darkness! (Matt. 6:22-23 NIV)

This verse is a play on words. Consider the context: the Greek word translated *good* in the phrase *if your eyes are good* literally means "if your eyes are single." Jesus has just said, "Be careful not to do your 'acts of righteousness' before men, to be seen by them. If you do, you will have no reward from your Father in heaven" (Matt. 6:1 NIV). In other words, Jesus is saying we must strive to be "God" pleasing rather than "man" pleasing. Jesus repeats this same message five more times in the verses that follow. All five of these are part of the introductory context to the twenty-second and twenty-third verses above. The first three are illustrations: giving (vv. 2-4), praying (v. 5), and fasting (vv. 16-18). With each of these illustrations, Jesus is stressing that if we seek to please man when we do these things, then we should seek to please man very well because our Father in heaven will no longer have interest in rewarding us for them. This is because our spiritual-looking attempts are focused on pleasing man, i.e., doing spiritual-looking things for man's approval rather than for God's. He follows these warnings by giving the same message through two parables. The first parable in verses 19-21 warns mankind to "not lay up for ourselves treasures on Earth but in Heaven" (v. 19). Why is that? It is because in the end, we have only one to please, the One who will judge all of our works—our Father in heaven. *In the end, it doesn't matter what man thinks of us.* The continual emphasis in this sixth chapter of Matthew that precedes the parable we are considering is that we are to strive to be God-pleasers rather than man-pleasers.

What Jesus is saying in this parable on the eye being the lamp of the body is a play on words. "If your eye is good [*single* in the literal Greek, i.e., knowing that you have only One to please], your whole body will be full of light [the light that comes from God]" (my paraphrase of verse 22). The good eye that brings true light (i.e., God's truth) to the body is the "single" eye. *We have only One we must please*—not God *and* man, but God only.

But that is not the point of this parable. It goes deeper than that. The point is "if then the light within you is darkness, how great is the darkness" (v. 23). Bad eyes leave us in darkness. But the greater darkness is to blend light from God with darkness from the world, to mix the two together. Following this parable is Jesus's warning conclusion to the first twenty-three verses. "No one can serve two masters; for either he will hate the one and love the other, or he will stand by and be devoted to the one and despise and be against the other. You cannot serve God and mammon [deceitful riches, money, possessions, or whatever is trusted in]" (Matt. 6:24 AMP). Jesus's point is clear. We are to live our lives to please God alone. If we try to gain the pleasure of both God and this world, we will live in *greatest* darkness, confused by mixed allegiances, stressed, and deceived. We have One to please. His name is Jesus. His name is *not* "the world." Everything you add to the "One" only complicates life and waters down true faith.

The Complication of Stinking Thinking (i.e., *Flesh*)

A significant problem with our thinking is that many of our basic beliefs have been formed during our impressionable childhood, a time when our thinking was immature and self-focused. Thus, adult man has much "stinking thinking" that was developed at a young age, thinking that now distorts the way he perceives his adult self and God. These basic beliefs formed during childhood have great influence on our adult self-perceptions. I can't reference the source, but I remember being taught in Psychology 101 in college that 80 percent of a child's personality is formed by the child's fifth year.

Furthermore, we tend to be "believing" critters rather than rational critters, and sometimes even to the extent that some of our present beliefs are irrational. An extreme example of this is anorexia. Girls, women, and some men literally starve themselves to death because they are convinced (believe) they are fat when they are actually emaciated. Anorexia is an extreme example, but there are irrational beliefs in many of us, if not all, that are not so extreme. Adults may still believe the curse from the mouth of a parent who, in a state of anger, called them worthless or dumb or told them they would never amount to anything. Children who have experienced rejection often tend to expect rejection as adults and to inaccurately read rejection into situations. More will be said about this in the chapter 5, "Handling Rejection in Christ."

Most of us like to *think* we are rational thinkers. To some extent, that is true. But it is also true that we are prejudiced, and prejudice is sometimes immature and irrational. We have strong beliefs and make presuppositions. What we believe can be distorted by childhood misperceptions. Furthermore, much of what we do is not carefully thought out. Instead, it is a reflex action. Consider your experiences in learning to drive a car. Your initial attempts involved much thought, some confusion, and most likely the emotional interjection of the thoughts and feelings of your driving instructor into your brain, especially if your driving instructor was one of your parents. Initially you thought, *How far do I turn the wheel? And which way?* But now, you probably have it down pretty good. You no longer drive thoughtfully, but reflexively. You don't think about how to drive anymore. Your brain has been *programmed* to drive without having to consciously think about it. It is now reflex. In fact, your mind is more likely focused on something other than your driving. Learning is, for all intents and purposes, over. You basically drive on automatic pilot unless the weather or traffic is bad, or an unexpected event triggers you into an aware state.

We Habitually Default Back to *Flesh*

That is often the way our mind works—by reflex. Once something is well learned, we tend to function on automatic pilot. When experiencing the familiar we *react* far more than we thoughtfully respond. Reflex thinking applies to matters of faith too. Even though we have become born-again Christians, we tend to react the way we always have, often to our disappointment and sometimes to our shame. Our *flesh* (as our automatic reactions learned from the world) remains largely unchanged. It can change, but the change comes slowly just as habits die slowly. In the meantime, anytime we react rather than respond, we can find ourselves habitually doing what we have always done (or reacting as we always have). Our default mode is after the *flesh* (i.e., corrupted, deceived, warped, etc.), after the way the world has programmed our minds. *If we do not make a* conscious *choice to choose to walk according to the Spirit of Christ in us, we will find ourselves* defaulting back *to acting in the old ways.* Experiencing this defaulting can be very confusing to us if we do not understand the nature of *flesh*.

An Important Reemphasis

There is something we must not lose track of in this discussion. It is this: *our Heavenly Father is perfect and is perfectly committed to us.* Be careful not to make the mistake of misjudging God and defining Him in terms of the failures of your earthly father. All human fathers fail us in some ways, just as their fathers failed them. If we must judge, let us judge our earthy fathers by our perfect Heavenly Father rather than the Heavenly Father by our earthy fathers. We are to know our Heavenly

Father via Scripture, not via our earthly fathers. Here are some things to keep in mind during your reading of this chapter:

1. Our Heavenly Father is totally committed to His children. He does not love us in accordance with what we do. He has adopted us into His family and could not be more committed to loving us than He already is. Furthermore, He loves us with the same love He has for Jesus (see John 17:23, 16:7; 1 John 3:1; Eph. 3:16-19).
2. We chose Him because He drew us to Himself. He sought us first (see John 6:44, 15:16, 17:2).
3. He is not passive toward us, but actively involved in our lives (see Phil. 2:13).
4. He desires that we would know His word so that He might bless our lives (see Rom. 12:2).
5. He loves us so much that He: (a) can be grieved by our actions (see Eph. 4:30, John 11:35-36); (b) laments over our rejections (see Matt. 23:36-38); (c) longs for us to return when we have gone astray (see Luke 15:17-20), and (d) rejoices when we come to our senses (see Luke 15:3-10, 21-24).

Summary to Date

We who are Christians are in union with Christ. His worth has been added onto us. We have been redefined in Him. We are to choose to "walk according to His Spirit," that is, to love Him back by walking in the light of the way we have been revalued "in Christ" so that we will reflect His values as we go about in the world. With true repentance and the ensuing "new birth" comes a heartfelt desire to walk in ways pleasing to Christ. As a result, we want to love Him back—to represent Him well as we go about in the world. But we have a most deceiving enemy. Our enemy is our *flesh*, for it has been programmed by our archenemy (Satan), this fallen world, and sin. If we are not *conscious* of who we are now as "new creations in Christ" (see 2 Cor. 5:17), then in any given moment, we can find ourselves reacting and thus *defaulting back* to old flesh patterns. We will react the way we have been programmed to act. Even though we are Christians who want to honor Jesus, we can still stink up the place, just like we used to do before we became Christians.

Let's now pictorially represent this "Summary to Date" paragraph above.

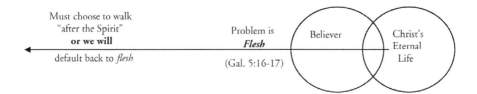

God has given His adopted children the most amazing presence and power, the person of His Holy Spirit, to dwell within us. With His Spirit comes (1) a wonderful promise: "**We can do all things through Christ who strengthens us**" (Phil. 4:13); and (2) a warning: "**Apart from Him we can do nothing**" (John 15:5). Thus, we must *choose* to let the Spirit of Christ within us express Himself through us because "**apart from Him we can do nothing**" (John 15:5).

Paul teaches us how to do this in Romans 8:6. "**For the mind set on the flesh is death, but the mind set on the Spirit is life and peace**" (NASV). In order to "walk after the Spirit," our minds must be set on (presently conscious of) our new identity "in Christ," or else we will habitually default back to the way our flesh has been programmed by the world. In one sense, choosing to "walk after the Spirit" is nothing more than obedience to the leading of the Spirit as the Spirit gives us understanding of God's Word. We are choosing to walk in new ways as God gives us new understanding rather than continuing to walk after our *fleshly* desires. Yet in another sense, "walking after the Spirit" is an empowering by God to walk in ways beyond our natural abilities. We sometimes find ourselves doing some things even though we know that we shouldn't. We need power from God to stop doing them. Perhaps this second sense of "walking" is best expressed as "walking *by* the Spirit." Both knowing how we are to walk and being empowered to walk in the new ways are necessary if we are to "walk according to the Spirit."

Will it always be this way? Not completely! Romans 12:2 teaches, "**Do not be conformed to this world, but be transformed by the renewing of your mind, so that you may prove what the will of God is, that which is good and acceptable and perfect.**" *By consciously choosing to "walk according to the Spirit," in due time we form new habits, but flesh will always be a problem. If we do not understand the problem with flesh and learn how to "walk according to the Spirit" as a means of combating* our flesh patterns, we will default back to flesh, be deceived, give up and, even though we are born-again Christians, live defeated lives. (This will be discussed in greater detail in the following chapters.)

The Foolish Galatian Warning: It's All by Faith!

Paul described a "foolish Galatian" this way:

> I do not set aside the grace of God, for if righteousness could be gained through the law, Christ died for nothing! *You foolish Galatians!* Who has bewitched you? Before your very eyes Jesus Christ was clearly portrayed as crucified. I would like to learn just one thing from you: Did you receive the Spirit by observing the law, or by believing what you heard? Are you so foolish? After beginning with the Spirit, are you now trying to attain your goal by human effort? Have you suffered so much for nothing—if it really was for nothing? Does God give you his Spirit and work miracles among you because you observe the law, or because you believe what you heard? (Gal. 2:22-3:5 NIV; emphasis mine)

Christians tend to fall into one of two errors: either we do not take our sin problem seriously enough to vigorously fight against it, or we feel hopelessly defeated by our inability to overcome sin—defeated because we have fought sin with our strength alone because we do not know how to (or sometimes want to) "walk by the Spirit." Sin is a powerful enemy that holds our *flesh* captive and causes us to do things that we really do not wish to do (see Rom. 7:8, 15-25). Sin's domination of our *flesh* is a very real problem, and faith is necessary if we are to overcome it. *Overcoming faith incorporates right thinking that is fully aware of our sin problem and knows there will be a struggle to overcome it, but also knows that the believer can prevail.* God's Word declares, "The Spirit who lives in you is greater than the spirit who lives in the world" (1 John 4:4 NLB) and "I can do everything through Christ, who gives me strength" (Phil. 4:13 NLB). When believers fail in their "walk," faith keeps believing, repenting, and receiving cleansing in accordance with 1 John 1:9: "If we confess our sins, He is faithful and just to forgive us our sins and to cleanse us from all unrighteousness." *We who are believers must know and act on the dual truths that we need help beyond ourselves and that God will supply the needed help.*

Faith keeps stepping out to obey God, doing what He asks, but also knowing that the work Christ would have us to accomplish cannot be accomplished in our strength alone. We who are believers must trust that when we step out to obey God's leading, then God's power will inhabit that step. Saul's army would not have been delivered from the rampages of Goliath if the boy David had not believed and then stepped out, hurling the stone at Goliath. Once David acted, God then empowered his action. Let us not be as the "foolish Galatians" (see Gal. 3:1) and try to "*flesh* out" spiritual work. Foolish Galatians (1) do not try what they cannot do in their own strength, (2) try to figure out their own solutions to their problems rather than seeking God's solution, and (3) are more interested in getting God to help them out with their own plans than they are in seeking to be involved in God's plans (especially when they could get hurt if they did). I heard one member of a downtown First Church say it this way: "We will always be around doing our thing, whether God is at work or not." *The greatest danger for foolish Galatians is that because they try to do God's work in their own strength, they will fail, become discouraged, and end up with watered-down faith. Kingdom work is supernatural work that God does through ordinary people who will believe and act. God then embraces the action and gives His people victory.*

A Picture of the Foolish Galatian Mentality

Below is a picture of what can happen when we are not choosing to walk after the Spirit and thus defaulting back to flesh.

"I am the Vine; you are the branches. Whoever lives in Me and I in him bears much (abundant) fruit. However, apart from Me [cut off from vital union with Me] you can do nothing" (John 15:5, AMP).

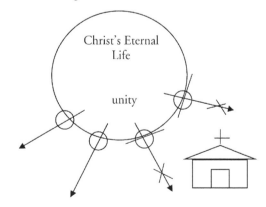

This diagram represents four Christians in union with Christ; the large circle represents Christ's eternal life (which is always available to us via the Holy Spirit), and the smaller circles represent the lives of individual believers. The directed arrows represent the goal for each believer, that being to choose to "walk according to the Spirit" and thus allow Christ-like life to be expressed through them. The two circles on the right represent two ladies who have been born-again Christians for forty years, who have been faithful in their church, and who have watched their church prosper to the point that a new church building was required. Then came the time for the carpet to be selected. The lady on the left thought it ought to be red, but the lady on the right thought it ought to be green. An argument ensued, the church took sides, and the result was a church split. Is this too far-fetched to believe? Could it happen? You know it can—and it has! The sins of individuals in the church can stimulate dissension, division, and broken relationships in the whole body of Christ. *But think about what is really going on when this happens.* Were both ladies walking "according to the Spirit"? Of course not! Their *flesh* had prejudices for red and for green, respectively. Their *flesh* had habits of controlling behavior, and *because they did not choose to "walk according to the Spirit," they defaulted back to flesh and stunk up the place.* Then the whole church body followed suit.

Though the story above has the ring of truth, it was only a made-up one. But consider a real one. The Reverend Jimmy Swaggart is a man that I believe loves the Lord deeply. As a young man, as he chose to "walk by the Spirit," God's power was displayed. Many were saved and miracles happened. The world was aware of his ministry. But then one day the world saw Rev. Swaggart fail to *choose* to "walk by the Spirit." As a result, he defaulted back to walking after his *flesh* and messed up badly. His moral failure made headline news. As far as I know, Rev. Swaggart has repented and is again walking after the Spirit. I have used him as an example only to show that even spiritual giants have *flesh* problems. Moral failures rooted in our past can happen to the best of us. They can happen to any of us and have happened to most of us, if not all. We all have *flesh* problems and we need to understand that. Even though I am a Christian, there have been times that I have walked independently of God, blocked off the flow of His Spirit through me, and stunk up the place. It has happened a lot. I'm not a betting man, but if I were, I would bet that my testimony of failure is your testimony too—even though you may have been successful at hiding your failures from the public eye. Hiding our sins is something we all try to do!

This problem of *flesh* in the believer is so severe that the unity Jesus prayed would happen among believers will occur only when one condition is met. We must get so sick of our failures and sin that we will be desperately determined to choose to "walk by the Spirit." Unless we reach that point, though unity may happen temporarily, it will quickly break down when our *flesh* biases begin surfacing.

Unity as oneness with God is an even greater problem than unity among believers. Our *flesh* not only caters to seek the misleading and deceiving blessings our fallen world baits us with, but it also tends to *use* God. *Flesh* approaches God for what we can get from Him rather than focusing on how we might be a blessing to Him. I think that if a course could be taught that could show us how to manipulate God to give us what we want, it would fill up quickly. Yet we will never discover the quality of life He pleases to give us until we learn to focus on what He wants for us. He is to be not only our Savior, but also our Lord. As long as we think we know what is best for us, we will never know God's full blessing.

Some *flesh* behaviors and attitudes do not appear as bad to the believer. In fact, we can sometimes view our *flesh* as righteous. One *flesh* pattern that I am speaking of is called prejudice. God's people are full of Methodist prejudice, Baptist prejudice, Pentecostal prejudice, nondenominational prejudice, racial prejudice, national prejudice, team prejudice, and on and on—things taught to them not by the Spirit of God, but by other persons whom they admire and want to be like. These *fleshy* biases affect understanding and perceptions of truth. Unity between persons of different denominations, races, nationalities, or sports teams is often difficult to achieve and maintain because of our prejudices. But when two Christians are walking according to the Spirit, these prejudices cease to matter. Christ alone is glorified, and they walk shoulder to shoulder in unity. "Christ in us" alone is our unity. *Flesh*, out from under the control of the Holy Spirit, will cause disunity.

Common Flesh Problems

Sylvia Gunter shares an inventory of "flesh patterns" on page 227 in her excellent book, *Prayer Portions*, which helps us to see how common and subtle negative flesh patterns can be. She lists things like

Anger	Hostility	Prone to Gossip
Anxiety	Idolatry	Rebellion to Authority
Bigotry	Impatience	Resentment
Bitterness	Impulsiveness	Restlessness
Boastfulness	Impure Thoughts	Sadness
Bossiness	Indifference	Self-Centered
Sowers of Dissension	Inferiority Feelings	Self-Confidence
Conceited	Inhibited	Self-Depreciation
Controlled by Emotions	Insecurity	Self-Gratification
	Jealousy	Self-Hatred
Controlled by Peers	Loner	Self-Pity
Covetousness	Low Self-Discipline	Self-Righteousness
Critical Tongue	Low Self-Worth	Self-Sufficiency
Deceitfulness	Materialistic	Sensuality
Depression	Negativism	Slowness in Forgiving
Dominance	Nervousness	Stubbornness
Envy	Opinionated	Too Quick to Speak
False Modesty	Overly Quiet	Unforgiveness
Feelings of Helplessness	Overly Sensitive	Vanity
	Overly Submissive	Withdrawal
Feelings of Rejection	Passivity	Workaholic
Gluttony	Prejudice	Worrier
Greed	Pride	
Hatred	Projecting Blame	

Each one of these items in the above list is a learned behavior or attitude that is fortified by strong, controlling emotions that have become an enemy of the activity of God's Holy Spirit in us. These all contend against the Spirit and can keep us from walking after His Spirit. You might want to circle the flesh patterns in the list above that you feel may be resident in you. But be sure to think of these as areas in your life where God wants to give you freedom, not as areas of God's condemnation.

God is not in the business of condemning His children (see Rom. 8:1-2). My prayer for you as I write this is that you will find God's help for walking out of these behaviors (*flesh* patterns) as you read through this book.

Adding color into Our Diagram

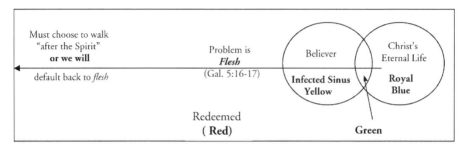

I think it would be helpful to you to add color to the developing diagram above. The purpose of the diagram is to place in picture format what it means to both be "in Christ" and to have "Christ in us." Color the circle labeled Christ's Eternal Life blue and, because He is the Lord of Lords and King of Kings, color His circle the royal shade of blue. Likewise, color the circle labeled Believer yellow and, so that it can adequately portray *flesh*, color it an infected-sinus shade of yellow (because we can really stink up the place even though we are Christians). I chose blue and yellow because when they intersect we have green, which connotes the appearance of "life." There is a greening up of our *flesh* when it intersects with the Spirit of Christ. Obviously, as we become more accomplished at "walking after the Spirit," the green area will cover more area in the believer, so think of it as dynamic and expanding. In Romans 12:2, Paul calls what I have pictured as the "greening of the *flesh*" the "renewing of the mind." This renewing happens when we choose to subject flesh to the leading of the Holy Spirit. *Theologically, we could call this "greening up of flesh" progressive sanctification. Practically, it is the tearing down of strongholds in our flesh that block the flow of Christ's Spirit through us.*

There are strongholds in everyone's *flesh* (strongholds of pride, shame, addictions, poor self-worth, etc. See Gunter's list of "flesh problems" in the section of this chapter that immediately precedes this diagram). Think of these strongholds as providing Satan a handle by which he is able to gain a strong hold on our lives, a grip strong enough that he can use it to figuratively sling us around, deceiving us and enticing us to stink up our world. Paul describes the fight against these strongholds in his second letter to the Corinthians: "We are human, but we don't wage war as humans do. We use God's mighty weapons, not worldly weapons, to knock down the strongholds of human reasoning and to destroy false arguments. We destroy every proud obstacle that keeps people from knowing God. We capture their rebellious thoughts and teach them to obey Christ" (2 Cor. 10:3-5 NLT).

We must think of these "strongholds" as old thought patterns that cause unholy reactions to the world's stimuli. Choosing to walk "after the Spirit" begins tearing down these strongholds in our minds so that Christ's Spirit may flow unimpeded through our lives into our world. Literally, "the greening effect" is the knocking down of these strongholds that have allowed Satan freedom to cause havoc (sin) in our lives. In order for strongholds to be demolished, we must learn to (1) recognize these *flesh* patterns (strongholds), (2) call them what they are (deceptions of Satan that enslave us to do his will), (3) repent (turn away from them and seek to honor Christ alone), and (4) step out to obey Christ. When we step out in faith and choose to seek to demolish these strongholds by choosing to "walk by the Spirit," we will then begin experiencing the Holy Spirit tearing down our strongholds and empowering our walk.

A Big Deception: Green Flesh Can't Walk the Walk Either

When we are viewing this diagram, we must not forget one very important thing: *green flesh cannot walk the walk any better than our contaminated, infected-sinus-yellow flesh.* Only "Christ in us" can walk the walk. "'Not by might nor by power, but by my Spirit,' says the LORD Almighty" (Zech. 4:6). The Spirit of Christ must flow through us as we *choose* to honor Him—as we step out to obey Him. It is then that we will experience the Holy Spirit empowering us to walk down a Christ-honoring path.

When we choose to "walk by the Spirit" so as to tear down strongholds, we are not perfecting our *flesh,* but rather freeing it of the clutter that hinders the flow of the Holy Spirit through us and out into our world. We make a big mistake when we pray and ask the Lord to zap us, i.e., perfect our *flesh.* That is just *flesh* praying for *flesh.* One of the characteristics of *flesh* is that it wants to look good and never to look bad. But *flesh* will not ever be perfected. We must not pray for our *flesh* to be made perfect, but instead pray for our perfect dependence on His Spirit in us. If God just zapped our *flesh*, we would only have a whole bunch of independent "good" people walking around. There would not be unity, and God would not be in control. We would still be in control. We would still be existing at a level far beneath the "oneness with Him" that Jesus prayed believers would experience, and we would probably still be full of ourselves. *Zapping flesh is not the solution to man's sin problem—dependence on the Spirit is.*

We must depend on the Spirit of God to set Himself against our flesh so that we might not do that which we please (see Gal. 5:16-17), for "apart from Him we can do nothing" (John 15:5). We need to join Paul in depending on Christ alone for our righteousness, being "found in Him, not having my own righteousness, which is from the law, but that which is through faith in Christ, the righteousness which is from God by faith" (Phil. 3:9). The Pharisees had spiritual-looking strongholds in their *flesh* that looked good on the outside but were putrid in the eyes of Jesus. Righteousness that is seemingly acquired independent of the work of the Holy Spirit in and through us easily becomes distorted into the pride that God opposes (see James 4:6). Pride then issues forth in judgmental attitudes toward others, stimulating us to "look down our noses" at people who fail to measure up to our standards. We should weep for the lost and the weak, not judge them.

Finally, the whole diagram needs to be shaded blood red, indicating believers are redeemed people. Christ came to redeem us, to set us free from the power and contamination of sin, not to judge us. "For God did not send the Son into the world in order to judge [to reject, to condemn, to pass sentence on] the world, but that the world might find salvation and be made safe and sound through Him" (John 3:17 AMP). When we fail, our failure is covered with the blood of the Lamb who takes away the sin of the world (see John 1:29 NASB). God is our encourager. As our loving Abba Father, when we stumble and fall in our attempt to "walk after the Spirit," He picks us up, dusts us off, and sets us to walking again. He is not focused on our failures, but rather on helping us to overcome sin.

We must learn how to "walk according to the Spirit," but we must understand our *flesh* patterns if we are to be able to do that. Our acknowledgment of our *flesh* problem should then cause us to desperately strive to "walk according to the Spirit." But we will not eliminate our *flesh* problem; instead, we must overcome our *flesh* by choosing to "walk by the Spirit." Our flesh is intended by God to keep us on our knees, for it is there that we are powerful. Pray not for perfect *flesh*, but for perfect sensitivity to the Holy Spirit. We serve a *living* Savior Who is ever ready to lend His strength through the Holy Spirit and Who even covers our sin when we fall. Our walk must be one of complete dependence on the Spirit. *Our desire to be independent and self-sufficient in matters of piety flows out of our flesh and is an enemy of both ourselves and God.*

It Is Not About Looking Good, but About Being Available!

Life in Christ is not about walking perfectly. It is about being available to Christ. Often, God uses our *fleshly* failures to get our attention so that He can bless us by accomplishing His work through us. That is what happened to Isaiah.

> In the year that King Uzziah died, I saw the Lord seated on a throne, high and exalted, and the train of his robe filled the temple. Above him were seraphs, each with six wings: With two wings they covered their faces, with two they covered their feet, and with two they were flying. And they were calling to one another: "Holy, holy, holy is the LORD Almighty; the whole earth is full of his glory." At the sound of their voices the doorposts and thresholds shook and the temple was filled with smoke. "Woe to me!" I cried. "I am ruined! For I am a man of unclean lips, and I live among a people of unclean lips, and my eyes have seen the King, the LORD Almighty." Then one of the seraphs flew to me with a live coal in his hand, which he had taken with tongs from the altar. With it he touched my mouth and said, "See, this has touched your lips; your guilt is taken away and your sin atoned for." Then I heard the voice of the Lord saying, "Whom shall I send? And who will go for us?" And I said, "Here am I. Send me!" (Isaiah 6:1-8 NIV)

"Here am I. Send me!" This response of Isaiah is the essence of walking after the Holy Spirit—being available to God so that Christ might express His heart through us as we choose to operate as His ambassadors to this world. At a minimum, God's will is that we represent Christ everywhere we go. Some do receive a special calling from God to go to places to which they would not go were they not called, but all of us are called to represent Christ as we go about in our world. We must understand our *flesh* problems that make us unavailable to God as we go about in our world, for they render us ineffective as witnesses and ambassadors. "Walking by the Spirit" is God's plan to loose us from the pull of the world so that we are available to Him and are empowered to represent Him well. We can do His will on earth, right now, if we will learn to "walk by the Spirit."

Summary of Chapters 1 and 2

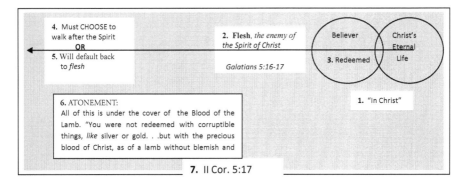

Let's try to pull the first two chapters of this book together by asking anew, "I am a Christian, but just who am I?" (The numerals below correspond with the diagram above.)

1. *You are as Mrs. Christ*, in union with Christ, the possessor of all that is His, made righteous, indwelt by His Spirit, adopted into God's family, and dearly loved. You are "in Christ"!
2. But *you have a flesh problem*. Your *flesh* sets itself against God's Spirit Who dwells in you. But even though He is within you, you still must *choose* to walk according to the Spirit in order for the Spirit to set Himself against your *flesh* so that you might not do that which your *flesh* pleases to do (see Gal. 5:16-17).
3. *You are redeemed*. When you fall, God does not condemn you but encourages you, covering your failure with His blood. That is why the whole diagram is shaded red, for our walk is established in a field of blood. Walking is a learned process, perfected by trial and error and full of bumps and failures until we master it. We all need encouragement and help, someone to pick us up and dust us off when we fail, and then

to encourage us to get going again. God has done that for us, allowing us to experience the life of Jesus so that we might know Him and imparting the indwelling Holy Spirit so that we might obey Him.
4. *You must choose to walk according to the Spirit.* You walk according to the Spirit by faith, by choosing to believe that Christ is in you and will prevail when you choose to walk in obedience to His Word, trusting His Spirit's empowerment to accompany your choice to step out in faith. That's what David did.
5. *You will find yourself defaulting back to flesh* if in times of temptation you are not presently conscious of who you are "in Christ." God does it this way so that we will depend on the Spirit. We need His help. Old habits die slowly.
6. *God is still committed to you when you fail.* You are His child. When you fail, He is still "for" you. "If we confess our sins, he is faithful and just and will forgive us our sins and purify us from all unrighteousness" (1 John 1:9 NIV). When you fail, the Holy Spirit convicts you to repent, believe, and confess your sins so that you may be purified from your acts of sin. Satan, the one who wants to destroy you, is the one who condemns—not God. Which of the two will you believe?
7. *This whole diagram is a picture of 2 Cor. 5:17:* "If anyone is in Christ, he is a new creation; old things have passed away; behold, all things have become new." You are a new creation—"in Christ." Your old relationship with the world has passed away. You are now a citizen of heaven: "But our *citizen*ship is in heaven. And we eagerly await a Savior from there, the Lord Jesus Christ" (Phil. 3:20). This is truth, but it must be walked out in faith by the power of the Spirit before it will shape us.

Knowing that I am "in Christ" and understanding my *flesh* problem, along with God's provision for it in the Person of the Holy Spirit, has finally enabled me to walk in victory! Understanding these two things was what was lacking for me, the something I testified I was missing in the introductory chapter. I pray that as you continue to read this book you too will find His grace sufficient for your every need. As you will see, He is Lord of our problems too, causing all things to work together for our good to grow us into Christlikeness (see Rom. 8:28-29)!

My prayer is that you are beginning to see yourself as a believer quite differently. The world gives you a totally different picture of yourself than the one God draws for you in His Word. It is very difficult for us to continually act and think differently until we clearly see what God has done to enable us to do so. The true faith that pleases God starts with right thinking (believing in the merits of Christ's work on our behalf) and is then followed by right acting (righteousness), acting made possible through God's provision of the Holy Spirit to indwell each believer.

We are "in Him," and He is "in us." If you are a Christian, you are greater than you know! Before you read the next chapters, I pray you will take to heart Paul's prayer for believers:

> For this reason I kneel before the Father, from whom his whole family in heaven and on earth derives its name. I pray that out of his glorious riches he may strengthen you with power through his Spirit in your inner being, so that Christ may dwell in your hearts through faith. And I pray that you, being rooted and established in love, may have power, together with all the saints, to grasp how wide and long and high and deep is the love of Christ, and to know this love that surpasses knowledge—that you may be filled to the measure of all the fullness of God. Now to him who is able to do immeasurably more than all we ask or imagine, according to his power that is at work within us, to him be glory in the church and in Christ Jesus throughout all generations, for ever and ever! Amen. (Eph. 3:14-21 NIV)

Things You May Ponder and Discuss with Others

1. When Jesus prayed that all believers would be "one" with the Father and Himself (see John 17:20-23), exactly what was He asking the Father for?
2. How has "life" worked out for you as you have sought to find identity through conforming to the world's standards and ideas? Are you satisfied?
3. Do you tend to try to get God involved in your agenda, or are you aware of and caught up in His agenda? Examine the way you pray as a means of determining this.
4. What do you think about the idea of accepting God's valuing of you as your true worth? What would you need to do differently

in order to start seeing your worth through His eyes, seeing yourself as "in Christ"? Who and what would you need to quit looking to as a means of personal worth so that you might fully receive the worth God wants to grant to you?

5. Looking back at the section in this chapter titled "Common Flesh Problems," which patterns did you circle as applicable to you? Again, as you acknowledge these flesh patterns, remember that there is no condemnation for those who are "in Christ" (see Rom. 8:1). The circling is only done so that we might recognize the flesh patterns that we need to overcome by the Spirit.

6. When you were born again and adopted into the family of God, heaven rejoiced over you.

   a. What do you think about the ideas that God could not love you more than He already does and that He could not be more committed to you than He already is?
   b. How do you think God feels when you are hurt, when you fail, or when you sin?
   c. Why does God discipline you? What forms does His discipline take?

7. How committed is God to helping you grow up spiritually?
8. Why does God want you to be a person of faith?
9. What things have happened to you that have hindered your receiving as truth God's revaluing of you when He placed you "in Christ" so that you might walk in the light of this glorious new identity?
10. Why does God want you to (a) succeed in your Christian walk, and (b) choose to be a worker in His kingdom?
11. Why does God want believers to "walk by the Spirit"?
12. What is your greatest hindrance in walking "by the Spirit"?
13. What areas of your *flesh* most strongly battle against the work of the Holy Spirit in you? What choices do you need to make so that the Holy Spirit will prevail?
14. How will knowing that you are redeemed by the blood of the Lamb be an encouragement to you in your Christian walk?
15. What have you learned in these first two chapters that you think will be the most helpful in enabling you to "walk by the Spirit"?

PART II

How to Experience God's Help When You Are Hurting or Struggling

CHAPTER 3: LIVING IN THIS WORLD "IN CHRIST"

WE ALL BEGIN looking for our true identity through this fallen world. It is the natural place for persons of flesh and blood to look for identity. As earth critters, we naturally compare ourselves to other earth critters to know who we are. After all, others have done that to us, i.e., compared us to others and then judged us in terms of how we measure up in those comparisons. Why wouldn't we do the same? We tend to copy other earth critters because we desire their affections. We want to fit in, and after all, that is what everybody does—or so we think.

Surprisingly, the apostle John found this idea of finding identity through the world's eyes to be repugnant. He wrote, "Do not love the world or anything in the world. If anyone loves the world, the love of the Father is not in him. For everything in the world—the cravings of sinful man, the lust of his eyes and the boasting of what he has and does—comes not from the Father but from the world. The world and its desires pass away, but the man who does the will of God lives forever" (1 John 2:15-17 NIV). James is even more adamant than John in insisting that we should not look to the world for our identity. He writes, "You adulterous people, don't you know that friendship with the world is hatred toward God? Anyone who chooses to be a friend of the world becomes an enemy of God" (James 4:4 NIV). What is their problem? Why are such strong words written against finding our identity from the world?

In the first two chapters, we asked "Who am I?" and looked to Christ for the answer. In this chapter, we will be asking the same question but will look to the world we live in for the answer. We will also contrast what the world teaches us about ourselves with what God's Word teaches us about ourselves.

Identity Crises

I count myself among the fortunate because my identity crises have come after childhood. For many, identity crises start much earlier than that and create lifelong confusion. I had a good start—loving parents, accepting friends, and natural abilities that gave me a sense of worth. My first identity crises came in college. I was there as the result of being awarded a football scholarship. However, that didn't work out for me. Looking back, I now see myself as having been either "too slow for my size" or "too small for my speed." But that is not the way I saw it then. I felt another player was elevated above me because he was a hometown boy. I no longer see that as true. But at that time, I needed to blame someone else for my failures so that I would be OK.

The problem was that somehow my identity was tied up in being an athlete, and that identity had now branded me a "failure." This failure affected me so severely that for a time I even rationalized that football was not a "good" game because so many players received bad injuries from playing it. It also affected my pride. I was proud of the fact that because I was on a football scholarship, my mom and dad would not have to pay for my college education. When the scholarship fell through, I refused help from them, determined to make it on my own. I developed quite a spirit of independence.

My second identity crises came after I had graduated from college, had received a master's degree in math, and had worked for five years. At the time, I was the assistant registrar at Kilgore Junior College. The understanding was that if my work proved satisfactory, the next year I would become the registrar so that the present registrar could be moved up the administration ladder. But my work was found unsatisfactory, and I was fired from that job. I wept for three days. This failure far exceeded my failure in football. It was devastating to my ego.

Who am I? If you had asked me this soon after I had been fired, I would have described myself as a failure. That was my identity. It wasn't accurate, but I didn't know that then, and that incident had a long impact on my "self" perception. I had a lingering sense of failure during my twelve years as pastor of the First United Methodist Church of Baker, Louisiana. Why? Because there were several churches that were larger and were growing faster. I asked myself, "Why those churches and not my own? What am I doing wrong? Why aren't we on the top?" Asking these questions may drive some to achieve success, but they can also drive some toward misery. Sometimes, both success and misery happen at the same time.

When men are asked who they are, they will often answer that question by telling you what they do to make a living. Others might answer that question by stating their successes in life or their education. Many women would tell you about their children. Below, in the diagram titled "Finding Identity through Our World," you will find a list of things that people commonly look to in their search for personal worth or identity. We want to be accepted and significant. We look for something that will make us secure. How do we get these needs met? We seek our identity in three places: (1) from the fallen world we live in, (2) from God Himself, and (3) from both God and the world.

Finding Worth and Significance through Our World

Somehow, our world conveys to us that we will find identity or worth through things like marriage, children, education, possessions, power, job, popularity, physical attractiveness, and affirmation. The arrows in the chart below are there to indicate that we tend to believe that these things will somehow trickle down and fill us with a sense of personal worth. Even though God's Word teaches something quite different, we who are Christians still tend to buy into this search for identity (i.e., meaning and purpose) through the world. Let's take a moment to focus on the following diagram in order to examine this idea that true and lasting acceptance, significance, and security will come to us through things like those in the diagram.

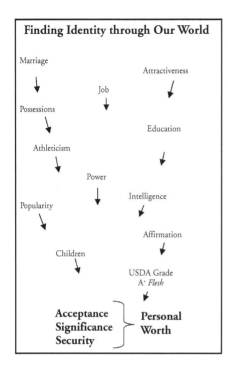

Explanation of Diagram

Suppose you were average in all of these things in this diagram to the left. Would you then gain acceptance, significance, and security? No, you would just be average—not significant. Yet we have been taught that 10% in our world excel (are A students), and the next 20% are above average (are B students). This means that 70% in our world are average or below. Thus, by this way of thinking, 70% cannot achieve any real sense of worth in this world. That doesn't sound right, does it? But that's where this way of thinking takes us. It promotes "worth" for the elite alone.

How is this working for you?

A Fading Glory

Furthermore, think about how time affects each of the things in the diagram. Do we hold our attractiveness? What happens to the worth that is derived from jobs and power positions when we retire? How long can we gain worth through our children? Do possessions really satisfy in the long term?

What happens to the significance we gain from friends and popularity when we (or they) move or even start running in different circles? What happens to our sense of worth when we move into a retirement or nursing home? Fifty percent of marriages fail. What additional percent is unhappy? How do failed or unhappy marriages affect our sense of worth? What happens to our sense of significance after the death of a spouse? The things the world normally holds up as things that would give personal worth are but a *fading glory*.

Could This All Be a Deception?

Could it also be that we are looking for worth or significance in ways that will not even produce it, but we just don't realize it? Think about it for a moment. If we buy into this diagram as a means of personal worth, we can be easily deceived. Many of us will conclude that we are not experiencing the measure of personal worth we would desire *because* we are lacking in some area; we might conclude we need more affirmation, or a better job, or more things, or children, or to lose a few pounds so we'll be more attractive, or even better, new clothes. We can work to achieve those. *But what if this diagram is a deception in the first place?* What if the things in this diagram will not trickle down and fill us with acceptance, significance, and security with the accompanying sense of personal worth we have assumed they will create?

What if this is all a deception? It would certainly be hard to realize that these things don't trickle down and produce lasting worth and significance because very few of us have all these things working for us at the level we desire. Thus, if they can't produce significant personal worth we would never know it because we will always be lacking in some area and just assume we aren't there yet. We can only conclude we need a little more of this or that rather than accurately conclude: "This just doesn't work. It doesn't produce the *worth* I am looking for."

These things do work to some extent, or they wouldn't be a deception. If they didn't have the appearance of working, we wouldn't seek after them. But even if we are partially fulfilled by this search, what happens to each of these things as time goes by? At best, the individual items in this diagram produce only a *fading* glory, even if we could attain them.

The Envied Few Who Have It All

A small number of people have been fortunate enough to have an abundance of all of the things in this diagram in their lives. King Solomon was one of those few. He intensely pursued the things of this world in his own search for personal worth and satisfaction with life and became a man of great power with huge resources. However, in his autobiographical account in Ecclesiastes, he wrote something quite interesting about his experiences in seeking significance through pursuing the things of this world:

I, the Teacher, was king over Israel in Jerusalem. I devoted myself to study and to explore by wisdom all that is done under heaven . . . . I thought to myself, "Look, I have grown and increased in wisdom more than anyone who has ruled over Jerusalem before me; *I have experienced much of wisdom and knowledge.*" Then I applied myself to the understanding of wisdom, and also of madness and folly, but I learned that this, too, is a chasing after the wind. For with much wisdom comes much sorrow; the more knowledge, the more grief. I thought in my heart, "Come now, I will test you with *pleasure* to find out what is good." But that also proved to be meaningless. They are as fruitless as chasing after the wind. "*Laughter,*" I said, "is foolish. And what does pleasure accomplish?" I tried *cheering myself with wine*, and embracing folly—my mind still guiding me with wisdom. I wanted to see what was worthwhile for men to do under heaven during the few days of their lives. *I undertook great projects*: I built houses for myself and planted vineyards. I made gardens and parks and planted all kinds of fruit trees in them. I made reservoirs to water groves of flourishing trees. I *bought male and female slaves* and had other slaves who were born in my house. I also owned more herds and flocks than anyone in Jerusalem before me. *I amassed silver and gold for myself,* and the treasure of kings and provinces. *I acquired* men and women *singers*, and a *harem* as well—the delights of the heart of man. *I became greater by far than anyone in Jerusalem before me.* In all this my wisdom stayed with me. *I denied myself nothing my eyes desired; I refused my heart no pleasure.* My heart took delight in all my work, and this was the reward for all my labor. Yet when I surveyed all that my hands had done and what I had toiled to achieve, everything was meaningless, a chasing after the wind; nothing was gained under the sun. (Eccles. 1:12-13, 16-18, 2:1-11 NIV; emphasis mine)

King Solomon had it all: wisdom, knowledge, laughter, wine, great projects, things galore, slaves, silver and gold, singers—even a harem. He denied himself nothing. Having it all, he could see through the deception of the world. It was all a "chasing after the wind," and wind is hard to catch up with. But we don't have to look only to King Solomon. Many of the world's most glamorous have had tragic endings. They seemed to have had the best the world offered, but it was "chasing after the wind" for them too. We could learn from them, but will we?

The world's way does not deliver what it promises. But we cannot see this deceit through our experiences because we are always lacking some pieces. There are always things most of us think we need to work on, or acquire, to gain the measure of life we are looking for. For all of us, there will be areas in this diagram in which we do not excel. Thus it is easy to conclude that we do not have the worth or significance we desire because we are still lacking some of the things in this diagram rather than to realize we are seeking significance through that which cannot deliver it. Then we die, still pursing this illusion that promises what it cannot deliver.

World-Based Significance Is Fragile and Can Be Lost!

There is another problem with finding worth and significance the world's way. Losing the things that have given us worth can leave us devoid of worth or give us an identity of "has-been." Our spouse can die—or a child. We can move. This can be a very hard event for some, and especially so for the children who are in school and for the spouse of the one who is relocated. We can lose our health and be forced to move from an independent to a dependent lifestyle. Any loss of a job is traumatic and can affect our lifestyle and our sense of worth. Retirement can be a very hard adjustment.

Sometimes a traumatic event can suddenly redefine our world. This happened to me when I was fired. It can happen through divorce or even the discovery that a spouse has been unfaithful. Our sense of worth and significance can be severely shaken and even lost by these life-changing events. As a result, we can feel ashamed, forsaken, or like a misfit.

A particularly damaging event in life is experiencing rape. A young woman can have everything going for her, but when she experiences rape, it is accompanied by feelings of humiliation, shame, anger, mistrust, disgust, contamination, and fear. It is a horrible indignity. Her world can come apart. Her sense of acceptance, significance, and security can be drastically altered.

God's Way of Granting Us Worth

I chose to risk offending your senses with the ugliness of rape only to help us gain a more accurate understanding of the magnificence of what God has done in order to grant to believers significance, acceptance, and security (i.e., personal worth). God has conferred on believers Christ's worth through Jesus's humiliation on the cross, a humiliation with all the earmarks of rape. Indeed, it can be thought of as the mother of all rapes. Jesus was not penetrated with a penis during His humiliation—only with a spear. Yet every other characteristic of a rape was there. He was belittled. He was used. He was spit on, laughed at, mocked, and struck. The cross was a place of humiliation and shame beyond our imagination. He was totally devalued—treated as though He were trash to be disposed of. He was nailed on a cross, which was likely no more than nine inches off the ground—at eye level. He was likely naked. The place of crucifixion was probably a public place, not a hill far away. Some would pass by and taunt him. Others would pass by and ignore him. Even worse, some probably passed by wondering what awful thing He had done that deserved crucifixion.

Why?

Why would God allow such shame and humiliation to come upon His Son? John 3:16 tells us the answer must lie in God's loving compassion for fallen man. As we saw in the first chapter, God allowed His Son to suffer on the cross so that He could transfer Jesus's worth to all who believe. Through His humiliation, believers have been declared by God to be saints, holy, blameless, beyond reproach, priests, ambassadors, etc., all of the things we saw in chapter 1 and more. "God made him who had no sin to be sin for us, so that in him we might become the righteousness of God" (2 Cor. 5:21).

Christ's Humiliation Has Become the Believer's Glory

His worth was conferred to all who believe. *Through union with Him ("in Christ"), believers have been made significant, accepted, and secure, and not just for now, but for all eternity.* As possessors of "His worth," believers have gained more significance than by any scenario that man could dream up. They have been made acceptable to even God Himself. The security of the believer lies in his union with Jesus, the Creator of the universe. The believer has a new identity.

God's plan is that the believer's need for acceptance, significance, and security are more than met "in Christ." Furthermore, the believer's personal worth "in Christ" comes through Christ's willingness to be shamefully crucified as our substitute (in our place)! Believers have a new identity; they are redefined by the cross. Christ's humiliation has become the believer's glory (see 2 Cor. 5:21)!

Summary: The believer's worth "in Christ" is glorious and eternal! On the other hand, the worth the world offers is (1) limited to a few, (2) a fading glory, at best, (3) fragile, (4) temporary (limited to our lifetime), (5) vastly inferior, producing far less valuing which is mostly limited to the prime years of our lives, and (6) a deception (it doesn't deliver what it promises).

Perhaps, you are not a believer. If so, now would be a good time to be eternally redefined "in Christ." Simply sincerely pray, "Heavenly Father, I am a sinner. I know I am unworthy of the benefits of Christ's humiliation. But I believe He is your Son, that He lived a sinless life on earth, and that His humiliation on the cross was for the purpose of being punished in my place for the sins I have done so that I wouldn't have to be punished. My sin made Jesus's death necessary. I am the guilty one. I am figuratively holding out my hands in the hope of receiving your gift of salvation through my belief that Jesus was punished for my sins so that I might live with you for all eternity. I desire to spend the rest of my life loving Jesus back by treating others the way He would have treated them were He in my shoes. Please forgive me of my sins, grant me a place in your kingdom, fill me with Your Spirit, and empower me to represent Jesus well on earth. Thank you for hearing my plea—and granting it. In Jesus's name I pray, Amen."

These Two Sources of Identity (or Worth) Will Not Mix

Satan knows that he cannot compete with the wonder of the "identity" (personal worth) that has become ours "in Christ" via the cross. So true to his nature, he tries to dilute its magnificence with another deception. Satan's deception is "the worth Jesus gives us is wonderful, but we need to add on worth from the world too." As all deceptions, this has the ring of truth, or it wouldn't be a true deception. But think about it. If it is Jesus's worth (His glory; see John 17:22) that has been transferred to us, how can it be increased? Is Jesus's worth not the ultimate? How can we possibly have more worth than that of Jesus?

But if the significance (or worth) we have been given "in Christ" cannot be increased, then any attempt to add to it will be like adding on a negative number. We can only take away from it, for what we try to add will substitute a temporary, lesser identity for the ultimate. Each substitution we then rely on for "identity" will only take away from our glorious, undeserved identity "in Christ."

The "And" Wall

The following diagram pictures *why* these two different ways of finding identity (personal worth) will not mix. Between the two sources of worth is a solid wall. I have drawn it as a brick wall and have named the wall the "And" Wall. The wall represents Satan's deception that we need Christ *and* the things of this fallen world if we are to have the greatest worth and significance. But the truth is that our greatest worth and significance (that which is true and eternal) comes only from clothing ourselves with the identity Jesus offers to all who will believe, a worth devoid of the world's contaminating clutter.

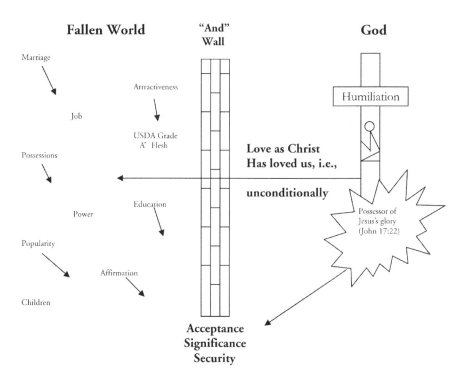

I believe Paul was speaking of the greatness of the personal worth Jesus had transferred to us (worth so great that it cannot be increased) when he wrote in his Epistle to the Philippians:

> But whatever was to my profit I now consider loss for the sake of Christ. What is more, I consider everything a loss compared to the surpassing greatness of knowing Christ Jesus my Lord, for whose sake I have lost all things. I consider them rubbish, that I may gain Christ and be found in him, not having a righteousness of my own that comes from the law, but that which is through faith in Christ—the righteousness that comes from God and is by faith. (Phil. 3:7-9)

Paul wanted no part of a sense of personal worth (or identity) that is separate from that which comes through Jesus's own humiliation on the cross. *In proportion to the extent we seek identity through the things of the world, we are robbed of knowing our ultimate identity in Christ.* Our true worth in God's eyes is not Jesus "and" anything; it is found in knowing the fullness of life that has become ours through Jesus's humiliation for our sakes, period.

The Severe Conflict

Seeking identity from "Christ *and* the world" is an exercise of severe conflict. In man's search for identity and worth, *flesh* is putty in Satan's hands. This is because *flesh's* focus is on this world where Satan reigns. Furthermore, *flesh* sets itself against the Spirit of Christ, Who is in the believer. The desires of His Spirit in us and the desires of our *flesh* are enemies (antagonistic to each other). Remember Paul's exhortation: "But I say, walk by the Spirit, and you will not carry out the desire of the flesh. For the flesh sets its desire against the Spirit, and the Spirit against the flesh; for these are in opposition to one another, so that you may not do the things that you please" (Gal. 5:16-17 NASB). *To the extent we walk after flesh, we are acting as an enemy of Christ. We need to get this truth straight in our minds.*

Transforming Our World

The last thing the diagram above depicts is that as participators in Christ's shared glory, we are to love in the world as Christ loved us, i.e., *unconditionally.* We are able to do this when we are conscious of the truth that our worth is not to come from the world but from Christ and, furthermore, that the worth Christ gives us is a far greater worth than the best the world could offer. This thinking empowers us to offer Christlike love to our world independently of the way the world treats us. The way we love is not to be a reflection of the way the world has treated us.

The "And" Wall is a deception of Satan intended to lessen believers' perception of the magnitude of the true worth God has granted them "in Christ." However, there is a proper "and" in our Christian life. We need to both look to Christ alone for our identity (worth and acceptance) and to *walk according to His Spirit*. Biblical faith never just "believes" in the modern understanding of "believe." True believing (faith) is always accompanied by seeking to "walk after the Spirit," which will result in living as we say we believe. As James says it, "So you see, faith by itself isn't enough. Unless it produces good deeds, it is dead and useless . . . . You say you have faith, for you believe that there is one God. Good for you! Even the demons believe this, and they tremble in terror. How foolish! Can't you see that faith without good deeds is useless?" (James 2:17,19-20 NLT)

We must choose to "walk after the Spirit." We must kneel in gratitude to God, acknowledge all that He has done for us by placing us "in Christ," and choose to represent Christ in this world as persons who are in the world, but not of the world. We are His ambassadors, His bride. We are to "walk after the Spirit" (Gal. 5:16): (1) *focused* on our identity "in Christ" rather than our identity from or in "the world" and (2) to be aware of our need for His power, if we are to represent Him well. Drawing on the abundance of life (significance and acceptance) Christ has given us, we are to be givers rather than takers, for the world can add nothing to who we are "in Christ." As Jesus said it, "Whoever finds his life will lose it, and whoever loses his life for my sake will find it" (Matt. 10:39). Whenever we, as Paul, (1) quit seeking life from the world ("Count it as rubbish" [Phil. 3:8]), (2) receive our worth from Christ alone, and (3) approach life in the world conscious of the worth we have "in Christ," we then experience true lasting life.

Life *lies in our union with Christ that makes us the possessors of the value (glory) that rightly belongs to Jesus alone, but glory that He has nevertheless lovingly shared with all who believe.* Accepting and walking in the light of this truth creates an intimacy with Him that is so empowering that it can stimulate us to express honor and allegiance back to Him for all eternity. The world cannot give this quality of "life." True lasting "life" comes from our union with Christ (from being "in Christ") alone. Furthermore, it is not a fading glory, but eternal!

Christians Are to Offer "Life" to the World Rather than to Seek "Life" from the World

As believers, we are to choose to let "Christ in us" transform our world experiences. *The world's way will not give true life to us, but we can share true life with our world and thus make our world better by the way we represent Christ in it.* Let me begin to explain this with an illustration from the life of my wife, Sally.

When God called me to attend seminary, Sally and I took our life's savings and placed them in an annuity that would make thirty-six monthly payments to us to help provide needed income for this time of training. Since I had extensive background with computers, we assumed I would find work to augment those savings. That didn't happen, but God faithfully provided at every point of need. Yet, when I began to pastor a church after seminary, things were tight. Since we now had only one car, which I needed for work, Sally was homebound and desired a second vehicle. To earn income to purchase a second car so she might become more mobile, Sally went to work as the church custodian. There, her most displeasing job was cleaning the restrooms. In the men's restroom there was a urinal mounted on the wall that evidently splattered urine on the floor, seemingly a common problem in all public men's restrooms. One day Sally was cleaning up the mess around the urinal, unhappily complaining about the seeming inability of men to keep from making such a stinking mess, when she sensed a word from God. Seeing Sally's unhappiness, God simply spoke to her mind. "Sally, will you start doing that job for Me?" With tears in her eyes, Sally responded that she would.

That was a transforming experience for her in the performance of that work. From then on, the time she spent cleaning that restroom was a sacrificial gift back to her Lord in response to all He had sacrificed for her. The job didn't actually change, but her attitude did, and thus the job was experienced quite differently too. *Her work had become a labor of love for her Lord.* "Christ in her" transformed the way she approached a formerly degrading job and, by so doing, also transformed her work experience. Yet that is what God's Word plainly says to all of us about the way we are to work: "Whatever you do, work at it with all your heart, as working for the Lord, not for men" (Col. 3:23 NIV).

Life Is Not to Flow from the World to Us, but from "Christ in Us" to Our World

We are to glorify God by our attitude in the way we perform work, thus choosing to let God give significance *to* our job rather than seeking significance *from* our job. Every job is important. Someone has to clean toilets or this world will become a stinking mess. Could it possibly be that your job, even if it feels like cleaning toilets, is a significant job and that you should see it as a ministry to Christ in your world rather than a means of gaining worth? Could it possibly be that *how* we do the things we do is as important as what we do? I expect we all know even pastors can do harm to the kingdom of God because of their attitudes. We also know those in seemingly lowly jobs whose attitudes bring glory to God as they daily go about their work. *Your job may not give you worth, but "Christ in you" can give worth to your job.* Do your work for Him. Our worth is to come from Him, not our job. Furthermore, the way we do our job is a declaration of the worth we have "in Him." *God's plan for Christians is that we do even menial jobs with a servant's attitude that brings glory to Him and makes this world we live in a better place.*

We must understand that we are not to seek worth from the things of the world, but instead to give worth to the things of our world by approaching them "in Christ." In so doing, everything will be experienced differently. Christ's life in us can transform our experiences in our world. Let's look at some of the other things the world offers as "life" to see how this same spiritual principle also applies to them.

Approaching Marriage "in Christ"

Because the whole next chapter deals with approaching our marriage "in Christ," I will try to be concise here. Marriages that are formed by two givers tend to be heavenly. Marriages between two takers tend to be hellish. When we "walk after the Spirit," we are givers, for we are walking like Christ. Our marriages are heartfelt. We love because we are loved, and people who perceive that they are loved just naturally love back. It's a wonderful, continuous cycle: loved people give love. God is the original giver; God loves so we can. What He gives to us, we are to give to others. When our eyes are on Him, we naturally give, and our world is transformed. But if God is not our focus, then the spirit of this world becomes our focus. In the fallen world, we experience rejection.

In the fallen world, loved people tend to love, but rejected people tend to reject.

If we are not walking "after the Spirit," we will *default back* to the ways we have learned through the fallen world. We can give for a season, but if there is no reciprocation, we tend to stop. We can give to get, but that is manipulation and will prove extremely unsatisfying in time. Eventually we all want to be wanted, and if we constantly have to manipulate our spouse in order to get love, we will become dissatisfied in our marriages. We can even become demeaning in our attempts to make the other person give us the love that we so desperately want from them. Marriages then dissolve into angry contentions. We are still living together, still legally married, but our lives together have become a farce. We are together, but we are not "together."

It was not God's intention that "life" would come through marriage. Rather, "life" is experienced when Christ's love flows through believers into their marriage relationships as they choose to "walk after the Spirit" and be love givers rather than love seekers. No matter how wonderful our spouses are, they do not make good gods. They are not perpetual "life" givers. They will run dry when "life" is continually sought from them and especially if it is not equally offered back to them. Spouses are not to be our source of "life." Good marriages are centered in giving, not getting. We must deliberately and constantly look to Christ as our source of "life." "Christ in us" must be the source of our giving. We must focus on Him (on how He has loved us), when we are choosing how to show love to our spouses because sometimes spouses (including us) just aren't very worthy of being loved. Our *flesh* guarantees that we can all be a "mess." *Life as marital bliss must flow from "Christ in us" to our marriage, not from our marriage to us.* Our marriages need to be centered on Christ—centered on loving our spouse as God through Christ has loved us. *When Christ is not our focus, but rather the performance of our spouses, then, our marriages can deteriorate. When God's love poured out to us "in Christ" is our focus, as unconditionally loved persons we are empowered to love unconditionally, and the norm is then to be loved back. All of us tend to love back those who are perceived as loving toward us.*

Personal Attractiveness "in Christ"

As we age staying attractive is hard work with increasingly fewer dividends. But should our worth come from the attractiveness or the athleticism of our bodies? Is that why God gave us bodies – to gain the world's admiration? If so, don't bother to get older, for beautiful or athletic bodies are a fading glory. (Actually, if our bodies never looked really good, then we wouldn't have to deal with the pain of becoming less attractive as we age. It is *really* hard work to keep them looking good, and discouraging, because we will never again look like we did at age twenty-one.) *Our bodies should be seen as the means by which we make the love of Christ known in our world.* When we see our bodies through God's eyes, we will take care of them but will no longer need to get our identity from them. We don't want our bodies to be repulsive, yet we are not to be defined by our bodies. *Our earth suits are not to be a means of worth, but rather a means of sharing Jesus's worth with other earth critters by the way we treat others.* People who freely give away Christ's love are often seen as beautiful, even when their earth suits aren't. Consider Mother Teresa: her earth suit was not special, yet everyone sees her as special! Her kind of beauty won't fade.

Friendships "in Christ"

Some would try to gain friends so that they might feel significant and accepted—even popular. But as persons who are already most significant and accepted "in Christ," believers can simply focus on being a friend. Amazingly, *persons who choose to be a friend attract friends.* We don't need USDA Grade A⁺ flesh to be significant. We simply need to *believe* in the worth that is already ours "in Christ," and then to act as persons of worth by loving others. Then we will discover that *people who love, encourage, and accept others tend to get loved, encouraged, and accepted in return* (see Matt. 5:46). However, this is not a way to manipulate people. This is something we do because we *are* loved and accepted in Christ, not something we do to gain love and acceptance. It is an outflow of life in Christ.

We who are believers should quit trying to get our worth from others. Instead, we should approach others in a way that values them, knowing that since we are "in Christ," we have been given worth and significance so great that it can't be added to. Others cannot give us more worth or significance than we already have "in Christ." Knowing this allows us to lose our fear of not pleasing people and frees us to be a blessing to them by loving them as Jesus would. When we are no longer needy, trying to get from others, we can freely give. "In Christ," we are persons called to be light and salt to our world. Christ in us gives life through us to our friends as we act in valuing ways toward them. *Our world comes alive and is transformed when we quit seeking life from it, but instead offer the benefits of Christ's life in us to it. "In Christ" life changes directions—we become life-sharers rather than life-takers or life-seekers.*

The things we tend to look to for life in this world are like moons. Although moons appear to be a light source, in truth, they are only reflectors of light. The things we look to in this world to light up our lives will disappoint us. They are temporary, a fading glory, and fragile. But when we approach each of these things knowing who we are "in Christ," we bring light to them that warms them, light that also reflects back to us and to others and warms us all. When the things of this world are energized by the light and life of Christ, they appear to have self-generated light. But do not be deceived. Remember that they are only reflecting back the light of Christ, the life-giver Who is in us. *God would have life to flow from the inside to the outside, from* Christ in us *out into our world. Choose to let your life change directions. Choose to offer* life *to your world rather than seek life from your world. You'll be glad you did—forever!*

"Out of This World" Worth

However, it is certainly possible that this fallen world may not attribute worth to believers and may even reject us. Because of this, it is absolutely essential that we who are Christians understand that we are citizens of heaven who belong to God. We should be looking to our Creator, alone, for our sense of worth. When we Christians look to the world to know who we are instead of to what Jesus has accomplished for us via the cross, we are belittling Jesus's sacrificial death on our behalf. In His prayer for all who would believe because of the witness of the apostles, Jesus reminded us that we have been made citizens of heaven: "They are not of the world, even as I am not of it" (John 17:16 NLB). Paul too plainly stated of believers, "Our citizenship is in heaven" (Phil. 3:20 NIV). We are citizens of heaven, sojourners on earth. Thus, we who are believers are to live our lives from the foot of the cross, gazing up at the sacrifice Jesus made for us in order to cover our sins and to transfer His worth to us. Our gaze toward His sacrificial love should be one of deep gratitude with full awareness of who Jesus has declared us to be. Jesus chose to be humiliated in order to transfer His worth to all who would believe. We are in this world, but we are no longer of this world. *We are redefined and overvalued "in Christ." This is a marvelous life-defining truth that should be reflected in all of our ways as we walk around in this temporary world.*

What Happens When We Let the Humiliating Things of This World Define Us?

As people with *flesh*, we can certainly be hurt by the world. Our minds must be renewed to think differently when we are hurt, to see life from a faith perspective. Let me share a sobering thought with you. *When we let our humiliation by the world become so large in our minds that it defines us, then we have also let Jesus's humiliation by the world become so small that it doesn't define us.* If we do not learn to think differently about our situations, then the old *fleshy* ways in which our minds have been programmed by the world will continue to give the world power to effectively override what Christ has done to redefine us. Our actions and attitudes will not flow out of Christ's love for us, but rather out of the world's hurt. When this happens, we have profaned the cross.

We may even find it easy to have a bitter attitude toward God, complaining, "If you love me, then why did you let the world treat me this way?" When we complain like that, I believe that if we had ears to hear, our Heavenly Father would lovingly reply something like this: *"My child, it was never My intention that you would gain your identity through this fallen world. I have always wanted to gloriously define you as mine. I have something much better in mind for you. Choose to be defined by my Son's humiliation by the fallen world you live in. My desire has always been that mankind would allow Me, alone, to define their worth, but they would not heed Me. Yet it is still My eternal plan that the humiliation Jesus has experienced at the hands of the world would redefine your 'self' image. I allowed Jesus to be humiliated as a means of passing His worth on to you. He suffered in your place so that you might spend eternity with Me as a person of great worth, fully knowing my love."*

Will you believe, or will you continue to let your humiliation at the hands of the world define you? *Jesus was humiliated so that He might transfer His worth to you.* Will you receive His worth as your own rather than break Christ's heart anew by declaring that if He loved you, He would not have let this humiliating thing happen to you? He does love you! He grieves over the sin running rampant in this world that has done you and others so much harm. If you will believe, He is able to redeem you from all that the world has done to humiliate you. Perhaps a more appropriate response than anger toward God would be to simply ask for God's forgiveness for your anger. Pray, *"Father, I believe. I don't deserve it, but I acknowledge by faith that you have given me worth that far exceeds anything the world could give to me. Forgive me for making my humiliation by this world so big that I let it define me and thus treated your humiliation by the world as inadequate for defining me. I have belittled the cross. Please forgive me. I choose to receive your righteousness as my own. By faith, I announce that I am "in Christ." Thank you. I pray this 'in Jesus's name,' Amen!"*

Bad things happen to good people in this world, and when they happen, we are sorely tempted to be defined by our circumstances rather than by our Lord. One of the problems is that our Father sees all things in the light of eternity, but we tend to see things in the light of this lifetime—or shorter. Because of this, even though God bestows multitudes of undeserved blessings on us for far longer than we can imagine, for eternity, we have a hard time getting our minds off *today*.

My father was a wonderful, godly man. He lived his life in service to others. Yet due to Alzheimer's disease, he had to retire prematurely from the pastorate at age sixty-two. He lived twenty-four years with that infirmity, in the end bedridden and not knowing anyone. It is a hard thing to watch this disease destroy a person's dignity. Many of God's people suffer undeserved indignities for a long time, but so does everybody else. That is a potential liability for everyone who is given life on earth. Jesus Himself warned, "In this world you will have trouble" (John 16:33 NIV). Hebrews lists in the faith Hall of Fame those who have been delivered by their faith, but also those who have been tortured and martyred in gruesome ways because of their faith (see Heb. 11:32-40).

Flesh Seeks Reward Now!

It is natural (of the *flesh*) for us to ask God to reward us immediately for the good we do. But He has chosen, instead, to overreward us for all eternity and to forgive us for the wrongs we have done. The trade-off is that we are overblessed for more than millions and billions of times longer than would be the case if blessings were in terms of this earth only. (Actually, it's better than that because eternity never ends. I cannot give you a constant multiplier that is large enough, so I just tried to give you a very large one for the sake of perspective.)

Yet we don't have to wait until eternity to be blessed. We can experience many blessings right now, *if we believe*. I know God's love now. Knowing God's love has enabled me to have faith that blesses me now in the midst of all circumstances. I love better "in Christ." I give better "in Christ."

I rejoice better "in Christ." The only thing I can't do better "in Christ" right now is sin. My marriage is better "in Christ." Friendships are better "in Christ." I have a new, blood-covered, cleaned-up *past* "in Christ." I have a far better, Spirit-led *present* "in Christ." I have a glorious *future* "in Christ." Life is far, far better "in Christ" right now – even though there is also trouble.

The Power of Praise and Thanksgiving

I experienced something wonderful while dealing with my dad's Alzheimer's disease. I discovered the power of praise and thanksgiving. God's Word tells us that praise is always in order, no matter what the circumstance: "For this world is not our permanent home; we are looking forward to a home yet to come. Therefore, let us offer through Jesus a continual sacrifice of praise to God, proclaiming our allegiance to his name. And don't forget to do good and to share with those in need. These are the sacrifices that please God" (Heb. 13:14-16 NLB). Praise in hard times may start off as a "sacrifice" of praise, but God soon makes our hearts glad, and praise then becomes easy. *Praise restores eternity to our perspective. It reminds us of who we are "in Christ." It renews the mind. It restores a spirit of thanksgiving.*

Because of the great things God has done on our behalf, it is only appropriate that we heed Paul's admonition to "pray without ceasing, in everything give thanks; for this is the will of God in Christ Jesus for you. Do not quench the Spirit" (1 Thess. 5:17-19 NLB). Praise and thanksgiving get our minds off our circumstances on earth and onto the excellencies of our Lord. It was only when I began to praise and give thanks that I found peace with Dad's disease. He is with the Lord now, and joy comes quickly with every thought of him. But in truth, He was with the Lord then. Long after he lost the ability to communicate with us (his family), he could still communicate with the Lord. He could still pray beautifully even after his communication with us no longer made sense to us. He was out of touch with us, but God was still in touch with him. The author of Hebrews expresses that truth beautifully: "God has said, 'I will never fail you. I will never abandon you'" (Heb. 13:5 NLT). In order to relate with Dad, we would sing hymns with him, softly, for he was in a nursing home. But he would sing with gusto. *He was in his right mind more than we.* Oh that we would always sing with such gusto!

Where Is the Church in This Diagram?

Which side of the "And" Wall does the church lie on? Obviously, the spiritual church is the body of Christ and thus to the right of the wall, at the foot of the cross. Churches, by divine purpose, seek to call us upward, out of worldliness and into Christlikeness.

But pragmatically, our churches are run by and attended by people who are far less than perfect. Though all who are "born again" can walk after the Spirit and represent God well, it is also true that all of us, including pastors, can default back to *flesh* and stink up the place. Our churches are made up of people who will sometimes disappoint and even hurt us, just as we sometimes act less than our best toward others and can disappoint and hurt them. Christians are a "work in progress" with some rough edges that can cut and bruise those who brush up against them. Yet our churches, because they are made up of individuals in union with Christ, will also bless us when her people "walk after the Spirit" and share their lives "in Christ" with us.

The bottom line is that we are not to look for life from the people of the church, but rather from the Christ of the church. All of us are in the church because we need God's forgiveness for the wrongs we have done and God's help if we are to stop doing wrong. We are not to look for a church with perfect people because there is none. Instead, we are to join with a group of people who need our help and care. In the church, we are to attempt to lose our "self" focus so that we might help and care for others while others are doing the same toward us. Our goal is to be the hands of Christ, members of His body, who touch one another "in Jesus's name." But we will sometimes default back to *flesh* and fail others, and others will fail us too. We're all in the same boat.

Churches are gathered people like us who have problems and need help. Our emphasis should be on helping one another grow into Christlikeness, not on being critical of others. Each of us has faults, and each of us has assets. Each of us, no matter how imperfect, has been given spiritual gifts to serve and bless our church. As Paul taught, "**Now to each one the manifestation of the Spirit is given for the common good**" (1 Cor. 12:7 NIV). The spiritual gifts the Holy Spirit has placed in "each" of us are not for the purpose of exalting ourselves or for making us look good, but rather for helping others like us who have needs that we can help to meet. God gives to us in abundance (see John 10:10b) so that we will have more than we need for ourselves and plenty to share with others.

The Word is quite clear that when we give, we get. As Jesus said, "**Even sinners love those who love them**" (Luke 6:32b NIV). We should rest "in Christ" and labor to give worth to others rather than to seek worth from others. Strive to remember always that our churches are established by God's will, but they are full of people who are a "work in progress" who very likely may not know who they are "in Christ." All of the persons in our church congregations are in the world, and unfortunately, many often act as if they are still *of* this world. We are to approach our church from the foot of the cross, offering unconditional love "in Christ" to her, doing our part to make her better. Too often, we approach our churches as criticizing "takers" when God would have us to be compassionate "givers." We must question our attitudes toward our church. Are we committed to giving our lives away to make our churches better? We must be careful not to seek "life" from our church. Our "life" comes from Christ alone, and His life is then to be expressed through us to our church, i.e., to the people who gather in the church buildings for worship. Strong churches are those who are full of people who know they have been abundantly given to by God and who want to give back to God by loving others.

As God's people, we should be focused on serving our churches rather than on looking for churches that would serve us. Personally, we must ask, "Will I look to my church to give me 'life'?" or "Will I walk after the Spirit and offer my life 'in Christ' to my church, continually choosing to be a bearer of His 'light' and 'life' to her?" Our churches will be transformed when a resounding "yes" to the second question becomes the prevailing attitude of the gathered people in our churches. Thankfully, while we are waiting for our churches to arrive at that point, we can still experience "life" in our church if we are choosing to offer Jesus's life in us to our church.

Functioning "in Christ" can make our interactions with the world a delight. We can experience His interjection of "life" into our world. Isn't that just like God—to inject new life into the ordinary? Everything in our world is made better when we are consciously aware of God's presence in us. He is the life-giver. But beware: sometimes life "in Christ" in the world can become so good that we forget the true source of the life! We must always strive to focus on the God who blesses, not the blessing.

What Will You Do?

It cost Jesus a lot to transfer His worth to us. He was stripped of everything on the cross. There, our sins were placed on His shoulders as He bore their punishment as if our sins were His own. But that is not the end of the story. He also placed His robe of righteousness on all who would choose to believe in Him for eternal life. *Will we continue to let the things of this world define us? Will we continue to be so satisfied with our status in the world that we do not bow before the cross, alone, to find our identity? Will we continue to profane the name of Christ, i.e., treat Him with irreverent commonness, which God's Word forbids?* (see Lev. 22-32). In so doing, we not only sin against the matchless Person of Jesus, but we also opt for an inferior identity to that which Christ alone would give us. Will you continue to seek Christ *and* the things of this world for "life"? You don't have to. Christ is in you. You are in Christ. You are greater than you know! Listen to Paul's prayer for you:

> I keep asking that the God of our Lord Jesus Christ, the glorious Father, may give you the Spirit of wisdom and revelation, so that you may know him better. I pray also that the eyes of your heart may be enlightened in order that you may know the hope to which he has called you, the riches of his glorious inheritance in the saints, and his incomparably great power for us who believe. (Eph. 1:17-19 NIV)

Things You May Ponder and Discuss with Others

1. What things in your life's experiences do you see as important enough to have made significant contributions in shaping your personal identity, i.e., the way you see yourself?
2. Which of the things in the "Finding Identity in Our World" diagram of this chapter have been important to you as a means of finding acceptance, significance, and security in your world? Are there others you would add? If so, what?
3. How has each of the things you identified in question 2 shaped you?
4. Have you experienced significant loss that has redefined your world? If so, what? In what ways has this loss reshaped your view of life?

5. Do you primarily see yourself as shaped by the cross or as shaped by the world? What areas do you see in your life that you have looked to as a source of life along with Christ? Have those areas truly given life to you or continually taken true life away from you? Try to explain your reasoning.
6. Has some hurt happened in your life that is so significant that you are mad at God for allowing it to happen? Is God wrong for allowing you to be hurt? Should He have protected you rather than allowing His Son to be hurt in order to give you a sense of worth that far exceeds the worth you would have if you had not been hurt?
7. Consider an area in your life that is presently causing you difficulty.

    a. How might you approach this area "in Christ," seeking to become a giver of life rather than a seeker of life?
    b. How could your attitude toward the situation change?
    c. How might you inject praise and thanksgiving to God into this situation?
    d. How is your *flesh* complicating and distorting your view of this area?
    e. Are you being personally defined in any way by what is happening, or is your identity "in Christ" defining the way you are approaching this area?
    f. How should you pray about this area? Remember: God's design is that life would flow from Christ in us to our world. If we see life as flowing from our world to us, we will not grow in faith in God, but rather in faith in our fallen world. The goal of faith, as God has designed it, is to quit expecting life from our world and to start expecting God to give us life as we "walk after the Spirit" as we go about in our world. Faith in Him should transform our life experiences in the world as we begin to see them through His eyes and follow the leading of His Spirit in the way we approach our world. We are citizens of heaven, and Christ is our life.

8. Are you looking for life from your church, or are you "walking after the Spirit" and offering Christ's life in you to your church? Examine your general attitudes toward your church.

Your attitudes will help you see how you are walking. God has gifted you to be a blessing to your church, though you must realistically understand that sometimes your "walking after the Spirit" will not be perceived as a blessing by some in your church. Nevertheless, your focus should always be on being a blessing rather than on being blessed. If you are encountering problems in your church, make your problems the subject of question 7 above.

Note: If your answers to these questions are troublesome to you, please consider making an appointment with your pastor or a Christian counselor to further consider them.

CHAPTER 4: ROOTING YOUR MARRIAGE "IN CHRIST"

THIS CHAPTER IS about making our marriages better, but it is not a comprehensive attempt to share what a Christian marriage should look like. Many things will be left unsaid. Some things that are said will not be pursued. This chapter's main purpose is to use marriage to illustrate how to effectively apply the last chapter's content to daily life. Life is to flow from "Christ in us" into our world as we go about our daily business. When our relationship with Christ defines how we approach our relationships with others, our relationships then become more precious, for they are infused with the life of Christ. Perhaps this is what Jesus meant when He said we are the salt of the world. "Christ in us" gives new, vibrant flavor to everything in our world and especially the people in our world. This is because others usually respond positively to the difference they see in us. Our world seems more alive, more fulfilling. But the source for that newness is God's honoring of us by placing us "in Christ" and empowering us to honor Christ in return as we choose to "walk by the Spirit."

This chapter is not about changing our world, although that can happen to a limited extent. It is about letting God change us so that we see and approach our world differently. When we recognize our fullness "in Christ," we are no longer driven to try to force our world to recognize us and offer life to us. Instead, we share the abundance we have "in Christ" with our world. When we do this, we have become "life" givers rather than "life" seekers. That's good, because the "life" this world offers is only a fading glory.

A Bed of Roses?

Marriage is not always experienced as a bed of roses depleted of thorns. Both are there—the sweetness that blesses and the prick that hurts. Over twenty years of doing marriage counseling has allowed me to see that marriage can be experienced as the heaven of heavens but also as the hell of hells. Sometimes, depending on the time being referenced, the same marriage can be described both ways. Marriage brings out both the best in us and the worst in us. I often find myself asking those I counsel, "If you treated anyone else the way you treat one another, would you even be friends?" The most common response is a sad no. It is not at all uncommon for couples to feel like they are hated when, in fact, they are loved. A root problem is the self-centeredness in our love. Let me to try to explain that.

The Blissful, Self-Focused Beginning

I think back to the days when I was seeking my marriage partner. You probably would not buy into the idea that I prayed, "Lord, show me the neediest girl on my college campus, the one that I could most bless and would make happy all her days." You would be absolutely right in not buying into that. Quite the opposite is the truth. Actually, I was looking for the best I could get with what I had to offer. I wanted a wife that looked good and made "me" feel good, one who would bless "me" all of my days. I was quite "me" focused. What about you?

During my senior year in college, I fell head over heels in love with Sally. I would come out of class, exit the building, and look for her from my elevated view at the top of the steps of the building. When I saw her, I would walk as fast as I could (without being obvious, of course) to try to catch up with her. It never occurred to me that she was slowing down so I could. Women can be quite adept at that, you know. I liked the way she made me feel. I loved her touch and her kisses. I loved her talk and the way she looked (still do!). I wanted her around me for the rest of my life. My youngest son, Michael, described young love well when he sheepishly said, "Dad, I'm not good for anything. I can't get my mind off Hannah [his wife, now]. I think about her when I'm in class and when I'm at work. I'm a mess—not good for anything." You probably know the feeling.

My attraction toward Sally was pretty much about what she did for me. Even though my eyes were on her, I was "me" focused in the relationship. You may have been that way also. The odds certainly lean heavily toward that being the case. Especially in America, we most often marry because of the special way our beloved makes us feel, and it is our expectation that they will make us feel that special way all the days of our life, or at least most of the time. They make us come alive. We try things we didn't try before. We open up. We are responsive to their needs. We are fully alive. We don't want such a good thing to go away.

Then Reality Sets in as *Flesh* Surfaces

It's a wonderful world when we're young and in love. But then we get married, and a new reality sets in. Commodes have to be cleaned. Bills have to be paid. We aren't always the highlight of our spouse's day. Eventually our spouse's eyes don't seem to "light up" like they once did when we first came into the room where they were. Now our spouses are often preoccupied with work or mothering rather than with us. They aren't always understanding, and they no longer seem to want to sit and talk for hours upon hours like they once did. They are often too tired for lovemaking (I guess that's probably more one-sided than the rest of these things—guys seem to stay ready!). They don't always make us feel special, and we don't like that. In fact, we soon discover that our spouse is quite capable of drawing out the worst in us. When they do, we tend to blame them for our bad attitude and behavior. When they confront us about our bad attitude, we may find ourselves angrily retorting, "I wasn't like that before I married you!"

No one has as much power to hurt us as our spouse does, simply because our expectations for others and our wants from others are not nearly as high as our wants and expectations where our spouse is concerned. We depend a lot on our spouse for affirmation. Criticism is just the opposite of what we want; we don't like it at all. When the person we most want to delight in us not only ceases to delight in us but also begins to treat us as common and sometimes even unkindly or worse, we are in uncharted territory. We can be quite surprised at how ugly we are capable of acting toward the one we love the most. Our response to their disapproval and anger has a way of reshaping us. Joy can leave, and sadness can dominate. We can become most miserable and pretty good at sharing our misery with our spouse.

When our marriage begins to hurt us, we can become resentful and even feel used or misunderstood and want to bail out. But rather than discard them, most often we decide to help our spouse act better toward us. We tell them how we are feeling, often coming across as critical and insensitive. At first, our frankness seems to help, but eventually, that too can become a frustrating experience. Even though criticism works for a season, the desired changes we see when we first make demands do not tend to last. Angry words are more commonly spoken, and even more unkind words are thought of than spoken (that's probably good!). When things get bad enough, we sometimes resort to seeking counsel.

Heading for Counsel

When we finally seek counsel, it is often the case that we don't even feel loved anymore. But the real problem probably is not that we are not loved. We still love one another or we wouldn't expose ourselves to the discomfort and risk of revealing our innermost self to a counselor, nor would we incur the expense of counsel. The real problem is that we are no longer being treated the way we want and expect to be treated, and that "feels" like we are not loved.

The things we then do to try to force the desired caring from our spouse to start happening again often results in countercriticism coming back to us. Rather than focusing on correcting *their* problems, our spouses often try to correct us and focus on our problems. We can all become quite ugly in our frustrated attempts to make our spouse act more loving toward us. Sadly, our attempts to force our spouse to express to us the loving behavior we so desperately want from them can be misunderstood and will then result in our spouse feeling that we no longer love them. Our criticalness of them can be interpreted as our not loving them anymore. In anger, we can even state that to be the case, which doesn't help.

When we decide to try counseling, the bottom line is that we want our spouse straightened out. But because we know that we have contributed to the problems between us, we are willing to change some ourselves. This is especially true if we think our change will be helpful in encouraging our spouses to change so that they will love us better.

Problems between spouses expose the self-centeredness that is a problem with all of us. Because we do not like the way we are being treated, we are ready for our spouse to be fixed. We start reading books on marriage. There are certainly a lot of them out there, for marriage can be a big problem. That's good! Most of us need to change some, and what more motivating force is there than trouble in our marriage?

Actually, I hope that you are experiencing some problems in your marriage as you are reading this. Problems placed in God's hands lead us toward growth and leave us with a testimony that can help others. If you aren't experiencing any problems in your marriage, you will most likely not be keenly interested in what God has to say about your marriage, will not read this material closely, and will not apply it to your marriage. As long as it is knowledge in your mind that somebody else might need rather than yourself, it is highly unlikely that you will be helped or your marriage strengthened. "Knowledge puffs up, but love builds up" (1 Cor. 8:1 NIV). May we all be more interested in building our spouse up in the Lord than in fixing them so they will respond by returning love to us in like kind. And may we be even more interested in becoming a better spouse "in Christ" than in getting our spouse fixed.

Should I Thank God for My Marriage Problems?

I believe that the most significant factors in my own personal spiritual growth were the things I had to learn about myself in order for my marriage to survive. My problems, placed in God's hands, became learning experiences that left me blessed and a better husband.

We all seem to know that God's Word says that God hates divorce (see Mal. 2:15-16). But God also hates the things we allow to go in our lives that undermine our relationships and will lead us down a path toward divorce. My love for Sally was full of selfishness and inconsiderateness because it was primarily "me" focused. It has always been easier for me to try to get Sally to adapt to my needs than it has been for me to look deeply into her needs and then respond unselfishly. I was fully aware of my needs, but not nearly as aware of her needs. I was quite capable of being insensitive to her while being very sensitive to others. Because she was strong and resourceful, I took her for granted. But I had expectations that she would not do the same to me.

I was a young pastor who, in theory, knew that God was to be first in my life, family was to be second, and church (my work) was to be third. That was what I believed, but it was not the way I functioned, though I didn't realize it until we went to counseling. I would be out visiting members of the congregation along toward our evening mealtime, look at my watch, and see that I could probably squeeze one more visit in before our agreed-on time to eat. Then I would get caught up in the visit and wind up coming home late to the meal that Sally had lovingly prepared but, to her chagrin, was now cold. I was sensitive to the needs of the persons I was visiting with, but very insensitive to my wife. Since our house was right behind the church, I would drop in at any time in the morning for a coffee break. I thought I was being considerate and spending time with my wife. Yet she was a young mother with little children and her own busy agenda of things that needed to be done. It was hard for her to just set everything aside when I would drop in at *my* convenience. I tended to be a workaholic. I was always on call. Yet what was she to do? I was a pastor. I was doing God's work. Since I seemed to be doing God's work, she felt like she shouldn't complain to me. So she remained silent. One definition of depression is "stuffed anger; anger turned inward."

I could see that she was unhappy, but I could not see how I was contributing to her unhappiness. I wanted her fixed, but I didn't know how to fix her. I desperately needed God to show me the error of my ways and to take my eyes off her errors. It took nearly losing my marriage for me to come to my senses and to be able to look at our relationship through her eyes too. In my case, I needed a godly counselor to help me do that. I thank God that he gave me Jim Craddock, the founder of Scope Ministries International in Oklahoma City.

During the process of seeing my contributions to our marriage problems and learning God's solutions as well as His plan for marriage, my marriage came alive. Jesus said it this way: "If anyone would come after me, he must deny himself and take up his cross and follow me. For whoever wants to save his life will lose it, but whoever loses his life for me and for the gospel will save it" (Mark 8:34-35 NIV). I, like so many, was looking for life through my marriage *and* Christ. When Sally didn't treat me in a way that gave me the sense of worth I desired from her, I would be upset. I was so self-absorbed that I failed to be sensitive to her needs, focusing on my own needs instead. But God turned things around for me. I was able to see that He alone is the life-giver. I am not to seek life *from* Sally. Rather, I am to look to Him for life so that I might have resources in Him to offer sacrificial and sensitive love *to* Sally that is not dependent on how I perceived she was treating me (which might have had quite a different look if I could have seen it through her eyes). When I began to love her the way God had intended for me to love her all along, she again felt loved and was then free to relax and love me back.

Once we felt loved again, we then naturally loved back. That's the way our marriage had started out. Now, because of adversity, our marriage has become stronger than ever before. We were more intentional in giving love and less demanding of love (because givers don't usually lack).

Doctors say a healed broken bone is stronger than it was before because it is thicker at the area of the break. When God heals a broken marriage, it is also stronger than before because our focus for loving our spouse is no longer on how our spouse treats us but on the self-sacrificing way our Lord has treated us. Our spouse now has the freedom to fail and still be loved. As a general rule, people given to naturally give back.

How does God pull off this mending of marriages? First, we'll look at what doesn't work.

The Christian Model for a Marriage That Doesn't Work

If you are like most Christians, your idea of Christian marriage is that you are to marry a Christian, faithfully do your part, and expect your spouse to faithfully do their part. The content of their part and your part is negotiable, but you are determined to love one another and work to do your part until death do you part. You feel like you can do that, and you feel and think your spouse will work to do likewise. You see marriage as a fifty-fifty proposition. Our thought process is, "You make me feel good, and I'll make you feel good. You treat me right, and I'll treat you right."

What I have said to this point has come mostly from my experiences. But if a good part of what I have said is also your experience, I am excited for you. I found the help I needed, and I want to share with you the essence of the help I discovered.

One day, as a young pastor, I found myself embarrassingly saying to my congregation, "Sally and I very much need help with our marriage. We are going to Scope Ministries in Oklahoma City to work on it, and we will be back when we get it straightened out." We both thought Sally had problems that needed fixing. That was true. But I never expected that the problem she had that most needed fixing was *me*. Even she was surprised. But this is the nature of relationship problems. Couples tend to defensively react to one another. Our reactions are often insensitive and inhibit needed communication. We can make *angry retorts*, punish by using the *silent treatment*, or *cry* when we feel criticized rather than listen with sensitivity. *Temper tantrums, the silent treatment, and tears are all communication killers.* We can use hurtful sarcasm and become critical and judgmental. Furthermore, we are sometimes quite blind to our own contributions to our marriage problems.

Christian Marriage Is Not a Fifty-Fifty Proposition

There are a lot of self-help books out there for marriage, but what I want to share with you is a God-help teaching. There is a problem with this fifty-fifty model of marriage that seems to be the model most Christians adhere to. The problem is *flesh*. We all want our spouse to ascribe worth to us with their words and actions, and we become upset when we perceive them as failing to value us enough to do this for us. Furthermore, our perspective of the relationship problems and their perspective of the problems do not always mesh. From our perspective, even if our spouse is wise enough to listen to our perspective, they often do not tend to be smart enough to agree with us. They can be very selfish and narrow-minded! (That's not a serious statement, but my attempt to state a very serious problem with tongue-in-cheek humor.) The diagram below illustrates what often happens to us.

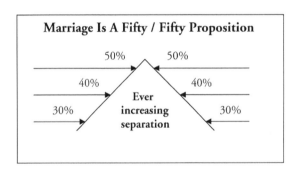

Explanation of Diagram

Initially, we both want to enthusiastically do our part, but when we perceive our spouse backing off in doing their part, we will then eventually back off too. That in turn makes our spouse want to back off a bit, which in turn makes us want to back off a bit more. The result is an ever-increasing separation.

Most Christians know that God's Word teaches that God hates divorce (see Mal. 2:15-16), yet they still get divorced at a rate at least as great as that of non-Christians. Some polls indicate that a marriage between Christians has a slightly higher divorce rate. I believe the reason for this is that Christians tend to have higher expectations for their Christian spouses than they would for a non-Christian spouse, and this greater expectation then leads to greater disappointment and frustration. Furthermore, when Christians then go to marriage conferences designed to help, they often come back with an even higher list of expectations for their spouse (and themselves too) that feeds into this pattern of disappointment with ever-increasing separation. *God has a different model in mind for His children.*

God's Model for Marriage Between Christians

There is a major flaw in man's way of approaching marriage as a means of happiness. *When we determine that it is our spouse's job to make us happy, it has also been pretty much determined that we will make them miserable.* First of all, it places the responsibility for our happiness on the wrong person. We are to be the determiner of our happiness, not someone else. Happiness comes from the choices we make. We must take responsibility for our happiness. What do you do when a child says, "I'm bored!" Don't you suggest things he himself might do to relieve his boredom? Are you responsible for his boredom, or is his boredom a result of the choices he is making? Are we to give our whole lives to entertaining our children? We do our children great harm when we let them passively lie back and expect to be entertained rather than take the initiative to change their own state of being. *We are not to place the responsibility for our happiness on someone else.*

Second, happiness is a relative state, not a permanent one. It is circumstantial. It comes and it goes, dependent on our circumstances. Sometimes it is hormonal. Sometimes it is determined by our thought life. Sometimes we find ourselves continually thinking back on times of hurt from our past. The result is depressed feelings now, even though the event that hurt us is long past. It's like putting our tongue in a newly discovered hole in a tooth. The hole doesn't go away because we keep sticking our tongue in it. We must deliberately choose to focus on something different. Happiness can be quite fickle. Old hurts must be forgiven. We will learn how to do that to the glory of God in chapters 7 and 8.

Third, continually turning to others to be made happy sucks life out of others. People must be refreshed as well as give. To continually try to gain life from another person without being equally determined to give life to the other will finally result in the destruction of the relationship. *Furthermore, what right do we have to demand that another focus their life on making us happy? Shouldn't their life have a greater purpose than that?*

God has a better plan for us. He tells us to look to Him for life. Jesus said, "If you cling to your life, you will lose it; but if you give up your life for me, you will find it" (Matt. 10:39 NLV). A state of true happiness occurs when we focus on honoring God with our lives. God's Word promises that if we choose to "walk after the Spirit," then something we highly desire will happen. The promise is this: the Holy Spirit will produce this kind of fruit in our lives: love, joy, peace, patience, kindness, goodness, faithfulness, gentleness, and self-control" (see Gal. 5:22-23 NLV). The "fruit of the Spirit" listed in that Galatian passage sure sounds to me like a state of happiness we would all like to have. But we look for happiness in the wrong places. The "fruit of the Spirit" does not happen for those who are seeking to fit in with the world, but rather to those who are choosing to walk in God-honoring ways.

Providing happiness is essentially God's job, and spouses do not make very good gods. Our job is to honor God by treating our spouse right, and then trust God for our happiness. If we do not understand that, then we can become quite miserable in our marriages and also make our spouses miserable at the same time by our attempts to force them to make us happy.

God's Word describes something totally different for Christians than the "fifty-fifty model for marriage" because He has something far better in mind for His children than merely a functional marriage. His plan not only creates oneness in marriage, but it is also designed to prepare us for life in heaven—to help mature us spiritually, to help eliminate our selfishness, and to teach us to be givers. His plan uses our circumstances in this world (even the negative ones) to build Christlikeness into us. **"And we know that God causes everything to work together for the good of those who love God and are called according to his purpose for them. For God knew his people in advance, and he chose them to become like his Son, so that his Son would be the firstborn among many brothers and sisters"** (Rom. 8:28-29 NLT).

We find God's plan to accomplish "oneness" in Ephesians 5:18-33. Surprisingly, this section of Scripture begins this way: **"And do not be drunk with wine, in which is dissipation; but be filled with the Spirit"** (Eph. 5:18 NKJV).

At first, it seems strange that a teaching on marriage would be set in this context of drunkenness, but as we shall soon see, it is not really strange at all but rather profound (just what we would expect from God). To be drunk with wine is to be so full of liquid spirit (alcohol) that it controls our actions and loosens our inhibitions. The result is that we act beneath ourselves. It is as if our life is poured out on the ground where it dissipates into the earth. Drunkenness is a waste of God-given life. When we are drunk, we act far beneath who God has created us to be.

Yet this is not a verse on temperance. It is a *contrast* intended to teach us a deep spiritual truth. Instead of being controlled by liquid spirit, we are to be controlled by God's Holy Spirit. We are to be drunk on the Holy Spirit, so to speak, so that our lives will be magnified, restored to all God intended when He created man. In like manner, just as liquid spirit tears down our inhibitions and causes us to act beneath ourselves, the Holy Spirit tears down strongholds of *flesh* so that we may love the way God intended. He wants us to overcome our self-protective inhibitions that keep us from treating others as more important than ourselves.

As you might expect, the result is relational: "Speaking to one another in psalms and hymns and spiritual songs, singing and making melody in your heart to the Lord, giving thanks always for all things to God the Father in the name of our Lord Jesus Christ" (Eph. 5:19-20 NKJV). *When we are filled with the Holy Spirit (drunk in Him), we are so caught up in our identity in Christ and in the way that He loves us that the way we love others is shaped by the way He loves us.* We encourage others and are in turn encouraged. We choose to be thankful in all things, believing that God will use them all (good and bad) to work His good through us into our world. Paul describes this truth in Romans 8:28, "We know that God causes everything to work together for the good of those who love God and are called according to his purpose for them" (NASB).

Submit *to* One Another Out of Reverence *for* Christ

There is another relational aspect of being filled with the Spirit (i.e., influenced by or drunk on the Spirit) that is especially critical for the marriage relationship. Because of His commitment to us, we are able to "submit to one another out of reverence for Christ" (Eph. 5:21 NIV). This verse is especially important because it is the verse immediately preceding the largest segment in the New Testament that speaks of the marriage relationship. This verse is so important that it could be thought of as foundational for true Christian marriage. Let's see why that is so.

The very next verse after this introductory verse begins, "Wives, submit to your own husbands, as to the Lord" (Eph. 5:22). However, though the Greek is translated as "submit" in both verses 21 and 22 in the original Greek, we have two *different* words that do not have the same meaning. We do not see that they have different meanings from their English translation because *submit* has many varied meanings in English that covers both of the Greek words that are used and thus removes the distinction between them. The Greek is more specific, and it is important to understand this difference and to know *why* God's Word makes this distinction. We will begin with the husband's submission, as He has been chosen by God to be the spiritual leader, and thus he should be the first to get his act together.

The submission in verse 21, which is for all believers, basically means to "defer to." *All* believers are called to submit *to* one another (i.e., defer to or treat as more important than ourselves) out of reverence *for* Christ. What should this submission look like for believing husbands? Paul writes, "Husbands, love your wives, just as Christ loved the church and gave himself up for her . . . . In this same way, husbands ought to love their wives as their own bodies. He who loves his wife loves himself" (Eph. 5:25, 28). *Submission* by husbands takes the form of Christlike unconditional love toward their wives.

Husbands, Love Just as Christ Loved the Church

Let's look more deeply at God's instruction for marriage to husbands as we focus on the twenty-fifth verse. "Husbands, love your wife *just as* Christ loved the church and gave himself up for her." That's pretty plain talk, but it's somewhat hard to do. Consider that command in the picture format below.

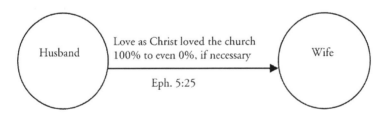

Christ gave Himself up for His church, period. Nothing was held back. What He gave was in no way determined by the worthiness of the bride. We, the bride, got all that was rightly His alone. He held nothing back. He came not to be served, but to serve; not to get, but to give. That is the same attitude God wants husbands to have toward their wives (God's daughters). Our Heavenly Father is quite clear about how husbands are to treat His little girls. Husbands are to give themselves totally to their wives, even if their wives are giving nothing back.

Believing husbands are to give to their wives the same sacrificial love Jesus first gave to themselves. But husbands have a flesh disposition that makes doing this difficult. Let me share an illustration with you that makes this *flesh* predisposition easily understood. Suppose a young husband, as a means of showing his wife he loves her, decides he would like to permanently begin cleaning up the kitchen after his wife's labors to prepare his evening meal. So he shares that idea with her, eagerly anticipating how excited and grateful she will be. But after she finishes eating her only response is to go sit in front of the TV, prop her feet up, and fully take advantage of her husband's labor of declared love. She never acknowledges the gift and just takes her husband's action for granted. How long do you think the husband will keep cleaning up the kitchen? Not long, you say? I think you're right!

But if he quits cleaning up just because she doesn't respond in the way he wants her to, was he really doing it for *her* in the first place? Was it not for himself? There are lots of reasons for washing dishes, and some of them are quite self-focused even though they have an outward appearance of being other focused. Unconditional gifts are much harder to give than manipulative gifts. If the husband keeps looking at the wife to judge if she appreciates or deserves his gift, he sometimes will not like what he sees and thus likely stop washing the dishes. That is the nature of *flesh*. It is "self" focused. *Because of this flesh problem, God wants the husband's eyes to be focused on Him when he gives to his wife.* God gives to us unconditionally so that we might do the likewise.

God's *to* and *for* Solution for the Husband's *Flesh* Problem

That is why God introduced this whole teaching on the marriage relationship with, "Submit to one another out of reverence for Christ" (Eph. 5:21 NIV). Surprisingly, the key words in this verse are *to* and *for*. Husbands are called to show Christlike unconditional love *to* their spouse *for* their Lord's sake. Husbands are to love their wives *"just as He [Christ] has loved them"* (v. 25).

The things we do toward our spouse are first to be seen as a gift *for* our Lord—a way we love Him back. Most of us husbands are so naturally self-focused that just loving our wives in ways that please God regardless of the way she is treating us in return is a hard thing. Even most wives do not expect to be loved by their husbands in such a Christlike way if they are not acting in ways worthy of that kind of love. This is God's idea! We husbands must remember that it is God Himself Who expects husbands to love His little girls that way. It is not their wife's expectation. We are to love our wife that way because God asks us to and because He is worthy of our offering of that kind of love to our wife. Here's a picture:

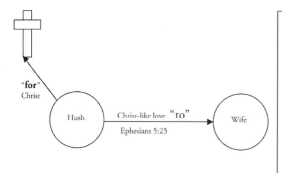

Husbands must keep their eyes on the Lord when they do deeds of righteousness "to" their wives. If they fail to do this, the things they do will become conditional. Husbands are to extend Christ-like love **"to"** their spouse **"for"** Christ, fully aware they are still doing less than what God has done for them.

God has a reason for requiring that husbands offer this unconditional giving of themselves to their wives. Two especially good things happen when husbands decide they want to show the kind of love that God desires for His little girl *to* their spouse *for* His sake. First, husbands discover God's empowerment for this kind of love. When husbands choose to walk according to the Spirit (in this case, stepping out [with no conditions attached] to obey God in the way they treat their spouse), they will discover the Spirit's empowerment to love beyond their own abilities, i.e., with no strings attached.

Second, as the wife experiences her husband continually loving her better than she feels she deserves to be loved, she will want to return that kind of love. The end result is two people striving to *give* 100 percent even when their spouse is failing to respond satisfactorily. If either spouse is choosing to give when the other is failing, someone is always picking up the slack. And as they do this, they are, at the same time, encouraging their spouse to do likewise. God's plan for husbands in marriage is far better than the fifty-fifty trade-off model from the world that so often ends in marital disaster (sometimes even murder of a spouse). Both are to be givers, giving *to* their spouse *for* their Lord. But it is the husband's job as leader to initiate this kind of love. If he will, the wife, a natural responder, will most likely follow his example.

We might picture God's plan for the way husbands are to treat their wives as follows:

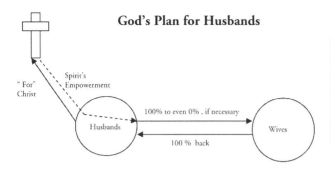

The diagram above shows a third reason for unconditionally giving 100 percent to even 0 percent, if necessary. That's the way God loves us. We are only loving Him back when we love our spouse unconditionally, but the end result is that our personal relationship with our Lord will also be strengthened.

When believers choose to love their spouses the way God loves them, they are "walking according to the Spirit," following His prompting. Humanly speaking, continual unconditional giving is tough and unnatural. But attempting it plugs us into the Holy Spirit's power source. Anytime we choose to do that, we will find the Holy Spirit empowering and energizing that choice. He initiates (in this case, by the written Word in Ephesians and perhaps by also tugging at your heart as you read this). We respond (choose to attempt to do what He asks), and He then empowers our walk (enabling us to do beyond what we could do in our own strength). That's "walking by the Spirit."

Husbands are to love their wives this way as a means of expressing trust in their Lord; they are loving Him back by obeying Him even if their wives never change. "Those who accept my commandments and obey them are the ones who love me. And because they love me, my Father will love them. And I will love them and reveal myself to each of them" (John 14:21 NLB). Husbands, if we will do this, even if our wives do not change, we will change, and for the good. *God has not designed marriage to make us happy, but rather to grow us up, to mature us in Christ and get us ready for heaven.* We are to honor God in the way we treat our spouses and trust that, as we honor Him, a general state of happiness and contentment will be the by-product. But we are not to seek happiness from our wives. Instead, we are to offer Christlike love to our wives. If we do that, happy marriages will generally follow.

God's Plan for Wives in Marriage

God's plan for wives in marriage is somewhat different in content (though not in style) from the husband's. Instead of loving *just as Christ loved the church* (the husband's requirement), she is called to submit. "Submit to your husbands as to the Lord" (Eph. 5:22 NIV). In this case, the Greek word translated in English as *submit* is not the same Greek word as in verse 21, where *submit* is properly understood as "a deferring to." This verse 22 word connotes submitting military-style. It has to do with responding correctly to established authority (in this case, the authority God has established and given to the husband in marriage).

The Amplified Bible says it this way: "Wives, be subject [be submissive and adapt yourselves] to your own husbands as [a service] to the Lord" (Eph. 5:22 AMP). This is a very hard requirement for the wife if her eyes are focused on her husband and looking to see if he is worthy of her submission. Every woman knows her husband is not always right, so following his leadership does not always feel right. But again, we must realize Who has asked wives to do this. This is a requirement from God. Most husbands do not expect this kind of submission from their wives. The issue is, will wives trust God enough to do what His Word asks of them? Does God, as our creator, know what makes marriage work best? When wives choose to honor God's command to them in the way they approach their husbands, they will then discover the Holy Spirit's empowering to do so.

They will also more than likely discover why God wanted them to do this; they will see their husbands changing. But that is not *why* wives are to do this. Wives are to do this as a means of expressing trust in their Lord, as a means of loving Him back by obeying Him, even if their spouse never changes. "Those who accept my commandments and obey them are the ones who love me. And because they love me, my Father will love them. And I will love them and reveal myself to each of them" (John 14:21 NLB). God gives special blessing to those who respond to Him by loving Him back, love made manifest by our obedience to His commands.

There is an old saying that goes, "What is good for the goose is good for the gander." So let me say the same thing to wives that I said to husbands. Wives, if you do this, even if your husbands do not change, you will change, and for the good. God has designed marriage to grow you up, to mature you in Christ, and to get you ready for heaven—not to make you happy. You are to honor God in the way you treat your spouse, and trust that as you choose to honor God with your obedience to His Word, a general state of happiness and contentment in your marriage will be the by-product. But you are not to seek happiness from your husband. Instead, you are to offer Christlike love to your husband. If you do that, happiness will generally come. A warning though: the exception to this is addicted persons who have become users of people. *Addictive behavior must be confronted with tough love.*

The Issue of Leadership in Marriage

Concerning leadership in marriage, the husband is to be the leader because God has delegated authority to him. But man's authority must be exercised under God's authority. The husband does not have the authority to command (nor the right to request) that his wife do anything that is in violation of God's expressed will for her.

Furthermore, this issue of leadership in marriage has nothing to do with one's value. Our value was established at the cross. *All* believers have been supremely overvalued through our union "in Christ." This means that both husband and wife have infinite value and that neither has greater value than the other. But they do have different functions, each being uniquely endowed by their Creator for their designated roles in marriage.

Marriage is about teamwork. How can a man and a woman best function as one? God has decreed that the man is to lead and has equipped him to do so. He has also made the woman to be a natural follower or responder. When the woman leads and the man follows, we most often have a recipe for disaster in the marriage and the family. The result will be resentment, rebellion, and withdrawal in the relationship by both the husband and the wife, and sometimes even divorce. A sense of "oneness" rarely happens when God's plan for leadership in marriage is reversed. It is not that the woman does not have the ability to lead; she can, and a man can follow. But when the wife leads in a marriage relationship, it is usually counterproductive (unless the husband has been injured and is unable to lead). That is why God does not ordain it. Every team needs a leader in order to be effective. God has chosen to equip the man to be the leader of the family.

However, the husband must know that God has only given him authority to be a *servant* leader. "Husbands, love your wives, as Christ loved the church and gave Himself up for her" (Eph. 5:25 NKJV). The husband is to make choices that best serve the team—the whole family. Furthermore, if he makes decisions without gaining his wife's input, then he has made a half-brained decision for two reasons: First, he has used only half the brains available to him (in my case, I make about a one-third-brained decision when I don't receive my wife's input, for she is a very perceptive lady). Second, he has made a half-brained decision because he has devalued his wife by not seeking her input. To put it simply, that is just not smart. It is neither a God-ordained nor an effective leadership style. Most women will find it quite easy to follow their husband's leadership if he is open to their input and has her best interests in mind—is a servant leader.

There is something else to think about in the area of leadership. The leader of the family is responsible for the family. That means the husband is responsible for taking care of the kids, for planning and cooking healthy meals, for cleaning the house (including commodes), for taking care of the yard, for providing adequate income, for running the household, for the discipline of the children—for everything. God has given husbands far more responsibility than they can possibly handle by themselves. But the good news is that He has also given husbands a helpmate to share this responsibility with him. Most wives are very willing to have areas of responsibility delegated to them. If that were not the case, I would not have time to write this book, be as available for ministry to others, play golf, or do a lot of things I do. In fact, were the wife not to pitch in and help the husband with his responsibilities, husbands would have so much to do that they would be overwhelmed and would probably not be effective at anything.

Do you think that maybe a husband ought to express appreciation often to his wife for all she does? As my friend Earl Ballard often says, "That folded underwear in your drawer didn't get there by accident." Not only are husbands to be servant leaders, those with sense will also be grateful leaders who know how to express appreciation. Husbands and all who are called to be servant leaders ought to take Ephesians 4:29 to heart: "Don't use foul or abusive language. Let everything you say be good and helpful, so that your words will be an encouragement to those who hear them" (NLT).

One last word of common sense: In today's world, where both husband and wife are working full-time jobs, traditional responsibilities should not necessarily be the norm. Too many women come home from a full-time job and still have another full-time job to do in the home. It is the husband's responsibility to provide. If the wife is sharing that responsibility, then the husband needs to be sharing equally in the home responsibilities. Talk together about this. Divide the responsibilities. You both have likes and dislikes. As much as possible, each should do what they are best equipped to do.

Summary Picture of God's Model for Marriage

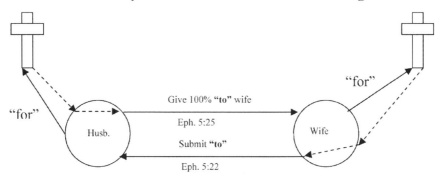

Above is the summary diagram of Ephesians 5:21-32. Both husband and wife are to honor Christ in the way they show love *to* their spouse. We all are to live our marriage *for* Christ, striving to love our spouse the way God has loved us. Our eyes are to be focused on Christ, not on our spouses or ourselves. In this way, both are givers, strengthened in their giving by the way Christ has given unconditionally to them. Both are to be committed to honoring Christ 100 percent of the time by the way they treat their spouse, even when they feel their spouse is unworthy of such treatment. That is the way Christ has chosen to love us, and He asks us to do the same.

If we will obey and choose to love our spouse God's way, He will then empower our choice. That is "walking by the Spirit" in our marriages. *There is nothing else as effective in changing a spouse as loving them better than they deserve to be loved so that they will want to do the same for you in return.* You will likely discover that if you change the way you approach your marriage, choosing to honor God and your spouse over yourself, your spouse will also change in response to your change.

Marriage is not about fifty-fifty; it is about 100 percent to even nothing, if need be—just like Christ's commitment to us. If both decide to live their marriage toward one another *for* Christ, it will very rarely ever be 100 percent to nothing. Even if only one spouse decides to do this, the marriage will seldom stay status quo. But this is not something we do to change our spouse. If we do it for that purpose, we will be engaging in unhelpful manipulation that will be resented. It is something we do to honor our Lord—to love Jesus back. It is our love gift to Him. As I have already repeatedly stated, if we do this, even if our spouses do not change, we will change, and for the good. God has designed marriage to grow us up, to mature us in Christ, and get us ready for heaven, *not* to make us happy. We are to honor God in the way we treat our spouses and trust that as we honor Him, a general state of happiness and contentment will be the by-product. But we are not to seek happiness from our spouses. Instead, we are to offer Christlike love to our spouses. If we do that, happiness will generally come. Life is to flow from Christ through us to our spouse. Do not seek life from your spouse. Instead, seek to be a giver of His life (a giver of Christlike and Christ-empowered love) without demanding a return in any way, and you will most likely find the kind of love you are offering being returned.

God's Summary Verse for Men

Look closely at God's summary verse for this whole section on marriage. "**Each one of you also must love his wife as he loves himself, and the wife must respect her husband**" (Eph. 5:33 NIV). Once again, since God acknowledges the husband as the leader, we will first look at God's summary statement for the husband, "loving his wife as himself." In order to put this verse in proper context, we will first consider verse 26. "**Husbands ought to love their wives as their own bodies. He who loves his wife loves himself**" (Eph. 5 NIV).

Husbands, Your Wife is "Bone of Your Bones, Flesh of Your Flesh"

Let me remind you once again of the Genesis 2 teaching concerning marriage that was first discussed in chapter 2 of this book. Man was created from dust (v. 7). Every other living creature was also created from the ground (v. 19). But Eve was created from the rib of man. Since every other living animal was created from the ground, why not Eve too? God wants *every* husband to understand something extremely important about marriage. He wants husbands to understand that his wife is to be seen as a part of himself, as an extension of himself, not as an independent, totally separate critter. Adam got it! He said, "This is now bone of my bones and flesh of my flesh; she shall be called 'woman,' for she was taken out of man" (Gen. 2:23 NIV). Somehow, since the "fall of man," this very basic foundation for the marriage God wants for His children has been lost. It shouldn't have been—the results have been tragic!

Let's now apply this basic foundational principle of marriage that sees our wives as a part of ourselves, an extension of us. Our hand is a member of our body, "bone of our bones and flesh of our flesh." If our hand is burned, it quickly shares its pain with the body. The body is sympathetic. The biceps contracts to rescue the hand, quickly bringing it to the mouth, which kisses it. Other parts of the body quickly take the hand to the sink and put cold water on it. The rest of the body shares in the hand's pain. The body may apply healing ointment to the hand and then bandage it. The hand may even be put in a sling so as to keep it above the heart. Our hands are treasured when injured. That is as it ought to be. That is how the body has been designed to treat an injured member.

Husbands, what do we do when our wives report their pain to us? Do we see them as a part of us? Are we sympathetic? Are we protective? Do we treat her as a member of our own body, with the same compassion we would have for our hand? Do we provide gloves for her hands in cold weather? Do we rub ointment on her blisters? Do we appreciate all she does to help?

Remember, if we are the leader, then we are responsible for everything: cooking the meals, buying the groceries, taking care of the children, cleaning—everything. In His mercy, God has given us a helpmate whom He has called to be committed to helping us with our responsibilities. She will tend to work diligently to help when she is *treasured* like a hand, i.e., as a member of our own body. We cannot spend too much time thanking God and thanking our wives for all they do to help us with responsibilities that would be overwhelming to us alone. *She is the most important person in our lives and needs to be acknowledged as such.*

The Power of Treasuring

When God, in His summary statement, tells husbands to love their wives as themselves, He is picking up on this basic understanding of marriage that "husbands ought to love their wives as their own bodies. He who loves his wife loves himself" (Eph. 5:28). If husbands choose to value their wives as a member of their own body, as "bone of their bones, flesh of their flesh," they will be treasuring her. Wives want to be treasured, to be appreciated for all they do. They don't wash every man's dirty underwear—just their husband's and children's. They don't clean everyone's commode. Those clean clothes don't get in drawers by accident, but by a labor of love. Husbands, how do you view your wife? Does God need to give you an attitude check? Do you want Him to treat you the way you treat your wife?

I know wives get out of sorts. I know they say no. I know they sometimes blow it in their actions and attitudes toward us and can be harsh and unkind. That's why God has placed husbands "in Christ." That's why He has valued us far above what we deserve. He has done it so that in those times our wives fail to value us, we can choose to focus on the way Christ has undeservedly overvalued us and thereby find needed help in valuing her in her unlovely times. As ones who have had great mercy extended to us, we are to extend mercy to our wives. In those times when our wives fail us, we need to think of the hurt Jesus suffered on the cross because of our wrong behavior. Then when our wives are blowing it, we are to love Jesus back by loving our wives better than we feel they deserve to be loved at that moment. Isn't that what we want her to do for us?

The Necessity of Forgiveness

When our wives hurt us, we are to look to Christ and the way He has valued us. Being strengthened by that perspective, we are to then treasure our wives as we would our hand when it has been hurt and is sharing its pain with us. When we fail to do that, we are to first approach God and ask Him to forgive us for being insensitive to our wife's needs. Then we are to go to her and tell her we are sorry and to ask her to forgive us for being insensitive to her needs. Seeking forgiveness is a very powerful healing agent. *If we don't learn to ask for forgiveness, the accumulation of little hurts can become a big, damaging hurt. Furthermore, as husbands, God has appointed us to be the leader, the initiator of reconciliation.*

We men don't naturally do this. Normally, we are defensive and insistent that we will be treated right (respected), whether we make this demand verbally, by visible unhappy reactions, or by simply seething on the inside. As believers, we must always strive to remember that we are "in Christ." We don't have to demand respect and right treatment from our wives (or others) when we are conscious that God has given us the ultimate respect. We must remember what God has done for us, for when we confront and make demands of our wives, we often belittle and devalue them. As persons who have received abundant, undeserved respect from God, we are to humbly treat our wives in the same manner, seeking to value them always. Then when things are not right between us, we are to initiate reconciliation by calmly sitting with them and speaking the truth in love, being as eager to listen as we are to speak. When we lead, our believing wives will normally follow. If we will do this, our wives will not only feel treasured, but will probably also consider us a treasure—and respect us for it.

God's Summary Verse for Women

Men desire to be respected more than to be treasured. Men may not be as good as women in expressing their feelings because they live in a competitive man's world that encourages men to shut down their feelings. But they know how to die for their woman and how to work hard. They may work long hours when their wives would prefer that they be home with their families. But they are normally doing this because they have a strong sense of wanting to provide well for their families. That is often not good, but they are usually doing it for respect—their self-respect as a provider and the respect of other men. That is why God's summary admonition to women is "the wife must respect her husband" (Eph. 5:33 NIV). God asks this of wives because He knows, as their Creator, that men need respect from their women.

The Amplified Bible helps us to more clearly see what respect looks like: "Let the wife see that she respects and reverences her husband [that she notices him, regards him, honors him, prefers him, venerates, and esteems him; and that she defers to him, praises him, and loves and admires him exceedingly]" (1 Pet. 3:2 AMP). Men may come across as tough, for they have to be in order to make it in a man's world, but they tend to be vulnerable to their women in their homes. I am more interested in what my wife has to say about my performance than anyone else. She has the power to build me up and to bring me down. I am not unique in that. However, it seems that most women do not understand the power they have in their tongues to discourage their men. Ephesians 4:29 is in order here for wives too: "Let everything you say be good and helpful, so that your words will be an encouragement to those who hear them" (NLT). Wives, using your tongues wisely (in the biblical sense) in your relationships with your husbands is as important as anything you do. The Proverbs declare, "The tongue can bring death or life; those who love to talk will reap the consequences. The man who finds a wife finds a treasure, and he receives favor from the LORD" (Prov. 18:20-21 NLT). Several translations of this twentieth verse render it as saying "the tongue has the power of life and death." Isn't it interesting that this twenty-first verse then links the tongue's power with finding a wife who is a treasure, a favor from the Lord?

The True and Eternal Treasuring

Most wives desire that their husbands would treasure them. Yet wives are not to look to their husbands for their worth. They are to see themselves as treasured "in Christ." If wives do not get this straight, then they will most likely use their tongues in disrespectful ways in attempts to get their husbands to treasure or value them. This can easily begin a negative exchange that affects the way their disrespected husbands relate to them. Husbands will then likely see themselves as separated from their wives, and failing to treasure them will be the result.

Wives need to take responsibility for the use of their tongue and disrespectful behavior rather than to just blame their husbands for their behavior. *The blame game is Satan's delight.* When the Holy Spirit convicts wives of failure, they should approach their husbands, confess the wrongness of their behavior, and seek their husband's forgiveness. When we choose to do things God's way by repenting and seeking our spouse's forgiveness, we will then likely find Christ restoring and growing our marriages.

Experiencing Treasuring through Respecting

It is not easy for wives to choose to respect their husbands when their husband does not value her like a member of his own body by loving her as himself. But to react to your husband's failures with disrespect only adds to the problem. Because of their *flesh* problems, husbands tend to respond to perceived lack of respect by withholding treasuring from their wives. Wives must learn to do things God's way, trusting that as our Creator and Designer, He knows how marriage works best.

I challenge you to strive to use your tongue to bless and respect your husband and see what God will do. Practice seeking forgiveness when you fail. He has placed you "in Christ," thereby treasuring you far more than your husband ever could. Furthermore, that treasuring is for all eternity, not just for an earthly lifetime. Focus on working on the things you have the power to change (which probably isn't your husband) and the ways in which you are acting beneath who you are "in Christ." Strive to let your actions, attitudes, and words flow out of Christ's treasuring of you.

Below is a diagram for the teaching of God's Word from the thirty-second verse of Ephesians 5, Paul's summary verse on how husbands and wives are to treat one another:

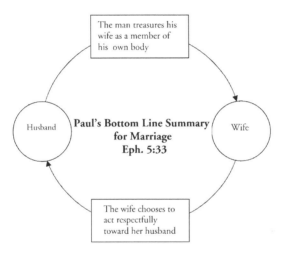

It is extremely easy to find ourselves focusing on the world around us and walking unaware of our identity in Christ. How blessed are the husband and wife who labor to be aware of who they are "in Christ" so that they can stand in the gap for their spouse when their spouse is being deceived by the world and acting beneath who they are "in Christ." Remember, our goal is 100 percent giving to even 0 percent, if necessary. Our *flesh* is proud and doesn't want to do this, but our Savior desires this for us. Paul writes, **"For the flesh sets its desire against the Spirit, and the Spirit against the flesh; for these are in opposition to one another, so that you may not do the things that you please."** (Gal. 5:17 NASB). Take comfort in knowing that *God fights for you.* He is willing to set His Spirit against your *flesh*. It's not all just up to you alone. God is with us and for us.

When one understands God's plan for marriage, it is easy to see what we are to do. When wives fail to respect, husbands are still to treasure. When husbands fail to treasure, wives are still to respect. This is not the natural thing to do, but it is the thing that promotes what we really need and want. We must learn to do just the opposite of what our *flesh* wants and is programmed to do when its wants aren't met. Do your part to honor God in your marriage. *He is much better at straightening out spouses than we are, and He does it with a lot less frustration on our part.*

God Uses Marriage to "Grow Us Up" into Christ's Image

It would be wrong to say that God does not care about the quality of our marriages. He does, and He has a plan for making them better—a plan that far exceeds even our best, most clever manipulations. But God is more interested in getting us ready for heaven. For all of us, that involves *some* change. For many of us, that involves *much* change. Change most often comes about through the pressure of problems. Without problems, we tend to be resistant to change.

I am convinced that God's most effective tool in growing us up into Christlikeness, in teaching us to care more about others than ourselves, and in teaching us to be givers rather than takers, is marriage. Problems in our marriages make us more open to change than anything else I know of. May you grow ever stronger in your covenant relationship with Christ so that you may enjoy the full pleasure of the marriage relationship God desires for you and your spouse!

> Be imitators of God, therefore, as dearly loved children and live a life of love, just as Christ loved us and gave himself up for us as a fragrant offering and sacrifice to God. (Eph. 5:1-2 NIV)

Christ gave His life up for us so that we might give our lives up for others. He would not ask us to do more than we can do. We can live a life of love toward others rather than living for ourselves. *"In Christ," we are greater than we know!*

Things You May Ponder and Discuss with Others

1. In our marriages, we can be self-honoring, spouse-honoring, or Christ-honoring. Which of the three kinds of honoring do you

think is most characteristic of you in your marriage? If all three are present, try to represent each category with a percentage. For example, you may defer to yourself 20 percent of the time, to your spouse 50 percent of the time, and to Christ 30 percent of the time.
2. Do you think that self-centeredness is a *little* problem for you in your marriage, a *moderate* problem, or a *big* problem? When pondering this question, please remember that sometimes what appears to be giving is only manipulation in order to get something you want.
3. Can you identify some ways God has used your marriage problems to mature your faith and teach you to be a giver? If so, list some of them.
4. How has the fifty-fifty model of marriage worked for you?
5. How deceived are you by the idea that (a) it is your spouse's job to make you happy, (b) and that it is your job to make your spouse happy? Who or what has influenced you to think and act the way that you do in your search for happiness?
6. How well have you done in living your marriage *for* Christ? What do you see as the key thing(s) you need to do in order to make Christ the focus of your marriage?
7. How do you view leadership in your marriage? Is your view biblical or just patterned after the way you were raised?
8. Do you tend to view your spouse as a part of you or as independent of you? Is your view made evident by the way you act toward your spouse?
9. When was the last time you *sincerely* said to your spouse after you had blown it, "I was wrong, will you forgive me?" Will you commit to doing that instead of your old form of behavior?
10. a. Wives, what do you do when you do not feel treasured by your husband? b. Husbands, what do you do when you do not feel respected by your wife?

CHAPTER 5: HANDLING REJECTION "IN CHRIST"

I. Rejection's Power to Shape our Thoughts, Feelings, and Actions

At least two things are certain in life: (1) you are going to experience being rejected, and (2) you won't like it—at least, that is my experience. You may be the exception, but I doubt it. I see bathroom scales and I feel rejection, even if I don't step on them. At sixty-seven years of age, I look in the mirror and guess what? Yep, that's right—rejection! My mom used to say, "I wouldn't be young again for anything. I couldn't stand to be that ignorant." That worked for a while, but before she died, she had quit saying it.

All rejection is big, but some is bigger. A significant percentage of persons we see in counseling have experienced childhood abuse (both physical and verbal) or traumas such as sexual molestations with the lingering effects that come with it, things like shame, humiliation, feelings of powerlessness, hopelessness, isolation, apathy, ambivalence, depression, and anger. Some of the men we see have been "picked on" by their peers, and the effects on their lives range from anger problems to insecurities. Divorce is devastating for both parents and children. Many to whom we minister report feeling they could never quite please their parents. This has had negative long-term lingering psychological effects on them, including feelings of defectiveness and sometimes worthlessness.

Other rejections aren't quite as big and can even not be perceived as rejection, things like being left out of the popular crowd, not liking what you see in the mirror, skinny boys, heavy girls—but all carry a toll to the psyche. Little things can bother us too: someone not speaking or maybe not smiling, being left out of a gathering or not being included in a clique, an angry look or even a bored one, or criticism. These are just a few of the myriads of the examples of rejection that could be listed. It is highly probable that you have experienced quite a few others that you could readily add to these that I have mentioned.

The Skunky Approach to Stopping Rejection

Because we don't like the pain of rejection, but were never taught how to deal with rejection as children, we form defense mechanisms to try and stop it from happening. One form of these defensive mechanisms falls under the general title of skunkiness, i.e., those behaviors that confront the rejecter by stinking up the place. We throw temper tantrums to warn others not to reject us. We throw inner temper tantrums too; we give them a three-day silent treatment. "You cross me, buddy, and I'll not speak to you for three days!" Tears can be quite effective in making people feel bad for rejecting us. We can develop critical spirits, criticizing others before they criticize us. This is an attempt to divert the negative attention onto the other person. We become judgmental, finding fault with others in order to feel better about ourselves. We belittle others. We practice one-upmanship: you tell me one thing wrong with me, and I'll come up with two things wrong with you. We complain or whine, thinking that if we do enough of this, we will be treated better. We become sarcastic, negative people. We can become vengeful, accusative, and condemning blamers, manipulators, and fierce competitors. *These all flow out of our woundedness and are an attempt to try to stop the pain of rejection.* This is not an exhaustive list. Feel free to add other special forms of skunky actions to it—things you have seen either in yourself or in others.

We may not think of it in this way, but all of the forms of skunky behavior are self-protective mechanisms used in an attempt to control the behavior of others in order to stop the pain of rejection. We do not necessarily want to be skunky; we're just trying to stop the rejection, and skunky seems to work. But think about what happens when people use these skunky, self-protective mechanisms on us. We reject them, don't we? *This skunky behavior is our attempt to stop rejection and the hurt we are experiencing from it, but it only perpetuates rejection and causes even deeper hurt to our psyches and hearts.*

All of us have experienced some unhealthy and unpleasant relationships and the accompanying rejection. Yet when we experience a healthy relationship and feel truly valued by the other person, we tend to believe that the other person doesn't really want to reject us. We also know that if we are doing something that makes the one we care about feel rejected, we would like to know about it. So we carefully communicate with our friend or loved one concerning the behavior we are finding offensive. Our hope is that they will consider our request and be willing to change their behavior toward us. We know that we would try to stop any offensive behavior we might be demonstrating toward them if we knew it bothered them. We communicate in order to make the relationship better and to keep it pleasant. But if every time (or even several times), when we share with them, we then get back a "skunky" reaction, we will soon stop sharing. When we stop sharing, we have then begun moving away from them rather than toward them. Our motivation in sharing was to strengthen the relationship because we value that person's friendship. But their response of skunky behavior will kill our efforts to make the relationship better and actually cause it harm, for we cannot be honest in the relationship. Whether our response to someone's effort to be honest with us is a display of anger, a withdrawal to silence, or tears, the result is the same. *Skunky defensive mechanisms perpetuate rejection, and wounded, defeated spirits are the result.*

Do you know anyone who enjoys being around critical people, judgmental people, belittling people, sarcastic people, complainers, or whiners? People are this way because they have been beaten down by rejection. They are trying to stop the pain that they experienced through rejection. But their chosen behavior to try to stop the rejection only perpetuates rejection. It does not bring about the acceptance, valuing, and approval they are trying to forcefully gain through their skunky behavior. The following diagram is a picture of the devastating cycle that is perpetually reinforced through skunky responses to rejection.

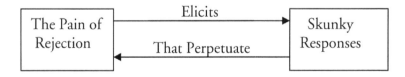

The Performer's Approach to Stopping Rejection

Skunky behavior is not the common mode of response to rejection in more polite circles, although everyone tends to be skunky at times. Our skunky behavior may even normally be limited to the home, where we tend to be more real than polite, if we have a choice.

Most people tend to use a much more socially accepted defense mechanism to stop rejection. We use "performance," but it is performance rooted in pretense and denial, an attempt to cover up felt inadequacies. However, performance done as a means of stopping rejection can be just as destructive to our psyche as skunky behavior. (Please note that I am making a distinction here, contrasting the performance that flows naturally out of one who feels accepted and valued with the performance that is an attempt to stop rejection by acting in ways designed to gain acceptance and valuing.)

A pattern we might easily recognize in this category is that of the "adult child of an alcoholic." The big problem with adult children of alcoholics is that alcohol was the center of the home rather than the child. Since the child is not given a sense of acceptance and importance by their parents, they tend to feel they must try to *earn* acceptance by their performance outside the home. There is a big emotional and psychological difference between a child who performs out of a sense of being accepted as compared to a child who performs trying to become acceptable. Since all children need to be accepted, if a child does not gain a sense of acceptance, comfort, and value from their parents or their primary relationships, they must then earn acceptance outside the home by *outperforming* others. This search for acceptance takes various forms. They may become a class clown so that people will laugh with them rather than at them. They may be driven to become a star athlete or a star student in an attempt to cover the shame they feel from home. Because their need is so great, adult children of alcoholics are *driven* to become very successful. Yet because their acceptance comes from their performance, they often feel at risk of failure and of losing acceptance. Thus, it is sometimes said of adult children of alcoholics: "They are the world's most successful people *and* the world's most miserable people." *They are driven to perform better than others just to be "okay" or acceptable.*

There is a little "performer" in each of us because we all experience some rejection by significant people in our lives. Because our performance is an attempt to gain acceptance and healing for our hurt, we attempt to eliminate the failure that has led to rejection. The child's thought is, "If I could perform better, then my rejecter (parents or peers, usually) would finally accept me and value me as one with worth." The process looks something like this:

The Performer:

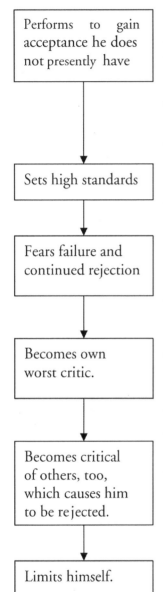

Explanation of Diagram

The problem is that the performer is trying to gain acceptance he doesn't sense he has. Therefore, he has to perform better than others so that someone will declare him acceptable. If he doesn't outperform others, he is still not acceptable. Thus, he is "driven" to always perform better than others. If he can't pull this off, he is still devoid of value. This is shaky ground for him.

Thus, the performance standards the rejected person establishes for himself will exceed normal standards. He is driven to *earn* acceptance by outperforming others.

The driving force is *fear* of failure and the resulting continuance of rejection. Anger can also be present, for no one likes to be rejected. Anger is a great motivator.

No one has to criticize the *performer* because he does plenty of that all by himself. Any critique he receives is perceived as personal criticism. He doesn't hear "bad job," but rather "bad person." It is hard for the performer to hear "You made a mistake" without feeling personal inadequacies.

One who is constantly hard on himself has problems with being hard on others too. He rejects them for their failures according to his standards. By so doing, he perpetuates his own rejection. We tend to reject back those who reject us.

The fear of failure, combined with the need to perform in order to be acceptable, can cause the rejected performer to start tasks he doesn't finish. The thought is "better to not finish (or even try) than to finish (or try) and be declared a failure." Thus, some things won't even be attempted because of the fear of failure. Other tasks are attempted but never finished for the same reason.

Sadly, the performer has listened to the lies of Satan and the fallen world. He doesn't feel loved and accepted and even has great difficulty in believing that a holy, sinless God would truly love and accept him when those who should value him have not found him worthy of love. Thus, he is programmed in his mind to even be closed to the worth that would be given to him by Jesus—inhibited in receiving because of his feelings and thought patterns (*flesh*). He can also experience much guilt for not being able to feel loved by God. Such is the nature of his woundedness.

The *Successful* Performer's Perpetuation of Rejection

Many rejected people have become quite capable performers and take pride in having done so. Their projected attitude is, "If I can do it, you can too." However, this comes across to others as, "Just pick yourself up. That's what I did." But some are so defeated that they are unable to "just pick themselves up." They then view this *successful performer* as arrogant and insensitive toward them. And what do you do with arrogant, insensitive people? You reject them, of course. Thus, even successful performers can perpetuate their rejection because of the attitude they project toward others who don't perform as well. This can then be very confusing to the ones who have overcome their rejection by their "performance." After all, they are not trying to hurt the one they are telling "Just pick yourself up." They are trying to help by sharing how they overcame rejection.

Yet something else is sad here. The performer has not really overcome rejection. They have only covered it up with performance so that it is hidden and denied. But their acceptance is now in their performance, not in their person. What will happen as they age and the time comes when they can no longer perform up to their higher standards?

The Unsuccessful Performer's Perpetuation of Rejection

What happens to those who try to perform as a means of stopping rejection but are unable to do so? Life tends to follow the following pattern for them. The pattern begins with their conclusion that the rejection they have received is their fault; they are to blame!

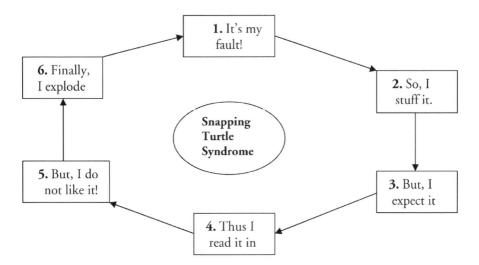

1. *It's my fault!* If a performer is unable to perform well enough, the natural conclusion with nearly every experience of rejection is, "If I were better, or had just performed better, or were more valuable, or if God had placed me in a different family, etc., then this rejection would not have happened." They have believed the lie that it's all their fault. This untrue "stinking thinking," which is based on wrong conclusions, then produces feelings of powerlessness, discouragement, fear, and shame. Furthermore, it becomes so deeply rooted in their thinking and emotions that believing otherwise is very hard.
2. *The rejected person stuffs their feelings.* They try to deny or ignore their hurt and go on. It feels bad, but that's just life. They tend to think that perpetual rejection is just their lot in life, and they have to put up with it. Yet their hurt is a malignant tumor in their soul that is in desperate need of eradication by the great physician, Jesus!
3. *But rejection is expected*, and the expectation often becomes a bitter, self-fulfilling prophecy.
4. *Rejection is often read into the actions of others toward them even though the action was not intended as rejection.* We all will likely experience what we expect. We see and hear through the filters of our past experiences. As we will see more clearly later in this chapter, we will often begin to think and feel in patterns that actually cause rejection to be perpetuated.
5. *But though the rejected person may expect to be rejected, he does not like it.* No one does! We get angry in the face of continued rejection, and we can only "stuff" so long until we reach our limit.

6. *As a result of this thinking, the rejected person will find themselves occasionally exploding in anger.* This explosion is not just about this perceived offense, but also about the whole history of the offenses against them that they have stuffed. The explosion is therefore disproportionate to the offense. This explosion might be external and vented on someone else, or internal and vented on themselves. Internal venting can result in ulcers, high blood pressure, anxiety, panic attacks, and depression. Either way, *the result, after the offended has cooled down, is that the "it's my fault" thinking is reinforced. The cycle has continued, and its hold on the thinking and feelings of the rejected has strengthened.*

Turtle Syndrome refers to the way a turtle, when he feels threatened, pulls his head and feet in and hides behind a thick shell. I call it the *snapping turtle syndrome* because sometimes, when the rejecter gets too close, the rejected "turtle" will pop out and bite the rejecter severely. This is especially true of those persons that are family members of the rejected, for it is with our families that we are normally most real and transparent.

Summary

The natural ways one responds to rejection, whether he is a controlling "skunk" or a performer (either the successful or the "turtle"), only perpetuate rejection. The very things most of us do to try to stop the pain of rejection only cause further rejection.

Rejection's Role in the Formation of *Flesh*

One of the most significant impacts of rejection on one's life is the way it shapes a person's thinking and feelings (or *flesh*), especially if the person receiving the rejection is quite young. Research has shown that not only the events, but also the emotions we experience during the event, are imprinted in our brains. Furthermore, those shaping events that are accompanied with severe emotional trauma are burned into our memories and have major impact on our lives. Experiences of severe rejection have a major impact on the psyche of the victims. (See pages 81-83 of *Discipleship Counseling* by Dr. Neil T. Anderson for a much more detailed discussion of the above paragraph.)

Let's consider the common thought patterns, attitudes, and behavior (*flesh* patterns) that can be formed in an individual's mind because of rejection. Though no one person will likely experience all of these patterns and attitudes of thinking, the following are *normal* responses to rejection. Pay close attention to this list. You may gain significant insight in understanding others whose behavior has been puzzling to you—or even your own behavior. You might want to place an initial by those that apply to you and your significant others. The following lists (of the common characteristics of the thinking, attitudes, and behavior normally formed as a result of rejection by significant others) have been derived mainly from the Victorious Christian Living Seminar notebook of VCL International and from *The Ins and Outs of Rejection* by Charles Solomon.

Common Thought Patterns, Attitudes, and Behavior (*Flesh*) for Performers (Both the Successful and the Snapping Turtle)

- They can be *filled with self-pity*, especially if they fall into the *snapping turtle* syndrome.
- Self-pity can be so bad that they feel *life isn't worth it*. Life is too hard!
- They can find themselves *self-preoccupied*. When they meet someone, they focus on what that person may think of them, perhaps sensing a need to make that person feel positive about them, or perhaps fearing that person will feel negative about them. Either way, the focus is on themselves and their needs rather than on the needs of the other person.
- They may have *problems expressing their feelings*. When they express their true feelings, they have made themselves vulnerable and subject to rejection. There is fear in that. The rejected person is normally more comfortable in remaining somewhat distant.
- They may find themselves *easily depressed*. This too has to do with the rejected person experiencing life as hard.
- They may *insulate themselves emotionally* so that no one can get close enough to hurt them. The more important a person becomes to them, the more power that person has to hurt them. Thus, they fear forming close relationships because this makes them more vulnerable.

- They may *focus on their feelings*. In fact, feelings may become reality to them. Instead of letting feelings give them insight into their thinking (by asking "Why do I feel this way?"), their feelings become their thinking, their reality.
- They may *continually examine themselves to see what is wrong with them*. They feel a strong need to perform better in order to stop rejection.
- They may become a *perfectionist*. They can't afford to fail, and thus they feel they *must* do the things they do very well. After they get started with a project, if they don't feel that they can do it well, they will quit, for they fear failure. At other times, they won't even try because they don't want to risk looking bad.
- They may be *lacking in self-discipline*. In an attempt to earn acceptance, they may start many things, but fearing failure, they easily quit.
- They may be *irresponsible or overresponsible*. They may not take on responsibility at all if they fear failure. If they have become quite successful at performing, then they may take on too much responsibility in an attempt to *earn* approval.
- They may be *filled with worries, doubts, and fears*. This would be quite common for a performer unless they have proved to themselves that they are quite competent.
- They may be *self-condemning*, especially if they have become a *snapping turtle*.
- They may *feel guilty*, but this is in a *vague* way. They can't quite put their finger on why they feel this way; they just do. They are quick to place the problem with themselves. If they had just performed better, perhaps it would not have happened.
- They can *try too hard to please*, for they are looking to others to give them the acceptance they never found in their formative years (or have lost in later years).
- *They answer back only what they think others want to hear*, instead of being truthful, because their need to gain acceptance by pleasing others is so great.
- *Their need for acceptance can override their own moral convictions.* They can even engage in what they believe is immoral conduct in order to gain acceptance from the others who are pushing them to engage in immoral behavior.

- *If they see two people talking, they can tend to feel they are being talked about.*
- They may have *trouble receiving constructive criticism.* They have gained acceptance through performance. Thus, when their performance is critiqued, they may feel as if their very identity is being attacked and can become defensive.
- *They can cling like a leech to the person who is able to accept them.* But eventually, their clinging will drive their accepter away.

Consider what you tend to do when you run into someone filled with the thought patterns and attitudes listed above. You tend to reject them, don't you? But where did these thought patterns come from? Right, from their rejection! Thus, rejection by persons that are significant to the rejected tends to create thought patterns in the mind of the rejected that will perpetuate the rejection. The cycle goes on and on, always getting stronger. Here's a picture of the rejection loop:

The Rejection Loop

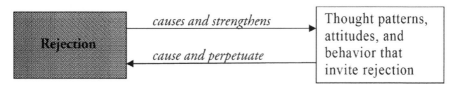

Just as there are predictable thought patterns for performers, there are predictable thought patterns for those who respond to rejection in skunky ways. Often, they are reflections of their own experiences with the rejection that is committed against them by other skunky people. This is especially true if those skunky persons are important to them. The following are *common* thought patterns and attitudes. No one person will likely have all of these. Again, pay close attention. You may gain valuable insights toward understanding yourself and others who are important to you. The following list of the *common* characteristics of the thinking, attitudes, and behavior of the skunky has been derived mainly from the SALT series of VCL International and from *The Ins and Outs of Rejection* by Charles Solomon. Place initials by those that apply to you or to your significant others.

Common Thought Patterns, Attitudes, and Behavior *(flesh)* of the Skunky

- They may be *resentful and thus easily offended*, especially if the ones who mistreated them are the ones who should have taken care of them and protected them.
- They may have a *bitter spirit* about them, a disposition that keeps others at a distance.
- They may *rebel against all authority*, especially if the authority figures in their lives rejected them.
- They may have *conflicting feelings of love and hate*. They love the person but hate what the person has done to them. Their feelings are thus unstable.
- They may *have trouble trusting anyone*. If the most significant persons in their lives have not proven trustworthy, trusting others can also be hard.
- They may have *difficulty accepting love* because the love they have received was manipulative and may have come with unpleasant and unwanted attachments.
- They may have *trouble expressing love* because it makes them more vulnerable to being hurt. When we really care about a person, we make their opinions and actions toward us important. Thus, our caring gives another person more power to hurt us.
- They may have *difficulty tolerating others*. This goes back to the trust issue and the pain that has become a part of the rejected person because of the rejection they have received. The pain brings about distrust of others and breeds a fear of people that can cause the hurt person to prefer isolation.
- They may *spend little time with the most important people in their lives*. This is because the people who are important to them may tend to take them for granted, whereas others are seen as more appreciative of them. Furthermore, the rejections of less significant others do not hurt as badly as the rejection of the near and the dear.
- They may *vent in hostile and punitive ways*. They are probably doing what was done to them or may just be possessors of an angry spirit and lose control when agitated. If so, this was very likely modeled to them by significant persons in their lives.

- They may *make open statements of rejection.* That behavior was likely modeled to them when significant persons in their life were displeased with them.
- They may *give verbal acceptance, but also emotional rejection.* For instance, they may say "I love you" but never spend time with you, or say "You're special" yet are very critical of you.
- In parenting, the rejected may *make too many decisions for their children or give too little guidance.* Both of these are extremes. They could be acting like their parents or acting the opposite of their parents. Either way, the result is that since they were parented with extremes, they parent with extremes. It may be the opposite extreme of their parents, but even so, it is an extreme.
- They may be *physically abusive.* Perhaps they are just doing as was done to them and hate it, but the latent anger that is just under the surface comes to the forefront when they discipline or when they are crossed.
- They may just *refuse to communicate.* When they were growing up, they may have always lost when it came to battles utilizing communication skills, so they tend to just shut down. They may shut down because they fear that the anger that might accompany their words would be harmful to the hearer, or they may shut down because they fear the rejection from others that tends to happen when they try to communicate. Thus they may fear hurting you, or fear being hurt, but either way, they are shut down.
- They may *give more importance to other people or things than their own family.* A husband may fix everyone else's things while his own home falls to the ground. Why? He may feel others are appreciative while his wife just takes him for granted. In his mind, it is better to go where he is appreciated.
- They may *intensely reject anyone who reminds them of someone who has rejected them.* This too has to do with latent anger and *flesh.* When something about another person reminds them of someone who has rejected them, they can respond as if the associated feelings that come with the remembrance are reality in the present. They should examine their feelings so that they might discover that the way they feel toward that person is irrational. But that is not the habit of the rejected. They are often controlled by their feelings rather than informed by their feelings. A dear

friend, upon reading this, told me about an experience that occurred when he was about twelve. An uncle from Brooklyn divorced a special aunt of his. He shared that to this day he has immediate prejudice toward anyone with a Brooklyn accent. *We are not always rational critters!*

Here's the cycle again. Rejection causes the above thoughts, attitudes, and feelings to form in the mind of the rejected. What do we all tend to do when we run into these resentful, bitter people who rebel against authority and don't trust anyone? We reject them. Our rejection then reinforces the thought patterns that the rejected have formed in their minds. These reinforced patterns are then strengthened and tend to invite further rejection. And so the cycle continues. *Our mind-set causes us to do the things that perpetuate the rejection we want to stop. It is a vicious cycle.* It looks like this:

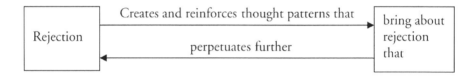

The Flesh Patterns That We Form in Response to Our Rejection Also Distort Our View of God

Obviously, in order to have an accurate picture of who God really is, we should read the Bible, where God has chosen to reveal Himself clearly. We are finite and limited. We cannot comprehend the Infinite unless the Infinite chooses to make Himself known. He has done that. But most of us haven't done our part in studying His revelation of Himself. The result is that our view of God is part Scripture, part hearsay, part observation, and part our natural interpretation of events in our lives from which we form judgments about God. The result of that is that *all of us have a partial understanding of who God is—partial because the finite cannot fully know the Infinite and partial because we haven't adequately searched God's Word to learn of Him.* Because of this, we are saddled with secondhand, deficient, and sometimes inaccurate knowledge of God. Furthermore, our rejection by other earth critters, and especially by Christians, becomes a big contributor to our misunderstanding of God. Thus, *our rejection misconstrues our perception of God. As a result of this*:

- *we* can to some extent partially *resist God's authority* because of the rejection we have experienced from the authority figures God has placed over us.
- for the same reason, we can find ourselves *having difficulty in trusting God*. After all, He created this world that has rejected and confused us.
- *we can see Him as a tyrant just waiting for us to fail*, just like everybody else seems to, and especially those critical, religious people.
- *we can become angry with God.*
- *we can reject God for letting us be rejected when He could have prevented it.*

Most of us do not literally reject God, but there is likely a little of the above in most of us. The deepest problem for the rejected tends to be in drawing near to, or feeling close, to God:

- *Our experiences with rejection can cause us to have little real fellowship or communion with God.* We don't feel close to Him because we have trouble feeling close to many people. We ask ourselves, "Why would a holy God love us when others who are far less holy than Him don't even love us?"
- *We can have trouble receiving God's love because we fear the strings that may be attached to His love.* That is what rejection has taught us. We may ask, "What is God trying to get out of me? If I love Him, will he make me do things I don't want to do?" There is a fear of being sent to places we don't want to go.

II. Breaking Out of the Rejection Cycle

How do we break out of this vicious cycle of rejection we sometimes find ourselves in? How do we quit doing the things that only perpetuate rejection rather than stop it? The way to do this is simple, but can be hard! *We must believe what God says about us rather than what this fallen world says about and to us. This can be hard because our flesh naturally caters to the world*. We have well-established habits that automatically cause us to focus on the world's view of ourselves. Furthermore, why would God require only that we would believe? Shouldn't there be more hoops to jump through than that? Isn't that a pretty shallow idea?

Why would God reward just "believing"? Consider this. Suppose you have a son you love deeply. You have supported him, gone to all his ball games, and have provided for his needs. You have shared joys and sorrows with him and always sought his best. You have sacrificed in order to provide well for him. You have paid for his education. But for some reason, he has misunderstood your attempts to love him. He has become a rebel, seeking his own way. He has run with the wrong crowd. He has forsaken you and your teaching. You have not heard from him in years. At first, you were mad. Now you are grieved, worried, and heartbroken.

Now imagine your rebellious son coming home one day and saying, "Mom, Dad, I have been a fool. I have rejected the things you taught me and have gone my own way. I know I have hurt you. I denied your wise counsel and have forsaken your instructions for life. I was so wrong! I believe you now! I want to live by the same values you have taught and shown me. I want to spend the rest of my days honoring you by walking with you down the path that you are walking. *Will you forgive me for my waywardness?*"

Your heart would leap for joy, wouldn't it? All of the sacrifices you have made are no longer in vain. Your faithful attempts at godly instruction are now rewarded. Your son has come home. It was all worth it. Your joy is even greater because it was preceded by your grief. What you have longed for has come to fruition. *You want to celebrate. Your son was lost, but now, he believes!*

That is what our loving Heavenly Father wants for us—belief! He longs for us to heed His words. His sacrifice is nothing compared to His joy over His children repenting and coming home. God's joy over our coming to our senses and returning to Him is beautifully pictured in the story Jesus told us of the prodigal son:

> But while he was still a long way off, his father saw him and was filled with compassion for him; he ran to his son, threw his arms around him and kissed him. The son said to him, "Father, I have sinned against heaven and against you. I am no longer worthy to be called your son." But the father said to his servants, "Quick! Bring the best robe and put it on him. Put

a ring on his finger and sandals on his feet. Bring the fattened calf and kill it. Let's have a feast and celebrate. For this son of mine was dead and is alive again; he was lost and is found." So they began to celebrate. (Luke 15:20-24 NIV)

Our believing is a big thing to God. It means life for His children! He greatly rejoices! Our belief moves us from death to life: "For this son of mine was dead and is alive again; he was lost and is found" (Luke 15:24 NIV).

So, What Are We to Believe?

Believe must have an object. We don't just believe; we believe in something. So let's focus on what we must believe in order to escape the rejection trap. In the first chapter, I talked about being "in Christ"—of our glorious union with Him. Let's add a verse of Scripture to compliment that teaching. Jesus prayed to the Father and said, "I have given them the glory that you gave me, that they may be one as we are one" (John 15: 22 NIV). *He has shared His glory with us!* Let me try to explain what that means.

He has chosen to join Himself with us in a covenant commitment like unto the marriage covenant so that, just as in the marriage covenant, all that is His is ours and all that is ours is His. We joke with others about marrying above ourselves; Jesus married below Himself, and that's no joke! Because of our covenant relationship with Him, He gets our sin (see 1 Pet. 2:24); we, in turn, get His righteousness—His right standing with the Father (see 1 Cor. 1:30). *We share in His glory!* In our covenant relationship with Him, we win! And because His heart is lovingly turned toward us and desiring the best for us, so does God!

For some reason that is beyond our ability to fully comprehend, our holy, self-giving, most powerful Heavenly Father desires to have fellowship with us self-centered, fickle, critical human beings. There is a reason for the gross unfairness to Him in this covenant relationship He has chosen to enter into with believers. *God wants us to be so caught up in the amazing wonder of His love for us and His shared glory with us that it profoundly shapes the way we live our lives on earth.* It is this unequal partnership that redefines our position in life. We have become the adopted children of the King of Kings. We are citizens of heaven. It is this *unequal* partnership that causes us to want to love Him back. *Properly understood, this unequal partnership elevates us and encourages us to leave our life of self-centeredness and to strive to mature into Christlike persons.*

Let us look at Scripture to see how our *unequal* partnership with Christ is purposed by God to breed attitudes that lead to wholeness in His children. Consider Paul's letter to the Philippians: "If you have any encouragement from being united with Christ, if any comfort from his love, if any fellowship with the Spirit, if any tenderness and compassion, then make my joy complete by being like-minded, having the same love, being one in spirit and purpose. *Do nothing out of selfish ambition or vain conceit, but in humility consider others better than yourselves.*" (Phil. 2:1-3 NIV; emphasis mine)

Here, Paul gives us the first attitude adjustment that is necessary for us to make if we self-centered human beings are to break out of the rejection loop. He wrote, "In humility consider others better than yourselves" (v. 3). There are two ways we can pull off treating others better than ourselves. The first is to be so beat-up, to feel so worthless, that we actually believe others are better than ourselves. But even if we believed that, we would seethe in anger below the surface and become miserable people. No one wants to be a "nothing," and we will always resent being treated as an inferior and being expected to act like an inferior. Thankfully, we know that attitude is not to be the basis for treating others better than ourselves because Paul says it is something we are to *humbly* do. If people are actually better than us, then we are not being humble if we treat them as if they were. That's not what Paul had in mind.

The other way to develop an attitude that would consider others as more important than ourselves is to believe that Jesus has truly shared His glory and worth with us. It is His gift to us through our covenant relationship with Him. But there is something extremely important we must realize here. *We do share in His glory,* but *we share in it as one who is totally undeserving of it.* We have been made high and lifted up, *but* not from our doing. The result of knowing that this high blessing is totally undeserved is deep gratitude to Jesus for the way He has lifted us up and a desire to want to spend the rest of eternity honoring this One who has so honored us. *When we fully realize what He has done for us, we just naturally want to love Him back for all eternity. And how do we do that?* By treating others as He would want us to, i.e., in the way He modeled treating others while He was on earth. We treat them as important and consider them as more important than ourselves.

You see, if I know I share in Christ's *infinite* worth, in His glory, then I don't need to manipulate you to try to get you to give worth to me by the way you treat me. I already have more worth than you can give me, and it is worth so great that it can't be added to. Because Jesus has shared His glory with me, I can love Him back by being concerned with valuing you, i.e., by declaring you as a person of worth by the way I treat you. There is power in that. Most people who perceive you as loving them naturally love you back. Jesus said it this way: "For if you love those who love you, what reward have you? Do not even the tax collectors do the same?" (Matt. 5:46 NKJV) Thus, Jesus taught that even the despicable will love back those who love them.

A Lesson from a Sack

Let me give you an analogy to try to help you more easily comprehend what Jesus did for us when He shared His glory with us. Let's say I line up five paper sacks on a table. One sack is new and crisp. One has been wadded up and thrown in the trash can but straightened out. The third is soiled. The fourth is one of those fancy sacks that you fill with gifts—instant gift wrapping. The fifth has been puked on but wiped off. If I were to ask you to come up and pick out the sack of your choice, I think I know which one you would pick, but I'm positive I know which one you would not pick. Now suppose I put one billion dollars in each sack and then requested that you come up and pick out one of the sacks for yourself. Does that change things? Would it bother you if you didn't get to pick first and thus had to receive your billion dollars in an inferior sack? It doesn't matter if the sack is old, soiled, wrinkled, plain, or new and crisp and pretty. The value of the sack itself has become negligible.

In this allegory, the believer is the sack. In like manner, God has placed His Holy Spirit in the believer and declared the believer to have the worth of Jesus, a worth far in excess of a mere billion dollars. "He has shared His glory with us." The condition of the believer (as the container or sack that Christ is in) does not determine the worth of the believer. *The believer may be plain, old, wadded up and seemingly thrown away, soiled, mistreated, abused, insignificant, or gift wrapped nice and pretty. But when the Holy Spirit of God is placed in Him, he has been totally revalued, made infinite in worth* (see 2 Cor. 4:7).

The value of believers is sealed in Christ. We have been endowed with infinite worth. *It is a sad state when we as believers look at the way the world has treated us to determine our value.* In the light of eternity, it doesn't matter what the world thinks our worth is. Some of us have been puked on by our world. Some of us have been wadded up and thrown in the trash can—treated as worthless. Some of us have come in a pretty package with a bow tied around it. Some of us are torn and battered, perhaps not looking so good. But *we have been totally revalued by God Himself.*

When we refuse to believe what God has done, it is like shaking our fist at God and shouting, "How dare you let the world treat me the way that it has. You don't love me, or you would not have let me be treated this way!" I need to remind us of one thing. No one has been as unjustly humiliated by the world as Jesus has. Yet consider why He let Himself be treated that way. He did it so that the guilt and shame of the sins of we who have believed could be placed on His shoulders. Paul says it this way: "God made him who had no sin *to be sin for us*, so that in him we might become the righteousness of God" (2 Cor. 5:21 NIV; emphasis mine). Everything believers have ever done wrong was placed on Jesus's shoulders. On the cross, He was punished as an adulterer, a liar, a thief, and a scoundrel. *He was thoroughly punished for things we have done, just as if He had done them, even though He Himself never sinned.* "He was made sin for us!" (2 Cor. 5:21). *Furthermore, not only did He allow Himself to be punished for the wrong we have done, He then replaced our shame with His glory.* That is totally unjust to God—it's the ultimate injustice!

Our Actions May Allow Satan to Laugh at Jesus

Satan must really laugh at Jesus when we get so upset about the way this fallen world (under his dominion) has treated us that we cannot get our eyes off ourselves so that we may clearly see what God has done to so richly revalue us. Because of our "self" centeredness, we have a hard time getting our focus off our soiled sack and the unjustness of the soiling, even though God has made believers of infinite value because we contain Christ. *We must learn to focus on what God has done to redefine us rather than on what the world has done to define us. We must believe God!* Will you do that?

Yet equally bad is getting so caught up with the glory of our USDA Grade A⁺ self, our packaging and the things we do, that we value ourselves in terms of our glorious self and our good works rather than according to Jesus's work on our behalf. Our sack may be nice and gift wrapped, with bow and all. But it's still an earthbound sack that, unless it holds Jesus, will rot in the grave and eventually be forgotten until it is resurrected to face the second death, an eternity in hell (see Rev. 20:14).

Sometimes it is better to have been humiliated by the world so that we are forced to look to Jesus for our worth rather than to have been so blessed in the world that we are satisfied with our situation in life. Satisfied people tend to just play around with Christianity as a peripheral of life rather than treasure Jesus as life itself. Jesus said that He is "the way and the truth, and the life" (John 14:6 AMP), not a peripheral of life. *I believe that Satan laughs at Jesus about that too, mocking Him because we who are believers often still choose to seek glory from this world rather than choosing to receive the glory that Jesus longs to share with us.* We must choose to not let our Savior be mocked by Satan, which is what happens when believers look to the fallen world for life rather than to the true "life" giver, Jesus, the Creator of all that we know. *We must believe!*

"Belief" in a Nutshell

Let me put what Jesus's disciples are to believe in a nutshell. We must know who we are. We are sharers in the worth Jesus earned by the way He lived His life on this earth. We need to choose to rejoice in that as fact and give Him praise. But so that we don't get full of ourselves, we must also know that we don't deserve that status. Instead of seeking our own glory, we should humble ourselves and honor Jesus. We love Him back by loving even the unlovely, *just as* He did. The unlovely may be our rejecters. We are still to treat them better than they deserve, just as Jesus has treated us. As those who have been given undeserved abundance by Jesus, we are to share out of our abundance with others! Jesus has shared His glory with us so that we can represent Him well to others, not seeking value from them but instead giving value to them. *It's not about the sack—it's about what is in the sack!*

That is what Jesus has done for us. We may think some others do not deserve this kind of valuing from us, but we do not deserve the valuing Jesus gives us either.

Four Things to Meditate on to Help Us Choose to Walk Out of Rejection

It is important for us to remember *how* we received Jesus's worth and *why* we received it. I want to share four things that believers need to seriously ponder.

1. *We received the glory of Christ up front.* We started sharing in His eternal life the moment we believed and made a faith covenant with Christ for our salvation. We didn't have to work to earn eternal life. It was a free gift that came the moment we believed. It came when we made our covenant relationship with the Savior (see Rom 6:23).
2. *His glory is 100 percent ours.*
3. His glory is *100 percent undeserved.*
4. *He gave us His glory so that we might quit trying to gain worth and significance from the world and choose to share His love with the world instead.* He has given us an abundance of worth, *much* more than we could ever need so that we would have plenty to give away. As encouraged people, we are to encourage. As forgiven people, we are to forgive. From our abundance of worth "in Christ," we are to become worth givers and to stop being worth seekers. If you are a believer, you cannot gain more worth than you already have, for your worth is now from Jesus, "in Christ." The ways we share Christ's love with others on earth are the treasures that we send on ahead of us to heaven (see Matt. 6:19-21). They are gifts we will lay at Jesus's feet. We come to Christ as sinners without personal merit. But He has prepared a way for us to go to heaven with personal dignity and bearing gifts.

But Just Having This Truth in Our Heads Is Not Enough

It is when we are fully conscious of these truths that we are mighty. When conscious of these truths we feel special. We are special always, but we don't always feel special. This is because Satan and his fallen world are quite good at creating situations in our lives that shift the focus of our minds off what Christ has done *for* us onto what the world is doing *to* us. When our mind is focused on our rejection by the world, we do not feel powerful "in Christ." We may even feel rejected by Christ. But when our mind is focused on who we have been made to be "in Christ" and on the way He has revalued us by sharing His glory with us for all eternity, we are then empowered to face and overcome rejection. Thus, *the key to handling rejection is our awareness of our identity in Christ—returning our focus to Christ.*

That is why we need to "walk after the Spirit" at all times. Notice what we are taught in Paul's letter to the Romans.

> For what the law could not do in that it was weak through the flesh, God did by sending His own Son in the likeness of sinful flesh, on account of sin: He condemned sin in the flesh, that the righteous requirement of the law might be fulfilled in us who do not walk according to the flesh but according to the Spirit. *For those who live according to the flesh set their minds on the things of the flesh, but those who live according to the Spirit, the things of the Spirit.* (Rom. 8:3-5 NASB; emphasis mine).

We Must Practice the Disciplines!

The way we walk is determined by what our mind is focused on in any given moment. When we are focused on what God has done by placing us "in Christ," we are powerful. When we are focused on the fallen world and what it has taught us, we are vulnerable.

That is why God has provided many disciplines designed to steady the focus of our mind on the things of God. The disciplines are things like praying, going to Bible study, being active in a local church, being in fellowship with other believers who will encourage and challenge us, preaching, reading Christian literature, singing spiritual songs, and meditating on the Word. But there is more involved than just focus.

Our Minds Must be Renewed

Our minds are a mess. They are *fleshy*, programmed in the ways of the world. Our minds must be renewing so that we can see ourselves and our situations through God's eyes. *We must labor to put off the old stinking thinking and to put on right or righteous thinking. If we do not labor to renew our minds, we will continue to default back to the mind-set we have learned from the world and, by so doing, often continue to act like the world has programmed us to act.* Paul speaks to this need in Romans 12:2, "And do not be conformed to this world, but be transformed by the renewing of your mind, that you may prove what is that good and acceptable and perfect will of God" (Rom. 12:2 NKJV).

Three key words in this passage (*conformed, transformed, and renewing*) are all in the Greek present tense. The Greek present tense carries a connotation that our English present tense does not carry. The Greek present tense connotes continuous or repeated action. If we say in English, "He is walking to town," we have no way of knowing whether that is the way he gets to town every day or whether it is an exception for today only. In the Greek, it is always repeated action. The Greek tense tells us that this is the way he normally goes to town. Thus we should understand *conformed* as "keep being shaped by," *transformed* as "daily becoming more like Christ in our thinking and actions," and *renewing* as "an ongoing, lifelong process of renewal." Thus, when the present tense connotation is factored in, we have "Don't keep on being being shaped by the world, but instead be being transformed into the image of Christ by the continual renewing of your mind" (Rom. 12:2a, my translation). *The continual renewing of our minds is necessary if our lives are to demonstrate the good, acceptable, and perfect will of God* (see Rom. 12:2b).

Another Thought That Should Help in Overcoming Rejection

Have you ever thought about how inappropriate it is for Christians to reject one another? Christians are loved, redeemed, and blessed possessors of the shared glory of Christ. Why would Christians ever reject one another or put one another down? We have been lifted up in order to lift up. Whenever we experience rejection at the hands of another Christian, or anyone for that matter, we must learn to recognize that normally the rejection we experience is not really about us. It is about our rejecter's own messed-up *flesh*. Our rejecter needs helpful ministry, not rejection back, just as we need helpful ministry to break out of our own rejection patterns. Rejecters have a problem, but we, as the rejected, are normally not the problem, even though it may feel like we are.

We need to have compassion for our rejecter rather than reject him back. But that is not an easy thing to do because when we are rejected, our *flesh* is not happy about it. Our *flesh* is normally programmed to take rejection personally and react in kind. But we *can* learn to do otherwise. As soon as we are able to reflect accurately, *we must remind ourselves that rejection normally reflects problems in the rejecter himself* (though we should also be open to the *possibility* that my rejecter is responding to the rejection I have first extended to him). Our rejecter is doing exactly what we can do when we are not aware of both our *flesh* problem and our identity "in Christ" and thus fail to choose to "walk by the Spirit."

The *root cause* of felt rejection lies in our failure to look to our Creator for our valuing. In truth, God is the only one that has the right to define our worth, for we are the product of His hands. But if we do not look to our Creator to determine our worth, we will then look to His creation for worth, seeking, and even demanding, that others would grant worth to us by the way they treat us. We might do this by trying to *control* others in order to force them to grant worth to us by the way they treat us. But that will feel like rejection to those we attempt to control—and is rightly perceived as such. Or we can be *judgmental*, unlovingly pointing out their errors when they fail to honor us in their actions toward us. However, that too feels like rejection to those we judge, and it is rightly perceived as such. Or we can do things designed to *manipulate* others to declare worth back to us. But people grow tired of manipulation and those who manipulate. *Our attempts to force the creation to grant acceptance to us often feels like rejection to others and will then be reciprocated in like kind.*

We would experience life far differently if we would only give our Creator the exclusive right to determine our worth. Then, as persons who have found incomparable worth "in Christ," we could choose to offer worth to others out of the abundance of worth (*much* more than we need for ourselves) that we have "in Christ." That's the most effective way to stop rejection. Most other methods we use only perpetuate rejection. Rejected people tend to reject back, but loved people tend to love back.

Rejection, both that which we receive and that which we reciprocate or initiate, is a big problem for mankind. We *all* need help in stopping it. We *all* need to look solely to our Creator for our identity so that we won't be so easily offended. We *all* need God's deliverance from our *fleshly* ways of handling rejection. An appropriate prayer for us when we experience rejection (or take offense) is the one that Jesus prayed on the cross in the midst of His agonizing rejection: "Father, forgive them; for they know not what they do" (Luke 23:34 KJV). Wouldn't that be a wonderfully different and potentially liberating way to respond to our rejection?

Things We Must Practice If We Are to Overcome Rejection

Paul reminds us that God's people need to prepare for battle, writing, "Be strong in the Lord and in his mighty power. Put on all of God's armor so that you will be able to stand firm against all strategies of the devil" (Eph. 6:10-11 NLT). We must never forget that because the devil is an avowed enemy of God he wants to steal from, destroy, and even kill those of us who are God's adopted children (see John 10:10).

If we are to compete well in a battle, we must prepare for the battle. *Our preparation should acquaint us with our enemy's tactics and prepare us to prevail over our enemy by giving us a plan for effectively combating our enemy's skills.* One of Satan's chief tactics to destroy us is rejection. God has a plan in place that will enable His children to prevail over this scheme of Satan, but we have to walk in it. God's plan is to transfer the worth of His Son to all who will believe so that *we are no longer rejects*, but rather *"the chosen of God, adopted into His family, and sharers in Jesus's glory." If Satan is to prevail, he must at least temporarily blind us to this fact.*

And Satan, being the chief deceiver he is, has done a pretty good job of blinding believers to truth. We often fail to walk in the light of our identity "in Christ." Isn't it interesting that when we are rejected, we don't focus on Satan, the true author of rejection, but on the person who is rejecting us? We get angry with them, not Satan. Rejection is of the fallen world where Satan reigns and wants to destroy God's people. Acceptance is of God Who would redeem us. But *instead of becoming angry with Satan, the father of rejection, we become mad at our rejecters and then act like them when we should be rejoicing in the marvelous thing Jesus has done for us and then act like Him.* We must diligently practice—seriously work at responding differently in the face of rejection—if we are to prevail over Satan's scheme to use rejection to blind us to God's truth. God's plan for enabling us to overcome rejection is that we will keep our eyes on Him rather than the world.

A Summary of God's Plan to Enable Believers to Overcome the Destructive Power of Rejection

A. The goal: Believe God for your identity rather than the world.
B. Preemptive work that must be done in order to believe God when we are under attack (experiencing rejection) rather than the world.

   1. *We must meditate on God's truth. Strive* to believe you are "in Christ." Believing God over the world is critical for victory. If you don't think you can win, you won't.
   2. *Strive to stay conscious of your identity "in Christ." Ponder often* the truths that (a) you were given this new worth *up front*, the moment you believed, (b) this new worth is 100 percent true, (c) this new worth is 100 percent undeserved, and (d)

this new worth was given to you as an unlimited resource for giving to others. You have so much "in Christ" that you can give to even the undeserving others (even your rejecters) and never miss what you have given away. You do not need to manipulate others so that they will give to you, nor do you need to fear what they might take from you. You *must* strive to believe this. The deceptions in our minds that have come about through the rejection we have received in the fallen world *must* be replaced with God's truth. It is through *believing* God that we are able to quit trying to gain worth from others (the creation) and to receive worth from God through Christ. *Only when you truly believe can you quit manipulating others to treat you better, stop being vulnerable to their opinions, and instead continually open your hands to receive the worth God wishes to grant you "in Christ."*

3. *Keep laboring to choose continuously to "walk by the Spirit" in order to resist the schemes of the devil.* These schemes are designed to blind you to the truth of who you are "in Christ" so that he may steal from you, with the hope of killing and destroying you (see John 10:10a). If you are to consistently choose to "walk by the Spirit," you must labor to stay *conscious* of who you are "in Christ."

4. *In order to stay conscious of your identity "in Christ" you must keep practicing the disciplines* that make you conscious of God's presence and your identity in Him. Our minds are in desperate need of renewal. Our failure to consistently choose to "walk by the Spirit" is rooted in not staying conscious of who we are "in Christ."

5. *Strive to let your sensing of rejection be a trigger to remind you of who your are "in Christ."* The power to act differently is *from* God and available to you *now*. His plan for you is sufficient for putting off the effects of rejection in your life. The goal of your practice is to stay so conscious of who you are "in Christ" that you will *choose* to take a first step of faith, a step that demonstrates to your rejecter and to yourself that you are "in Christ," a step that values yourself *and* your rejecter rather than reacting in like kind to your rejecter.

6. Spend time thinking about the rejection you have received in the past and about how you might have responded differently

to it had you been conscious that you are "in Christ." God will use that practice to empower your attempts to make that first step, and you will have begun the journey that leads to God's victory over the pain (and sometimes devastation) of rejection. *Because you are "in Christ" and the possessor of the Holy Spirit, you can learn to choose to walk "by the Spirit" when rejected rather than continuing to react after the flesh.*

7. Strive to keep remembering that overcoming rejection is a *process* that involves the renewing of your mind with truth from God. Hang in there! You can do all things through Christ who strengthens you (see Phil. 4:13).

8. Do not seek to perfect your *flesh*—instead seek to perfect your dependence on Christ by learning to "walk by the Spirit." I wish God would just zap me and make my *flesh* okay, make it pleasing to Him. But remember, *flesh* won't zap. "The carnal mind is enmity against God; for it is not subject to the law of God, nor indeed can be. So then, those who are in the flesh cannot please God" (Rom. 8:7-8 NKJ). I like the way this passage from the New King James Bible ties together the *carnal mind* and *flesh*. *Flesh* is an enemy of God. It looks to God's enemy, this fallen world, for life. Thus, it seeks worth from the creation and most often functions independently of God, ignoring the Creator.

Flesh will always have a root problem of enmity with God, for it has been programmed by this fallen world under Satan's influence. Our job is not to seek to perfect our *flesh*, but rather to recognize it for what it is—an enemy of God. We are then to choose to "walk according to the Spirit," to let the Spirit of Christ in us (i.e., the Holy Spirit) set Himself against our *flesh* so that we might not do that which we please (see Gal. 5:16-17). *We are not to perfect our flesh, but rather to perfect our dependence on Christ by "walking according to the Spirit."*

C. The victory: letting rejection teach us how to "walk according to the Spirit"

If we will cooperate and learn to "walk by the Spirit," God will use rejection to grow us up into a full experience of salvation. We can be defined by God alone rather than by His creation. Why should we, in any way, let the world water down the worth God conferred on His children when He placed them "in Christ"? We shouldn't, you say. Yet that is exactly what we do when we, in any way, look to God *and* the world to know who we are.

The following diagram is designed to help us understand how God can actually use our miserable experiences with the world's rejection of us to bring us face-to-face with our true identity "in Christ" and then keep us looking to Him alone for life. The diagram will appear complicated at first glance, so let me make a couple of statements that will help prepare you to understand the diagram better. First, notice that there are four lines across the page in the diagram, the fourth line being much shorter. These lines are to be seen as a continuation of one another. That's why the last entry on each line is also the first entry on the next line. Second, the numbers are not necessarily an ordered sequence of events, though they are for the most part. They are meant to be a reference to guide the explanation of the diagram, which follows after the diagram.

Learning to Handle Rejection "in Christ" Is Progressive in Nature

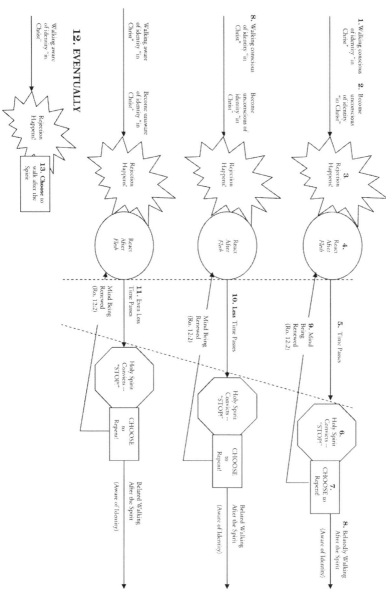

Like newborn babies, you must crave pure spiritual milk so that you will grow into a full experience of salvation. Cry out for this nourishment, now that you have had a taste of the Lord's kindness. (1 Peter 2:2, NLB) *"Those who live in accordance with the Spirit have their minds set on what the Spirit desires"* (Ro. 8:5, NIV)

YOU ARE GREATER THAN YOU KNOW ~155~

Explanation of the Diagram

Rejection can become a blessing if it leads us to remember who we are "in Christ" and results in loosing us from seeking identity through the creation rather than from the Creator. If we are to overcome rejection, we must learn to keep our minds set on our identity "in Christ" and the glorious, undeserved worth He has ascribed to us.

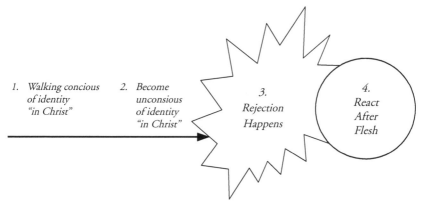

1. This diagram begins with the believer *"walking aware of (conscious of) his identity 'in Christ.'"* But it is not easy to stay aware of our identity "in Christ" because the world is always clamoring for our attention.
2. It is just a matter of time until *we will find our minds shifting, focusing back on the world,* the place it has habitually focused.
3. The good news is that when we do this, *God allows rejection to happen to us.* We can actually think of this experience of rejection as God using the world to bring about natural discipline. Hebrews teaches, "The Lord disciplines those he loves, and he punishes everyone he accepts as a son" (Heb. 12:6 NIV). The *purpose of this discipline* is to grow us up into a full experience of salvation (see 1 Pet. 2:2). In this case, "salvation" is being delivered from the ways in which the world has used rejection to deceive us, making us unconscious of our identity "in Christ" and thus ineffective in "walking by the Spirit." God will undo Satan's schemes and use rejection to grow us up "in Christ" if we will learn to "walk by the Spirit" when we sense we are being rejected.
4. Since our mind is not focused on our identity "in Christ" when this rejection happens to us, we will likely *default back to flesh*

and try to handle it just like we did before we discovered our identity "in Christ."

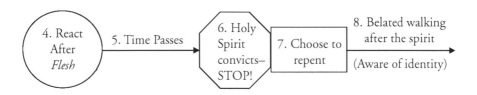

5. We will most often continue in that state, walking after the *flesh*, until the Spirit of God graciously intervenes.
6. When intervening, the Holy Spirit will *convict* us. John teaches, "**When he [Holy Spirit] comes, he will *convict* the world of guilt in regard to sin**" (John 16:8 NIV; emphasis mine). He is not condemning us (see Rom. 8:1), but rather becoming involved in helping us to overcome by reminding us that we have not made a right (righteous) response in the face of rejection, that we have not chosen to look to God alone for our identity.
7. Choosing to repent when the Spirit convicts is the most critical point of the whole process of overcoming rejection. To *choose to repent* is to *agree* with God that we are *reacting* to our rejection by walking after our *flesh* rather than choosing to be defined by Christ's painful and degrading work on our behalf—the cross. We are to agree with the Spirit that this is what is happening and then to turn back to seeing and doing things His way. If we are going to be successful in learning to walk after the Spirit, then we must learn to get our identity from God alone. Basically, we should respond to the Holy Spirit's conviction by praying, *"You are right, Lord. I have been focused on the way the world is treating me and have been oblivious to the way Jesus was wrongly treated for my sake. I am not focused on the humiliation Jesus received by the world so that He could transfer His worth to me. I let my humiliation by the world become so big in my mind that I treated your rejection and humiliation by the world as insufficient to define me. Forgive me, Lord! That is wrong! Thank you for your ultimate valuing of me by placing me 'in Christ.'"*
8. This *choice* to "walk after the Spirit" is obviously late (belated), but the important thing is that we have finally made that choice

so that no spirit of bitterness can set up in us and cause us to continue to sin against our brother and thus continue the cycle of rejection. Paul commands believers in Ephesians, "**Get rid of all bitterness, rage and anger, brawling and slander, along with every form of malice**" (Eph. 4:31 NIV). The Holy Spirit graciously convicts us so that our experiences of rejection will not continue to give Satan strongholds in our thinking that will naturally lead to sinful acts toward others. Our rejection can then become a blessing to us as it results in our refocusing on our identity "in Christ."

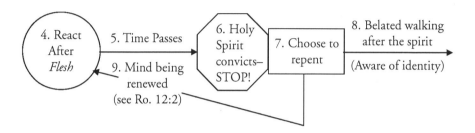

9. There is still another important benefit in belatedly choosing to "walk by the Spirit" when rejected. Responding rightly to rejection begins renewing our minds. Just as our old experiences with rejection have been stored in our minds, this new way of responding to rejection by consciously overriding our old *default* behavior is also stored in our mind, even though it was a belated response. *This new response then becomes input for the renewing of our minds.* But this is only *one* incident of choosing to respond differently to rejection. It is not yet ready to carry the day and to become our primary reaction. The old way will still dominate, but only for a season. Our victory will come as we persevere in making right choices even though they are belated choices. As Paul says it, "**For the one who sows to his own flesh will from the flesh reap corruption, but the one who sows to the Spirit will from the Spirit reap eternal life. Let us not lose heart in doing good, for in due time we will reap if we do not grow weary**" (Gal. 6:8-8 NASB).

Second Line

The second line of the diagram on p. 155 is meant to be seen as a continuation of the first line. "Walking after the Spirit," the first entry of the second line, is the continuation of the "walking by the Spirit" that ended the first line of the diagram. In the second line, we see that line 1 is repeated and has the same result—defaulting back to *flesh*. The difference between line 1 of this diagram and line 2 occurs at reference #10.

10. Because we have *begun* the *process* of choosing to "walk after the Spirit" when rejected, we can now more quickly sense the Holy Spirit convicting us to "Stop!" Thus, the amount of time that passes between our wrong reaction when rejected and our embracing of the Holy Spirit's conviction is shorter. Note also that since line 2 is a continuation of line 1, when you combine the time we are conscious of our identity "in Christ" in line 1 with the continued consciousness in line 2, you can see that the time spent in actually being conscious of our identity "in Christ" is increasing with our choices to walk by the Spirit following each rejection.
11. *Line 3* shows us being able to sense the Spirit speaking to us even more quickly. Thus, the pattern becomes an ever-quickening response to the Spirit's conviction. With each conviction by the Spirit, we have chosen to repent, and as a result, our mind is being renewed by the new data.
12. Eventually, rejection will happen while we are walking in awareness of our identity "in Christ."
13. Because we are aware, we can choose to "walk after the Spirit" even though we are still experiencing rejection. *Amazingly, when this happens God has actually used our rejection by the fallen world to remind us of His acceptance of us.*

A Goal "in Christ" Is to Choose to Be Thankful When We Experience Rejection

Peter taught, "So get rid of all evil behavior. Be done with all deceit, hypocrisy, jealousy, and all unkind speech. Like newborn babies, you must crave pure spiritual milk so that you will grow into a full experience of salvation. Cry out for this nourishment, now that you have had a taste of the Lord's kindness" (1 Pet. 2:1-3 NLT). Since Paul tells us to get rid of evil behavior, and we know that he is not just taunting us, we also know that we can change the way we respond to rejection. Therefore, *by faith, we can begin to choose to be thankful for rejection as God will use it to grow us up into a full experience of salvation.* Eventually, we can reach the point that by faith we can even look forward to our next rejection, for we will expect God to use it to bring us back into awareness of who we are "in Christ," to being made strong in Him rather than through our *flesh. Through this process of learning to let rejection make us conscious of who we are "in Christ," our minds can be "renewed" so that we will no longer be giving others the power to make us perpetually miserable.*

Learning to handle rejection "in Christ" is a necessity if we are to attain the "full experience of salvation" that God desires for us to attain. Paul prayed this for us: "I kneel before the Father, from whom his whole family in heaven and on earth derives its name. I pray that out of his glorious riches he may strengthen you with power through his Spirit in your inner being, so that Christ may dwell in your hearts through faith. And I pray that you, being rooted and established in love, may have power, together with all the saints, to grasp how wide and long and high and deep is the love of Christ, and to know this love that surpasses knowledge—that you may be filled to the measure of all the fullness of God" (Eph. 3:14-19 NIV). *We will never be able to be "rooted and established in God's love" and "filled to the measure of all the fullness of God" until we learn how to put aside the rejection that Satan sends our way through this fallen world.*

Rejection happens in this world. But though we are in the world, we are not of the world. We are "in Christ." May you choose to walk out of this world's ever-continuing cycle of rejection and to be defined by Christ alone as you strive to let rejection be a trigger to make you consciousness of who you are "in Christ"!

We Must Understand the Progressive Nature of Sanctification

If we do not understand that walking after the Spirit is a learned behavior with progression, we will soon find ourselves defeated by Satan. Instead of seeing failure as an opportunity for belated obedience and growth, we will instead become discouraged, lower our expectations, and find ourselves easily made victims of sin. The Amplified Bible states the key verse for this diagram above this way:

> Like newborn babies you should crave [thirst for, earnestly desire] the pure [unadulterated] spiritual milk, that by it you may be nurtured and grow unto [completed] salvation. (1 Pet. 2:2 AMP)

I do not think it a coincidence that Peter prefaces "growing unto completed salvation" with talk of babies. It takes babies a long time to learn how to walk. Likewise, it takes time to learn how to "walk after the Spirit" when we are rejected. Like babies, we will fall. We will get hurt. We will need encouragement, and to God's praise, He gives it! Our failure is covered by the blood of Jesus while the Holy Spirit is at work in us to grow us up in this *process* of learning to handle rejection through "walking by the Spirit."

We need to know that we will sometimes fail. But even more, we need to know that we don't have to keep failing. If we keep trying we are eventually going to "walk by the Spirit" in the face of rejection. *We can learn to receive our identity from Christ's work on our behalf rather than from our failures. In time, babies get walking down pretty good. Likewise, in time, we can get "walking by the Spirit" down pretty good too!*

> For he who sows to his flesh will of the flesh reap corruption, but he who sows to the Spirit will of the Spirit reap everlasting life. And let us not grow weary while doing good, for in due season we shall reap if we do not lose heart. (Gal. 6:8-9 NKJV)

The key to success is laboring to keep our minds focused on our identity "in Christ," for "those who live in accordance with the Spirit have their minds set on what the Spirit desires" (Rom. 8:5 NIV). When we are conscious of all He has done to redefine us, rejection is like a little Chihuahua barking at us from the corner of a room. This tiny dog makes a lot of noise; it can nip at us and perhaps hurt us, but it can't really harm us.

We have all received some rejection from this fallen world, and some of us have received so much rejection that we might properly be labeled as "rejects" if we continue to look to the fallen world for our identity rather than to our Creator. May we not let this happen, for though we are in the world, we are not of the world. We belong to God, and only He has the right to define us. If we learn to look to God alone to know our true identity (the eternal identity He gives us "in Christ"), we will see ourselves differently, and as a result of the subsequent renewed thinking about ourselves, we can then experience this world differently. We do not have to keep conforming to the old patterns of thinking that perpetuate the rejection cycle. God promises that our thinking can be transformed so that we might know His good, pleasing and perfect will. "Don't copy the behavior and customs of this world, but let God transform you into a new person by changing the way you think. Then you will learn to know God's will for you, which is good and pleasing and perfect" (Rom. 12:2, NLT).

God's Goal for Us Is that Ministry Will Flow out of Our Rejection

Remember, we do not need to pray for our rejection to be taken away, but rather to learn to respond to it "after the Spirit" so that God may then use it to mature us spiritually. Jesus did not pray for his disciples to be placed in a bubble or taken out of the world, but rather that we might overcome the evil one (see John 17:15). Furthermore, it is as we learn to handle perceived rejection "in Christ" by "walking by the Spirit" that we then also become equipped to help others do the same (see 2 Cor. 1:3-4). *As disciples of Christ, we need to know the truth and then apply the truth to our lives, and we also need to share the truth with others. That's what disciples of Christ are called to do!*

Hear these words from the Bible that express God's true attitude toward His chosen ones:

> The LORD your God is with you,
> He is mighty to save.
> He will take great delight in you,
> He will quiet you with his love,
> He will rejoice over you with singing. (Zeph. 3:17 NIV)

All of us have been somewhat deceived by the rejection we have received at the hands of the fallen world. In fact, most of us, including me, have trouble receiving Zephaniah 3:17 as truth. This is because our experiences in the fallen world have programmed our *flesh* in ways that cause this truth from God's Word to "feel" as if it is not true. Nevertheless, we are not rejects. We are the chosen of God, redefined "in Christ," and loved far beyond our ability to fully comprehend it all. *You are greater than you know! Will you believe?*

Things You May Ponder and Discuss with Others

1. What do you think about this statement: "Christians who reject others need ministry. Rather than 'walking after the Spirit,' they are reacting without consciousness of the deceitfulness of the world's shaping of them, blind to what God has done for them, and are thus unavailable for what God wants to do through them."
2. When you sense rejection, or even the threat of rejection, do you tend to react in: (a) skunky ways, (b) as a successful performer, or (c) as a turtle who sometimes snaps? How has the way you tend to respond to rejection worked for you?
3. As you have read this chapter, have persons come to mind who exhibit skunky or performance based behavior and perhaps even rub you the wrong way? Have you gained insights that will enable you to bless them by choosing to minister to them instead of reacting to them? If you are in a group where there is confidentiality, those who are willing should share their insights in order to help the group gain better understanding of how to best handle the rejection that inevitably comes our way.
4. Your response to perceived rejection can become a choice. But to be able to make a godly choice, you must quit looking to the world (creation) to know who you are and start looking to Christ alone. This chapter has talked about a lot of things that you can choose to do when you sense rejection. You can learn to overcome rejection. You can be empowered by the Spirit to make *choices* when sensing rejection rather than continuing to *react* and thus defaulting back to the old behavior your *flesh* is programmed to exhibit. Learning to respond differently to rejection is like breaking a bad habit. We must change the way we think and then persistently work to overcome our habitual reactions when sensing rejection. Look again at the section in this chapter titled "Things We Must Practice if We Are to

Overcome Rejection." Which of the truths listed do you think are the most important for you to labor to believe so that you might act differently when experiencing rejection?
5. Read through the section of this chapter titled "Common Thought Patterns, Attitudes, and Behavior (*flesh*) of Performers." Place a check mark by the bullets that seem true of you. *As you identify with some of these, please do not condemn yourself for having these thought patterns. The Holy Spirit does not condemn, but rather convicts so that you may choose to trust Him with your history and be empowered through Him to be delivered from these thought patterns and attitudes.* Also, remember that these patterns are normal for persons who experience rejection by significant people in their lives. But they are not thought patterns and attitudes that you need to keep holding on to. After identifying the bullets that apply to you, jot down some ideas as to why the thought patterns and attitudes that you checked are now inappropriate for you since you are now "in Christ." Let me encourage you to make the time to do this work. You will discover it to be time well spent. Your answers to questions 5-8 will also be used in chapters 8 and 9 of this book to enable you to experience God's deliverance from the effects of past rejection in your life and to limit the harmful effects of future rejection.
6. Read through the "Common Thought Patterns, Attitudes, and Behavior (*flesh*) of the Skunky" bullet list and do the same things that were requested in question 5.
7. Read over the section in this chapter that is titled "The Flesh Patterns That We Form in Response to Our Rejection Also Distort Our View of God." In what ways do you suspect the rejection you have experienced in your past has distorted your view of God?
8. Who has hurt you? How has the hurt you experienced from them impacted your thoughts and actions as you have matured? Know that even though the person did not necessarily act in malice toward you, their actions (or inactions) and their words can nevertheless impact the way you approach and experience life. You can be loosed from the impact of the rejection you have perceived from them, but you need to first recognize what has happened in order to facilitate God's loosing process.

9. Ask God to allow you to (a) experience rejection very soon, (b) be aware of how the rejection affects you, and (c) recognize how you naturally tend to handle it. This will give you the opportunity to begin handling rejection differently as you clearly see how it impacts you, and then choose to "walk by the Spirit" to overcome it. Walking "by the Spirit" when you experience rejection is learned behavior and takes practice, so you need opportunities for practice, and the sooner the better. You do not walk out of rejection just by reading how to do it. Consider journaling your experiences in handling rejection. If you have a chance to share your experiences with someone else, that will be better still. Another thing you can do that will be helpful to you is to think of past rejections and how you might have handled them differently. That would be practice that will help you to make a choice the next time you experience similar rejection rather than just continuing to react.
10. Why is our choice to repent when the Holy Spirit *convicts* us of our wrong reaction to rejection the most crucial step in the process of learning to "walk after the Spirit" when we experience rejection?
11. Why is extending thanksgiving and praise to God when we have been rejected an appropriate and important expression of faith?
12. Why must we understand that overcoming rejection is progressive in nature?

CHAPTER 6: OVERCOMING THE POWER OF SIN

LISTEN TO THE pain the apostle Paul feels as he struggles with sin and *flesh* and concludes that he is a "wretched man":

> For what I am doing, I do not understand. For what I will to do, that I do not practice; but what I hate, that I do. If, then, I do what I will not to do, I agree with the law that it is good. But now, it is no longer I who do it, but sin that dwells in me. For I know that in me [that is, in my flesh] nothing good dwells; for to will is present with me, but how to perform what is good I do not find. For the good that I will to do, I do not do; but the evil I will not to do, that I practice. Now if I do what I will not to do, it is no longer I who do it, but sin that dwells in me. I find then a law, that evil is present with me, the one who wills to do good. For I delight in the law of God according to the inward man. But I see another law in my members, warring against the law of my mind, and bringing me into captivity to the law of sin which is in my members. O wretched man that I am! Who will deliver me from this body of death? I thank God—through Jesus Christ our Lord! So then, with the mind I myself serve the law of God, but with the flesh the law of sin. (Rom. 7:15-25 NKJV)

We are given a new heart when we are born again, a desire to live pleasing to God. Because of that, we want to abstain from sin. Nevertheless, do you, as did Paul, sometimes experience conflict within—an inner struggle against doing what you know is the right thing to do? Do you sometimes lose the struggle and do what you know is wrong? It's a common dilemma for all Christians, not just Paul. This is a dilemma brought about by sin's domination of our *flesh*.

Even though we are Christians, much of the content of our minds is the programming that comes from our interaction with this fallen world that so powerfully represents to us the deceptive influence of sin and Satan. This deceptive programming of our minds by the fallen world is called *flesh* and is an enemy of God's Holy Spirit within us (see Gal. 5:16-17). *Flesh* is a present tense problem for all believers, but it is an old message from our old identity, and it can be overcome as we learn who we are "in Christ" and choose to "walk by the Spirit."

As a young Christian, I struggled with lust. I was convicted by the Holy Spirit and knew the way I was viewing women was wrong. I was grieved by it. I prayed and struggled to renew my mind. All of these were important things to do, but they were also inadequate by themselves to break my stronghold of lust. My breakthrough came when I grew to understand that enemies from without, Satan and his forces of evil, were triggering my struggle within. It is as Paul wrote, "Now if I do what I will not to do, it is no longer I who do it, but sin that dwells in me" (Rom. 7:20 NKJV). *I needed to take authority "in Jesus's name" over the thoughts, recognizing that since they did not reflect my true desires, they were not really my thoughts but old flesh patterns.* I found relief when I began to pray out loud this way: "By the blood of the Lamb, I order you, Satan, and every deceiving spirit, to leave me and go wherever Jesus tells you to go." I had to pray out loud because Satan cannot read our minds as God can. When I prayed this prayer, the thoughts would flee, and lust was overcome.

The "law of sin" (v. 25) in this Romans 7 passage should not be thought of in terms of an act but rather as a *power* that lures, and sometimes drives, one to act. *Flesh* gives Satan a foothold by which to establish his control in our lives. *Flesh* is an ever-present, potentially destructive nuisance that contends against our choosing to walk as Christ did. *Flesh* allows temptation housed in our mind, rooted in our past, and fortified by emotions to beset us. Temptation can be so strong that we find ourselves succumbing to it and then crying out with Paul, "O wretched man that I am! Who will deliver me from this body of death?" (Rom. 7:24).

Christians must learn to recognize *flesh* for what it is and believe that they are "in Christ" so that they experience God's power (in the person of the Holy Spirit) to stand against it. Believers, though they must struggle against sin and *flesh*, do not have to live in defeat. Paul finished his lamentation about being a "wretched man needing deliverance"

(Rom. 7:24) with a great affirmation of faith: "I thank God—through Jesus Christ our Lord!" (Rom. 7:25). *It is the intent of this chapter to show how we can join with Paul and gain victory "in Christ" to overcome the temptations and subsequent actions that leave us feeling wretched about ourselves.*

When thought about rightly, there is something good about this state of wretchedness that is in all of us. While we may lament this ugliness within our minds that spills out in unacceptable behavior, it nevertheless has an important function. It reminds us of our need to be dependent on Christ.

Flesh Can Have the Appearance of Righteousness

Flesh can desire righteousness, though it is righteousness that comes from our own doing. We might think that something distorted by the evil one would have no pretense of righteousness. But let us never forget that Satan masquerades as an "angel of light" (see 2 Cor. 11:14). *Flesh* can have a religious manifestation, as it always wants to look good and never wants to look bad. But this is a self-merited "goodness," a pretense of true "goodness" that is independent of Christ and the power of the Spirit. We must be wary of this manifestation! We need to join with Paul in seeking only the righteousness that comes through faith "in Christ" alone (see Phil. 3:9) rather than the righteousness that looks good to outsiders but, in truth, is only Pharisee-like behavior that earns Jesus's condemnation. Jesus declared to the Pharisees, who were outwardly very religious and proud of being so, "**Woe to you, scribes and Pharisees, hypocrites! For you are like whitewashed tombs which indeed appear beautiful outwardly, but inside are full of dead men's bones and all uncleanness**" (Matt. 23:27 NKJV).

Sin Must Be Dealt With in Its Entirety

Sin has two parts: (1) *acts of sin* and (2) the *sin principle within*. *Acts of sin* are the wrong things we have done. By God's grace, the things believers have done wrong have been dealt with through Jesus's substitutionary death in our place. But there is also the *sin principle within* or *state of sin*, the powerful allure of sin that draws and enslaves unbelievers into the state of doing wrong.

William Barclay, who was excellent in breaking down Greek words in order to present deep spiritual truths, writes of sin:

> *"Hamartia"* is the commonest NT noun for "sin"; it occurs in Paul's letters 60 times: and *"hamartanein"* is the usual verb for "to sin." . . . *In the NT "hamartia" does not describe a definite act of sin; it describes the state of sin from which acts of sin come.* In fact in Paul sin becomes almost personalized until *sin could be spelled with a capital letter, and could be thought of as malignant, personal power which has man in its grasp.* (Barclay 1974. *New Testament Words.* 118-119; emphasis mine)

Sin is more than something we do. In its noun form, sin is presented as a personification of evil that must be overcome or, as Barclay said, "a malignant, *personal* power." When tempted, believers need greater resources than just their natural ones if they are to overcome sin. So believers must learn to "walk by the Spirit," to be dependent on the Holy Spirit's power (which God makes readily available to believers), if they are to consistently overcome sin in its noun form (the *sin principle within* or *state of sin*). That is one of the main reasons Jesus said, "Apart from Me you can do nothing" (John 15:5).

Paul offers a most sobering view of the *sin principle within us* (sin in noun form) in Romans. He calls this *sin principle within us* the law of sin, writing, "But I discern in my bodily members [in the sensitive appetites and wills of the flesh] a different law [rule of action] at war against the law of my mind [my reason] and making me a prisoner to the law of sin that dwells in my bodily organs [in the sensitive appetites and wills of the flesh]" (Rom. 7:23 AMP). Barclay writes, "So basic is the hold of sin over man that sin is not merely an external power which exercises sway over a man; it has gotten into the very fibre and centre and heart of his being until it occupies him, as an enemy occupies an occupied country. The result is that we can be said 'to be slaves of sin'" (pages 121-122 New Testament Words). Paul said, "We know that our old [unrenewed] self was nailed to the cross with Him in order that [our] body [which is the instrument] of sin might be made ineffective and inactive for evil, that we might no longer be the slaves of sin . . . . But thank God, though you were once slaves of sin, you have become obedient with all your heart to the standard of teaching in which you were instructed and to which you were committed" (Rom. 6:6, 17 AMP).

Paul states in the above passage that the believers he is writing to are no longer *slaves* to sin, but warns us that the "law of sin" is still a powerful warrior against the Spirit of Christ Who resides within the believer. Thus, Scripture clearly teaches that we no longer *have* to walk after sin. Nevertheless, experience has shown us that we *can* sin and that we often *do. Even though Christians are no longer slaves to sin, their flesh is still programmed in accordance with sin's desires, and thus when believers do not choose to "walk by the Spirit," they should not be surprised to find themselves defaulting back to fleshly habits and thought patterns.* The difference is that slaves have no choice but to walk after sin. Believers, however, are not slaves to sin. Believers *can* still walk after sin, but they *have a choice* as to whether or not they will. Yet *if the believer does not learn to "walk by the Spirit," he will continue to defer to the* sin principle within *and will then commit acts of sin.*

The Person of the Holy Spirit

Jesus told the disciples, "You will receive power when the Holy Spirit comes on you; and you will be my witnesses in Jerusalem, and in all Judea and Samaria, and to the ends of the earth" (Acts 1:8 NIV). The Holy Spirit is the Third Person of the Holy Trinity, a part of the Godhead. The presence of the Holy Spirit brings power to the Christian, but He is a person, not some power or *force* that can be referred to as an "it." The believer is to personally interact with the Person of the Holy Spirit.

Just as Jesus came to reveal His Father to man so that we might know the Father intimately, in like manner, the Spirit makes Christ known to us. Following in a brief biblical introduction to the Holy Spirit:

- Jesus taught us that the Holy Spirit is like Himself, *another Helper*, who will dwell in us and help us to discern truth. "And I will pray the Father, and He will give you another Helper, that He may abide with you forever—the Spirit of truth, whom the world cannot receive, because it neither sees Him nor knows Him; but you know Him, for He dwells with you and will be in you. I will not leave you orphans; I will come to you" (John 14:16-18 NKJ).

- This *Helper* will teach us truth about Jesus. He comes to make Jesus known. "But when the Helper comes, whom I shall send to you from the Father, the Spirit of truth who proceeds from the Father, He will testify of Me" (John 15:16 NKJ). "But the Counselor, the Holy Spirit, whom the Father will send in my name, will teach you all things and will remind you of everything I have said to you" (John 14:26 NIV).
- As Jesus made the Father's will known to us, so will the Holy Spirit make Jesus's will known to us. "However, when He, the Spirit of truth, has come, He will guide you into all truth; for He will not speak on His own authority, but whatever He hears He will speak; and He will tell you things to come. He will glorify Me, for He will take of what is Mine and declare it to you" (John 16:13-14).
- Every *believer* has the Holy Spirit within himself. His personal relationship with God comes through his interaction with the indwelling Holy Spirit. The Holy Spirit not only makes Christ known to the believer, He is also so identified with Jesus that He is declared the *Spirit of Christ*: "But you are not in the flesh but in the Spirit, if indeed the Spirit of God dwells in you. Now if anyone does not have the Spirit of Christ, he is not His" (Rom. 8:9).

Summary: The Holy Spirit makes Jesus known to us. He takes what is Christ's and makes it ours. His presence empowers us to walk as Jesus walked. He is *another Helper*—as Jesus in us now—the One who has come so that we would not be left as orphans without a Shepherd. He takes Jesus's place. Though Jesus is now with the Father in heaven, we still know Him and have a relationship with Him through the indwelling presence of the Holy Spirit. Christians are to be full of the Spirit, under His influence and controlled by His presence, much like an alcoholic who is under the influence of and controlled by liquid spirits (see Eph. 5:18).

There is much controversy in Christian circles as to whether or not the baptism of the Holy Spirit is a second work of grace, but there is no controversy as to whether or not a Christian has to be empowered by the Spirit in order to walk as Christ walked. Even those who are of the persuasion that the baptism of the Holy Spirit is a "second work of grace" see progressive sanctification as both preceding and following this "second work." Thus, there is an agreement among all that if they are to overcome sin and the *flesh*, every believer must spend the rest of their lives learning how to be empowered to overcome the *sin principle within* via the presence of the Spirit of Christ within by continually choosing to walk "by the Spirit." It is as the angel declared in Zechariah. "'Not by might nor by power, but by My Spirit,' says the LORD of hosts" (Zech. 4:6).

Why Do Christians Fail So Often in Walking in Christlike Ways?

Peter admonishes us: "Like newborn babies, you must crave pure spiritual milk so that you will *grow into a full experience of salvation*. Cry out for this nourishment, now that you have had a taste of the Lord's kindness" (1 Pet. 2:2-3 NLB; emphasis mine). Many, despite the Bible's admonitions, do not seek "to grow into a full experience of salvation" because they are satisfied with the way things are for them now, and holy living would not comfortably fit in with their lifestyle. Others want holiness of life, but sadly, they have fought temptation with their own inadequate strength and have thus been so defeated by sin's power that they have lost hope for holiness. Failure will also be experienced by believers who have an inaccurate understanding of the Holy Spirit and therefore will not yield to the Spirit's influence because they fear exhibiting weird behavior if they do so.

Victory in our Christian walk comes only through our desperate dependence on the Person of the Holy Spirit. Jesus said it this way: "I am the Vine; you are the branches. Whoever lives in Me and I in him bears much [abundant] fruit. However, apart from Me [cut off from vital union with Me] you can do nothing" (John 15:5 AMP). We will grow toward a lifestyle of holiness only as we *learn* to be dependent on the Spirit. So *if believers are ignorant of or resistant to the role of the Holy Spirit in overcoming sin's power, then they will experience failure in their Christian walk.*

In his letter to the church at Galatia Paul chastised Christians who attempt holiness of living in their own strength, calling them "bewitched and foolish Galatians." He wrote: "You foolish Galatians! Who has bewitched you?" (Gal. 3:1 NSV). Let us examine these verses concerning the foolish Galatians so that we might better understand why Paul labels some believers as "foolish." The Amplified Bible expands on the term "foolish" Galatians, representing *foolish* with the synonyms *poor, silly, thoughtless, unreflecting,* and *senseless*.

> O you poor and silly and thoughtless and unreflecting and senseless Galatians! Who has fascinated or bewitched or cast a spell over you, unto whom—right before your very eyes—Jesus Christ [the Messiah] was openly and graphically set forth and portrayed as crucified? Let me ask you this one question: Did you receive the [Holy] Spirit as the result of obeying the Law and doing its works, or was it by hearing [the message of the Gospel] and believing [it]? [Was it from observing a law of rituals or from a message of faith?] Are you so foolish and so senseless and so silly? Having begun [your new life spiritually] with the [Holy] Spirit, are you now reaching perfection [by dependence] on the flesh? Have you suffered so many things and experienced so much all for nothing [to no purpose]—if it really is to no purpose and in vain? Then does He Who supplies you with His marvelous [Holy] Spirit and works powerfully and miraculously among you do so on [the grounds of your doing] what the Law demands, or because of your believing in and adhering to and trusting in and relying on the message that you heard? (Gal. 3:1-5 AMP)

Later in this chapter, we will more fully deal with these verses. But here is the point for now: *in His grace, God gives believers the Holy Spirit to take Jesus's place in helping them overcome sin's power and allurement. Just as in salvation, we are to overcome sin's power by believing in God's provision for our weakness.* At the time of our salvation, we believed in the effectiveness of Jesus's shed blood to cover our sin problem. Once saved, the believer is to trust in the power of His ever-present Spirit to be able to walk in ways pleasing to God. It is all by faith (believing). But faith must have an object, a focus.

Faith that overcomes the allurement and power of sin must focus on Jesus's promise to send the Holy Spirit to believers: "I will send the Holy Spirit, just as my Father promised. But stay here in the city until the Holy Spirit comes and fills you with power from heaven" (Luke 24:49 NLT). Just as we asked for salvation, *we must continually ask for the Holy Spirit's empowerment rather than trusting in our own abilities.*

When we ask, God promises to grant our request. As Jesus said it, "If you then, evil as you are, know how to give good gifts [gifts that are to their advantage] to your children, how much more will your heavenly Father give the Holy Spirit to those who ask and continue to ask Him!" (Luke 11:13 AMP)

The Holy Spirit Can Be Resisted, Even Grieved (Like Any Other Person)

Like Jesus, the Holy Spirit is a person Who must be responded to. He desires intimacy with us, *but* we must *choose* to relate to Him. *He has emotions and can be grieved*: "And do not grieve the Holy Spirit of God" (Eph. 4:30 NIV). *He can be insulted*: "Just think how much worse the punishment will be for those who have trampled on the Son of God, and have treated the blood of the covenant, which made us holy, as if it were common and unholy, and have *insulted* and disdained the Holy Spirit who brings God's mercy to us" (Heb. 10:29 NLT; emphasis mine). Like any other person, including Jesus, *He can be ignored*. He will not dominate. *He wants to bless us, but He can be resisted.*

How Do We Draw Upon the Holy Spirit So That We May Walk in Holiness?

John writes, "He who is in you is greater than he who is in the world" (1 John 4:4). Paul admonishes, "I can do all things through Him who strengthens me" (Phil. 4:13). *We do not have to walk in defeat.* Because of what Christ has done, we do not have to keep being brought low by Satan, *flesh*, and this fallen world. Because Christ is effective and powerful in us through the Person of the Holy Spirit, we can be overcomers. *Even though Satan is always tempting us to be less than what we have been called to be "in Christ," we can turn his temptations (that appeal to our flesh) against him by learning to respond to temptation "in Christ." We can choose to "walk by the Spirit" rather than yield to temptation.* We cannot overcome without the Spirit's help, but the believer has a *necessary* part to play in that overcoming. James says, "So be subject to God. *Resist* the devil [stand firm against him], and he will flee from you" (James 4:7 AMP). Weight lifting teaches us that struggling to overcome resistance makes us strong. Knowing that we are "in Christ" and persistently choosing to "walk by the Spirit" in order to resist Satan when temptation comes are the keys to being made "spiritually" strong. Even though we may experience temporary failure, our *persistent* struggle to depend on the Spirit in resisting temptation will eventually make us strong in the Lord. That is why Paul writes, "Consider it pure joy, my brothers, whenever you face trials of many kinds, because you know that the testing of your faith develops perseverance. Perseverance must finish its work so that you may be mature and complete, not lacking anything" (James 1:2-4 NIV). Becoming strong in the Lord is the long-term, persevering effect of abiding in Christ so that sin, the *flesh*, and Satan might be overcome.

Let us examine the following chart to more clearly understand how God will strengthen us by *using* against Satan the very temptations Satan and this world have designed to destroy us. *Isn't that just like God. He used Satan's attempt to destroy Jesus to grant salvation to all who will repent and believe, and now He uses Satan's attempts to destroy the believer to make the believer strong in the Lord.* The following chart is a slight modification of the chart developed in the last chapter. Its purpose is to chart the steps and rationale necessary to overcome the temptations that Satan continually uses to lure us away from being defined "in Christ," to lure us back into being defined by the fallen world so that we will be robbed of the Spirit's power for walking in victory. It is as Jesus said, "The thief comes only in order to steal and kill and destroy. I came that they may have and enjoy life, and have it in abundance [to the full, till it overflows]" (John 10:10 AMP).

This diagram on the right is very similar to the diagram in the previous chapter on "Handling Rejection in Christ" because both temptation and rejection are appeals through Satan's fallen world to our *flesh* that must be resisted by choosing to "walk by the Spirit." We must never forget Jesus's warning to all believers as recorded in the Gospel of John:

> Dwell in Me, and I will dwell in you. [Live in Me, and I will live in you.] Just as no branch can bear fruit of itself without abiding in [being vitally united to] the vine, neither can you bear fruit unless you abide in Me. I am the Vine; you are the branches. Whoever lives in Me and I in him bears much [abundant] fruit. However, apart from Me [cut off from vital union with Me] you can do nothing (John 15:4-5 AMP)

If we are not in vital connection with Jesus through the Spirit, i.e., aware (conscious) of our need and presently depending on His Spirit within us for power to act in accordance with His known will, then we will default back to old *flesh* patterns. We will find ourselves acting the way this fallen world has programmed our mind to react. Let's look at the chart in detail, using the numerical guides to work through the diagrams that are designed to show how we can overcome the power of sin. We overcome the power of sin by choosing to "walk by the Spirit" when we are tempted to act beneath who we are "in Christ."

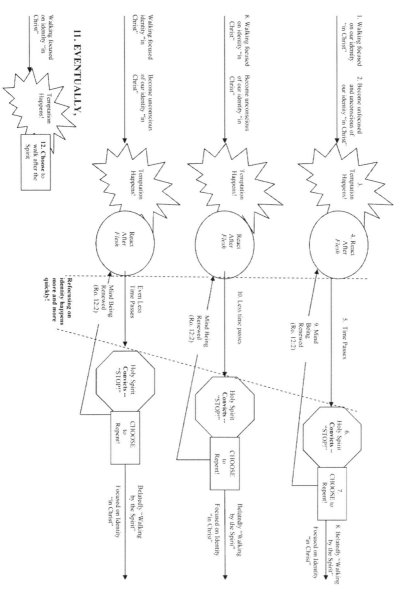

YOU ARE GREATER THAN YOU KNOW ~177~

1. We Need to Walk in Constant Awareness of Our Identity "in Christ"

1. Walking focused on our identity "in Christ"

⎯⎯⎯⎯⎯⎯⎯⎯→

Our need to subject ourselves to God's provisions for the *renewing of our mind* (see Rom. 12:2) cannot be overemphasized. *Our foremost tool for the renewal of our minds is God's Word.* There God's will is stated clearly in black-and-white (and red in some bibles). We must labor to know God's Word so that we can understand who He is and His "good" plan for prospering us: "'For I know the plans I have for you,' declares the LORD, 'plans to prosper you and not to harm you, plans to give you hope and a future. Then you will call upon me and come and pray to me, and I will listen to you'" (Jer. 29:11-12 NIV).

We need to be exposed to God's Word by reading it, but also through many other mediums such as Bible study helps, anointed teachings, and writings. But teaching alone will not suffice. Checking the word of teachers against the Bible is always in order. In the Acts of the Apostles, we read, "Now the Bereans were of more noble character than the Thessalonians, for they received the message with great eagerness and examined the Scriptures every day to see if what Paul said was true" (Acts 17:11 NIV). If what you are reading here (or anywhere else) is not in harmony with Scripture, then throw out what you are reading. Never take a speaker's word over the revelation of the Bible. Our final authority must always be what God's Word clearly teaches. We must become students of God's Word. If we sense that God is leading us toward something that is not in harmony with God's Word, we can be sure that our sense of leading is not of God and that we are most likely being deceived.

Fellowship is important too. Paul warns us in Hebrews 14:20, "And let us not neglect our meeting together, as some people do, but encourage one another, especially now that the day of his return is drawing near" (Heb. 10:25 NLT). We need the encouragement and fellowship of other believers. We need to learn from their experiences, and they need to learn from ours. An old saying I first heard through the lay witness movement says it well: "We're just one beggar telling another beggar where we've found bread." Just as a blazing log in the hottest fire will grow cold if separated from the fire, so also can we grow cold when we are out of fellowship. We need to rub against other believers who are alive (hot) in the Lord (see Rev. 3:16).

Don't forget music and worship either. They are God's special gift to touch our hearts. Pay close attention to the words. Time has shown music to be an inspiration, combining word and heart.

Furthermore, look around and give thanks—often! God's creation is marvelous, from the largest, most vast aspects, to the minutest. Take time to be amazed by the genius of God's creation. Offering thanks to God is appropriate in all circumstances and is especially important in helping us to rise above the negative circumstances of life. Thanksgiving and peace go hand in hand. Paul connects thanksgiving with peace, writing, "Do not be anxious about anything, but in everything, by prayer and petition, with thanksgiving, present your requests to God. And the peace of God, which transcends all understanding, will guard your hearts and your minds in Christ Jesus" (Phil. 4:6-7 NIV). Persons who often express thanksgiving to God tend to be conscious of their identity "in Christ" and aware of God's presence. There is much power in that awareness. How good are you at being quick to offer thanks to God? *Expressing thanks to God often is a simple habit that makes a tremendous difference in our awareness of God's presence.*

Finally, there is prayer. Prayer is speaking your heart to God, but it is listening to God's heart too. Almost all of us talk too much in prayer! We must learn to be silent before God, to listen for His heart expressions to us. Combine prayer and Bible reading. Meditate. Combine prayer and singing. It's all a love language.

2. But We Often Become Unconscious of Our Identity "in Christ"

1. Walking focused on our identity "in Christ" → 2. Become unfocused and unconscious of our identity "in Christ"

It seems that once we have discovered God's glorious good news of our identity "in Christ," we would never fail to walk in the light of this truth. But both our experiences and the Word of God tell us that this is not so. We have listened to Satan's voice through this fallen world for so long that our minds have been programmed to react in the ways of the world. Thus, it is easy for us to lose our conscious awareness of God's presence and who we are "in Christ." He is always with us, but we're often not conscious of His presence.

Once saved, we receive a new heart, and we will not suddenly fall away from God. But if we once again become preoccupied with this fallen world, then we can find ourselves once again attracted to this world and out of fellowship with God. This can happen bit by bit, so slowly that we are unaware that it is happening. That is why Hebrews warns, "We must listen very carefully to the truth we have heard, or we may drift away from it" (Heb. 2:1).

This idea of being more and more conscious of the continuous presence of Christ in us cannot be overemphasized. It is the essence of "walking after the Spirit." When we are conscious of our identity in Christ, we are also fortified to be mighty. He is always available and always "mighty to save" (Isa. 63:1 NASB), but when we are not conscious of His presence, we most often habitually handle things in our own strength. *Satan's most effective strategy against believers is to divert our thoughts to things of this world so that our minds are not fixed on our identity in Christ.* We can then become preoccupied with this world and vulnerable to its attractive deceits. Thus we must struggle to stay aware (be conscious) of who we are "in Christ"! *Growing in the amount of time we are consciously aware of His abiding presence is essential to learning to walk in His strength.*

3. When We Are Unconscious of our Identity "in Christ," Temptation Can Clobber Us

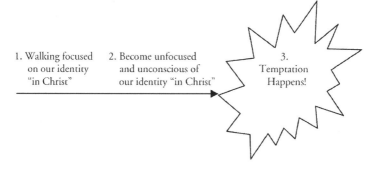

"Temptation" in this diagram should be thought of as not only something that temps us to act beneath who we are "in Christ," but also as anything that entices us to move away from dependence on "Christ in us" as our strength for holy living. We fall to temptation when we walk in our own strength rather than in dependence on the Holy Spirit. Satan is always tempting us to

focus on this fallen world to find our identity, meaning, and significance. His goal is to keep us unconscious of who we are "in Christ" for greater and greater lengths of time. *Therefore, our goal needs to be to stay conscious of who we are "in Christ" for greater and greater lengths of time.*

Satan's greatest asset for accomplishing his destructive mission is our deceived *flesh*, which naturally focuses on this fallen world to find identity, meaning, and significance. God places His Spirit within us so that we can withstand temptation (see 1 Cor. 10:13). But if we are not conscious of His Spirit (Who is ever ready to help us when we are tempted), then we will try to resist in our own strength. After all, that is our habit pattern. We have done it that way most of our lives (both before and after we became a Christian). Furthermore, we would keep doing it that way if it worked. But it doesn't! The result is not only failure in resistance but also a watered-down view of God's strength within us. We become as "foolish Galatians." Let me explain.

In his letter to the Galatians, Paul reminds believers of the futility of resisting Satan in their own strength. He writes, "I do not nullify the grace of God, for if righteousness comes through the Law, then Christ died needlessly" (Gal. 2:21 NASB). In Romans 3:20, he is quite clear about what that means, writing, "No one will be declared righteous in his sight by observing the Law; rather, through the law we become conscious of sin" (NIV). The "Law" cannot save man. This is because the unsaved do not possess the Holy Spirit and thus are powerless to overcome the power and deceitfulness of sin and keep the Law. All the Law does for the unsaved man is make him aware of his need for a Savior by holding before him standards he cannot keep by his own strength. It is as Jesus declared, "I am the vine; you are the branches. If a man remains in me and I in him, he will bear much fruit; apart from me you can do nothing" (John 15:5 NIV). Thus, Paul is reminding us that God, in order to save us, had to send Jesus to die for our sin and thus prepare the way for the Holy Spirit to indwell us.

But in the very next verses, Paul then reminds us that we still cannot keep the Law in our own strength even though we are saved. He writes,

> You foolish Galatians! Who has bewitched you? Before your very eyes Jesus Christ was clearly portrayed as crucified. I would like to learn just one thing from you: Did you receive the Spirit by observing the law, or by believing what you heard? Are you so foolish? After beginning with the Spirit,

are you now trying to attain your goal by human effort? Have you suffered so much for nothing—if it really was for nothing? Does God give you his Spirit and work miracles among you because you observe the law, or because you believe what you heard? (Gal. 3:1-5 NIV)

We can keep the Law only through the Spirit's help. That was true before we were saved. That is true after we are saved. Yet man is so used to walking in his own resources that he just naturally tries to *keep* the Law with his own resources after he is saved. But that doesn't work, does it? Christians must *learn* to "walk by the Spirit."

Good News about Temptation

Hear some good news: God wants to use the temptation we experience in the world to grow us up in our Christian walk. James shows how God uses temptation to expose the inadequacies of our *flesh*, writing, "Let no one say when he is tempted, 'I am tempted by God'; for God cannot be tempted by evil, nor does He Himself tempt anyone. But each one is tempted when he is drawn away by his own desires and enticed. Then, when desire has conceived, it gives birth to sin; and sin, when it is full-grown, brings forth death" (James 1:13-15 NIV). James has declared that man is tempted because of "his own desires and enticed." We are undone by our *flesh*. Let's now add Paul's teaching in Galatians 5:16-17 to James: "But I say, walk by the Spirit, and you will not carry out the desire of the flesh. For the flesh sets its desire against the Spirit, and the Spirit against the flesh; for these are in opposition to one another, so that you may not do the things that you please" (NASB). God's part in helping us overcome our problem with the desires of our *flesh* is the indwelling Holy Spirit. But we have a part too. We must learn how to "walk by the Spirit."

God allows temptation to beset us in order to show us the inadequacies of our flesh and the necessity of "walking by the Spirit." Flesh tempts us to seek to be good by our own strength, but fails. Thus, it plays into God's hands. God has given believers a new heart that desires to please Him. Now, through the conviction of the Holy Spirit, temptation exposes the "wretched man" in our *flesh* that cannot please God, calls attention to the inadequacy of even USDA Grade A$^+$ *flesh* to prevail in spiritual matters, and thus forces us to consider learning to "walk by the Spirit" so that we might please God (see Gal. 5:16-17). If we don't learn to "walk by the Spirit," we will default back to our old ways, become frustrated, and feel like a failure as a Christian (wretched man). Because our religious *flesh* hates to fail too, God has now used our *flesh* to get our attention. *Satan intends temptation for evil; God uses it for good. He uses it to point out our need to learn to "walk by the Spirit" so that we can please Him with our lives.* "God is working in you, giving you the desire and the power to do what pleases him" (Phil. 2:13 NLT). Satan means temptation to cause us harm; God uses Satan's schemes that are intended to destroy us to work His good for us and into us.

God the Father allowed even Jesus to be tempted. "Then Jesus was led [guided] by the [Holy] Spirit into the wilderness [desert] to be *tempted* [tested and tried] by the devil" (Matt. 4:1 AMP; emphasis mine). The Amplified Bible gives us insight into why Jesus was tempted. It refers to temptation as being "tested and tried." Being tested and tried is God's way of making us strong, just as bodybuilders are made strong by pushing against ever-increasing weight.

Paul clearly saw how God the Father used temptation to strengthen him when he wrote, "We do not want you to be uninformed, brothers, about the hardships we suffered in the province of Asia. We were under great pressure, far beyond our ability to endure, so that we despaired even of life. Indeed, in our hearts we felt the sentence of death. But *this happened that we might not rely on ourselves but on God*, who raises the dead" (2 Cor. 1:8-9 NIV; emphasis mine).

Let's add 1 Corinthians 10:13 to this to help us understand this process. "For no temptation [no trial regarded as enticing to sin, no matter how it comes or where it leads] has overtaken you and laid hold on you that is not common to man [that is, no temptation or trial has come to you that is beyond human resistance and that is not adjusted and adapted and belonging to human experience, and such as man can bear]. But God is faithful [to His Word and to His compassionate nature], and He [can be trusted] not to let you be *tempted* and tried and assayed beyond your ability and strength of resistance and power to endure, but with the temptation He will [always] also provide the way out [the means of escape to a landing place], that you may be capable and strong and powerful to bear up under it patiently" (1 Cor. 10:13 AMP; emphasis mine). *Choosing* to "walk by the Spirit" is "the way out" when we are tempted. *God does not allow us to be tempted so that we will fail, but rather so that we might learn to depend on His Spirit.* God's plan not only saves us from the temptation, but it also grows us (makes us stronger) by forcing us to depend on the Holy Spirit.

Consider Paul's experience as recorded in 2 Corinthians: "And lest I should be exalted above measure by the abundance of the revelations, a thorn in the flesh was given to me, a messenger of Satan to buffet me, lest I be exalted above measure. Concerning this thing I pleaded with the Lord three times that it might depart from me. And He said to me, 'My grace is sufficient for you, for My strength is made perfect in weakness.' Therefore most gladly I will rather boast in my infirmities, that the power of Christ may rest upon me. Therefore I take pleasure in infirmities, in reproaches, in needs, in persecutions, in distresses, for Christ's sake. For when I am weak, then I am strong" (2 Cor. 12:7-10 NKJV). Because of the great revelations God had given him, Paul could easily have become proud and resisted God (see Matt. 23:12, 1 John 2:15-17). So God gave him a problem he couldn't handle in his own strength and wouldn't take it away even though three times Paul requested this of Him.

Jesus spoke a truth to Paul that we all need to hear: "My strength is made perfect in weakness" (v. 9). *Flesh* doesn't want to be weak. As persons of *flesh*, we Christians don't want to be weak. But the only thing that will make us strong is learning to acknowledge our weakness and depend on God's Holy Spirit for strength, for "apart from Him we can do nothing" (see John 15:5). *There should be no proud Christians, only desperately dependent ones. Proud* combined with *Christian* is an oxymoron. In our own strength, we fail. We could save ourselves a lot of pain if we would go ahead and burn that truth into our brain. Paul understood that so well that he responded, "Most gladly I will rather boast in my infirmities, that the power of Christ may rest upon me. Therefore I take pleasure in infirmities, in reproaches, in needs, in persecutions, in distresses, for Christ's sake. For when I am weak, then I am strong" (2 Cor. 12:10).

There is something worse than failing. It is succeeding in our own strength and being deceived into thinking that is the way to follow Christ. If we start thinking like that, God can never do anything big through us. We will be limited to our own resources because those are the resources we habitually depend on. God had something bigger for Paul to do than Paul could do in his own strength, so God had to teach Paul to quit trying to *flesh out* the Christian walk. That's true for you and me too! We are limited because we focus on ourselves and rely on our strength when we should focus on Christ and rely on the strength of His Spirit within us.

4. When Tempted, We Naturally React After Our *Flesh*

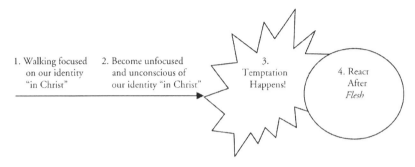

We all tend to start our Christian walk as "foolish Galatians." We do not seek the Spirit's power to do the task we feel *called to* or *asked to do*; we just naturally try to do it in our own strength. That soon becomes discouraging, for we fail—a lot. Thus, the cycle begins. We sin. We confess. We sin. We confess. We get *discouraged. Then, we begin to water down our expectations, to misunderstand God's purpose for us, and push Him, His Word, and His Church away. And Satan gloats!*

We all experience failure. We all think wrong thoughts, and we do wrong things. This is because we are reacting according to the way our *flesh* is programmed. Satan is a keen observer of fallen human nature. He knows how to ring our bell and get our attention, to effectively tempt us so that we fail. But it becomes even worse than that! Satan no longer has to be around once our *flesh* is programmed. We carry out his will habitually and reflexively and thus continue to live beneath who God declares us to be.

Our trust is not to be in our own natural abilities—our USDA Grade A⁺ *flesh*. We need to transfer our trust from ourselves to the Spirit of Christ in us so that we can be effectively used by God. We need God to intervene. And He does. "for it is God who works in you to will and to act according to his good purpose!" (Phil. 2:13 NIV). God is involved in helping us learn to "walk by the Spirit."

5. God Allows Us to Walk After the *Flesh* for a Season, and There's a Reason for This

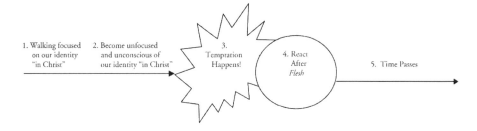

There is a reason for all things. God wants us to learn the futility of trying to do spiritual things in our own strength. *We need to be broken from self-sufficiency.* Our own efforts need to fail so that we, as Paul, can experience God's strength through our weaknesses (see 2 Cor. 12:8). In times of failure we are more likely to listen to God. Because we have first tried and failed in our own strength, we become more inclined to seek His strength. But our *flesh* doesn't want help. It wants to be independent. So "God is at work in us to will and to act according to his good purpose" (Phil. 2:13 NASV). He patiently waits for us to come to the end of our own resources so that we might fully seek His strength and be made truly strong. He waits, and when the time is right, His holy Spirit *convicts*. As we learn to respond, He will convict again and again, more quickly each time as we make progress in learning to rely on His strength. But *flesh* is very resistant, and since it takes on the appearance of our own thoughts (though it is really the programmed reactions from old thinking), we find ourselves reverting back (defaulting back) to our old self-sufficient ways. And if we don't understand the *process* of the "renewing of the mind" (see Rom. 12:2), we will soon become discouraged. *Instead of concluding that we have failed because we weren't walking dependent on the Spirit, we will conclude that we are failures who just can't walk pleasing to God. When that deception sets in, we will then focus back on the world in an attempt to find happiness there. We are deceived, and Satan gloats. But God is faithful.*

6. Then the Holy Spirit Convicts!

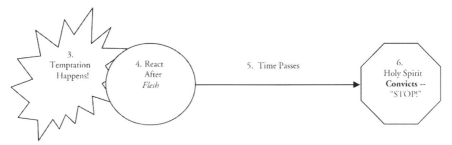

Jesus told believers that when He went away He would send another counselor, the Holy Spirit, to be with us always (see John 14:16). The Holy Spirit will make Jesus's will known to us. (see John 16:13). He will be faithful to convict us when our Christian walk is depending on self-sufficiency rather than Holy Spirit sufficiency. He may even be doing that for you right now, helping you to see through the "schemes of the devil who takes you captive to do his will" (see 2 Tim. 2:26).

> If you love me, you will obey what I command. And I will ask the Father, and he will give you another Counselor to be with you forever—the Spirit of truth. The world cannot accept him, because it neither sees him nor knows him. But you know him, for he lives with you and will be in you. I will not leave you as orphans; I will come to you. (John 14:15-18)

Convicting us of our sin is one of the most powerful and gracious things the Holy Spirit does for believers. "And when He [Holy Spirit] comes, he will convict the world of its sin, and of God's righteousness, and of the coming judgment" (John 16:8 NLB). The Holy Spirit is at work to contrast God's righteousness with our sin. We want to obey God because He shows us the beauty of His righteousness (utter goodness) and contrasts it with the ugliness of our sinfulness (our "wretched man" condition). Jesus used the word *convict* in John 16:8. The word *convict* carries within its meaning the quality of redemption. The Holy Spirit makes sin known to us so that we may escape sin's destructive deception. The Holy Spirit "convicts" us of sin in order to lift us up and away from sin, not to "put us down" (which is what condemnation does). The good news is that the Holy Spirit does not expose our sin in order to condemn us, but rather in order to free us of the ugliness of the sin in our lives. The Holy Spirit "convicts" so that we might not be overcome by the power of sin. Thus, if we do not respond to the Spirit's conviction with repentance, we hinder God's work in cleaning us up. Furthermore, we sow seeds for continuing the deception that Satan has designed for the destruction of our souls (see John 10:10a).

In essence, the Holy Spirit is saying, "Stop! Stop living beneath who you are 'in Christ.' Stop living in ways that trust in your own strength. Depend on Me. Turn away from your *fleshly* desire to attain righteousness independently of Me."

7. We Must *Choose* to Repent

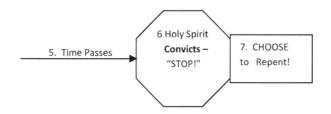

Our proper response to the conviction of the Holy Spirit is repentance. Repentance involves both a change of direction and a change of heart. It is a change of direction with "attitude."

The change of direction may not be obvious at all to an outsider. It is the difference between being God-directed and self-directed. We can be self-directed, doing spiritual-looking things, and appear to be God-directed, but it's a sham. It is only *flesh* deceiving us by looking spiritual. I remember a man who was very active in his church, a tireless worker who was seemingly eager to serve. But when convicted by the Holy Spirit, his confession was "I did all of these things to keep from doing what the Holy Spirit was leading me to do—preach." He appeared to be walking after the Spirit, but he was really walking in rebellion, substituting what he was willing to give God for what God wanted for him. But we could not know that from observing the way he was walking. He was walking in the right direction, but with a wrong attitude. He had the appearance of walking after the Spirit but, in actuality, was walking after the *flesh*.

True repentance includes a turning from "our" way to "God's" way. The Holy Spirit says, "Stop doing things your way and start doing them

God's way!" There is a verse in the Psalms that describes this turning: "I thought about my ways, and turned my feet to Your testimonies" (Ps. 119:59 NKJ). When the Spirit convicts, the truly repentant person stops doing what he was doing and starts doing that which God wants.

True repentance also involves a change of heart (attitude). The Amplified Bible describes repentance as "to change their minds for the better and heartily to amend their ways, with abhorrence of their past sins" (Luke 5:32). The heart of the repentant is no longer interested in fitting in with this fallen world but is now *desperately* interested in walking in ways pleasing to God. The man who was called to preach but chose to do everything else instead looked good from a worldly perspective, but he was a rebel from God's perspective. He was not obedient. If believers do not learn to be obedient to the Spirit's direction in their lives, they will experience the absence of the Spirit's power and, sometimes, the presence of God's discipline too. God's Word clearly states, "For the Lord corrects and *disciplines* everyone whom He loves, and He punishes, even scourges, every son whom He accepts and welcomes to His heart and cherishes" (Heb. 12:6 AMP; emphasis mine). The bottom line is this: *God will not mightily bless the work of the unrepentant because they are not wholeheartedly doing their part. They are holding out from God, holding on to personal control.*

True Repentance Is a Choice!

Repentance is a *choice.* God will not repent for us. He will send His Holy Spirit to convict us, but we must choose to respond. God is at work (Phil. 2:13), always initiating through the Holy Spirit, but man must choose to be responsive—to obey.

Walking after the Spirit often begins with our repentance. We must say "no" to our way and "yes" to God's way. In essence, when the Word declares that our works will be judged, it is also declaring that our obedience will be judged, for "apart from Him we can do nothing" (John 15:5). It is our obedience to the Holy Spirit that leads to intimate fellowship with God and God-honoring works.

Consider Paul's teaching on reward in 1 Corinthians 3: "For no other foundation can anyone lay than that which is laid, which is Jesus Christ. Now if anyone builds on this foundation with gold, silver, precious stones, wood, hay, straw, each one's work will become clear; for the Day will declare it, because it will be revealed by fire;

and the fire will test each one's work, of what sort it is. If anyone's work which he has built on it endures, he will receive a reward. If anyone's work is burned, he will suffer loss; but he himself will be saved, yet so as through fire" (1 Cor. 3:11-15 NKJV). The building materials we use could be thought of as a description of our "heart" obedience. True, heartfelt obedience to God offers Him our best for His use, "our best" being symbolized by gold, silver, and precious stones. If our "heart" is not in it, we will build with leftovers: wood, hay, and straw. *Heartfelt obedience to the Spirit's leading yields "works" that will persevere when tested by fire, and the result will be eternal reward. Self-focused, partial obedience is devoured by fire and has no eternal reward.*

Paul teaches us about the sorrow we should experience when convicted by the Holy Spirit concerning our wrongdoing: "**The kind of sorrow God wants us to experience leads us away from sin and results in salvation. There's no regret for that kind of sorrow. But worldly sorrow, which lacks repentance, results in spiritual death**" (2 Cor. 12:10 NLT).

Being sorry for doing wrong is a necessary part of repentance, but sorrow is not the same as repentance and does not necessarily lead to repentance. We can be sorry for the pain that our actions have caused to ourselves or to others but yet be without heartfelt sorrow toward God for our failure to honor Him in the way we were walking. *True repentance focuses on God's heart too, on what it cost God to cleanse us and how much God wants us to enjoy freedom from the power of sin.* True repentance is truly sorry for disobeying God, but it goes even further. It is redemptive; it not only turns us back to honoring God by the way we live on earth, but also removes the taint of our wrongdoing and motivates us toward "right-doing."

8. Belatedly, We Have Chosen to Walk by the Spirit

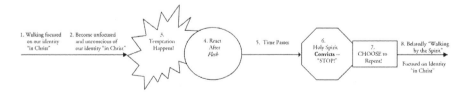

When we have chosen to repent in response to the Holy Spirit's conviction, we are once again ready to "walk by the Spirit." Ask God to

fill you anew with His Holy Spirit. God will be pleased to do that because He does not focus on our past so that He might condemn us, but on our future so that He might bless us. As John stated it, "If we say that we have no sin, we deceive ourselves, and the truth is not in us. If we confess our sins, He is faithful and just to forgive us our sins and to cleanse us from all unrighteousness" (1 John 1:8-9 NKJ). God is not like man. When others sin against us, we tend to go away from them. When we sin against God, His Holy Spirit seeks us out, wanting us cleansed. *God is far more interested than we are in our choice to "walk by His Spirit."* Just as we want the best for our children, God wants the best for His children and is at work to bring about our best (see Phil. 2:13).

9. Our Obedience Then Results in Our Minds Beginning to be Renewed

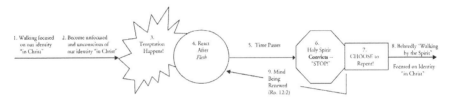

One more very important thing happens when there is true repentance. We have begun a new pattern, a pattern of depending on "Christ in us" rather than on self-sufficiency. We have taken an important step in turning away from the mind-set that keeps looking for identity from the world and the things it values. *We have begun learning to look to God alone for identity.*

Paul describes this as the "renewing of the mind," writing, "And do not be conformed to this world, but be transformed by the renewing of your mind, that you may prove what is that good and acceptable and perfect will of God" (Rom. 12:2). In order to form new habit patterns that will override the mind's old *reactions* to the world's stimuli, we must *consciously* decide to act in new ways in response to the Spirit's *conviction*. Even though we have first reacted in the old ways, *the fact that we have now chosen to respond "dependent on the Spirit" is the beginning of establishing a new mind-set that will honor God over the ways of the world.*

In chapter 2, the mind's reflex reaction was referred to as "defaulting back to flesh." Much of what we do is a learned response that has basically become a reflex action. The reaction is not so much something that we "choose" to do right now as it is something we have chosen to do in the past that has present tense reflex liabilities. This reflex action is demonstrated by our ability to drive a car when our mind is on something other than driving. It is the reflex ability to hit a fastball, something that happens so fast that it cannot be consciously thought out.

Now, "in Christ," we need to consciously develop new ways of thinking that will lead to different learned mental patterns. Our goal, though, is not to rationalize our faith (there is far too much *flesh* to overcome for that to fully happen). Furthermore, that rationalization would still result in "self" being in control rather than in the Holy Spirit being in control. We do not need self-help; we need God's help. *We need deliverance from this fierce self-reliance that is so rampant in us.* Our goal should be to prayerfully seek to respond to the Spirit's conviction and leadership so that we will consciously make choices that reflect our identity "in Christ." That process begins with our first choice to repent in response to the Spirit's conviction but must be followed by many subsequent choices before it becomes the dominant pattern in our minds.

"Walking by the Spirit" is a "choice." That choice is a response to the Holy Spirit Who is at work in us to will and to act according to His good purpose (see Phil. 2:13). It is a choice that we are actively involved in. God does not control us. He helps us by first convicting us of sin and then empowering us to respond after the Spirit. His Spirit is involved in our lives. *We do not have to always be controlled by the flesh patterns that bring us grief, but if we do not choose to "walk by the Spirit," we will be.* Consider Peter's admonition:

> Therefore, prepare your minds for action, keep sober in spirit, fix your hope completely on the grace to be brought to you at the revelation of Jesus Christ. As obedient children, do not be conformed to the former lusts which were yours in your ignorance, but like the Holy One who called you, be holy yourselves also in all your behavior. (1 Pet. 1:13-15 NASV)

If God's Word says to us "Do not be conformed to the former lusts which were yours in your ignorance, but like the Holy One who called you, be holy yourselves also in all your behavior" (v. 15), then (1) either we don't have to be conformed to our former lusts *and* we can be holy in all our behavior (v. 15), or (2) God is a sadist who enjoys deceivingly lying to us and then mockingly laughing at us for trying to do the impossible. It is hardly the second proposition! But you must also see in these verses that we are actively involved in God's deliverance from these "former lusts" (of our flesh) that have been established in our minds in our ignorance (i.e., before we knew of all that was available to us "in Christ.") We are to "prepare our minds for action, keep sober in spirit, and fix our hope completely on the grace to be brought to you at the revelation of Jesus Christ" (1 Pet. 1:13 NASB).

Many verses of Scripture declare this same warning: (1) "Therefore do not let sin reign in your mortal body so that you obey its lusts" (Rom. 6:12); (2) "But put on the Lord Jesus Christ, and make no provision for the flesh in regard to its lusts" (Rom. 13:14); and (3) "Flee from youthful lusts and pursue righteousness, faith, love and peace, with those who call on the Lord from a pure heart" (2 Tim. 2:22).

God grows us into Christlikeness as we learn to respond to His Spirit and discover that He is "renewing our mind" as we choose to "walk according to His leading." *The "renewing of our mind" involves both the work of God and our work—our joint efforts:*

1. The *renewing* requires our becoming aware of our identity "in Christ."
2. It requires that we will labor to know His Word so that we will also know His voice so that we might gain protection from Satan's clever deceptions.
3. It requires the conviction of the Holy Spirit when we face temptation.
4. It involves our repentance when we fail. God is always the initiator of renewal through the Spirit, but we must respond to the Spirit and do our part so that our mind will be "renewed."
5. It involves our "labor of love" to return the love Jesus has freely offered to us. Both God and the believers must work, but the believer's labor is always in response to God's initiative. Thus Paul admonishes us, "Work out your salvation with fear and trembling; for it is God who is at work in you, both to will and to work for His good pleasure" (Phil. 2:12-13).

Lines Two through Four of the "Handling Temptation in Christ" Diagram

We have now finished going over the first line of the "Handling Temptation in Christ" diagram and are ready to consider the rest of the diagram. Look back at the whole diagram, which is found on page 177. Notice that the second line is identical to the first with the exception of the numbered reference points and the length of the arrow connecting the "React after *Flesh*" circle and the "Holy Spirit Convicts" octagon. Reference point #8 on the second line is meant to call attention to the fact that this second line is a continuation of the first line. The second line begins with the continuation of that walk. That's why the reference numerals are identical. In fact, the 2nd, 3rd, and 4th line are all a continuation of the line that precedes them.

Unaware Again

Learning to stay focused on our identity in Christ is a hard thing. So only one experience of being convicted by the Holy Spirit and our subsequent repentance will not carry the day. The pattern of the first line will repeat itself several times. Even after we experience conviction and subsequent repentance we will still find ourselves drifting back to the things of the world and becoming unconscious of our identity in Christ.

10. But Now Less and Less Time is Passing Before We Choose to Respond to the Spirit's Conviction

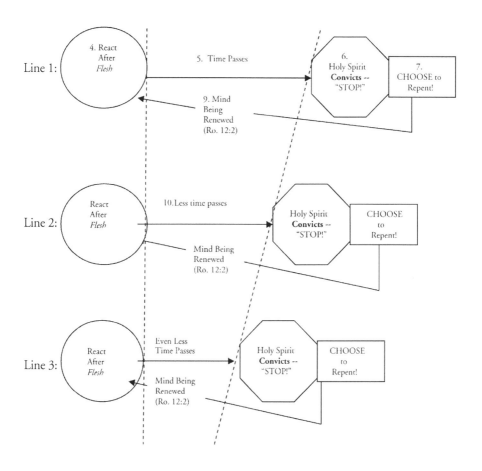

The good news is that God will be at work to make His conviction a *many* times experience so that it will eventually carry the day. God is at work in believers to help them break strongholds. The most important emphasis for lines two and three (which represent numerous repetitions of the pattern of line one) is that the time between reacting "after the *flesh*" and the Holy Spirit's conviction is decreasing and the instances of the resultant renewing of our minds through repentance are increasing.

Learning not to respond in old *flesh* patterns is rarely done quickly. Yet *the good news is that the very same temptation that worked against us will eventually work for us.* More and more quickly, we will find ourselves repenting when the Spirit convicts and thus belatedly "walking by the

Spirit." Remember, this is not about perfecting our *flesh*, but rather about perfecting our turning to the Spirit for God's help when we are tempted.

11. Eventually We Will Be Conscious of Our Identity in Christ When We Are Tempted and, (12) When That Happens, We Will Be Able to Choose to "Walk by the Spirit"

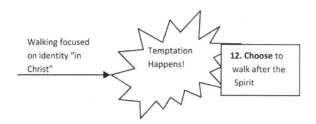

The key for victory lies in being conscious of who we are "in Christ" when the temptation presents itself. Then instead of reacting we will be able to *choose* to walk "by the Spirit." In so doing we have not perfected our *flesh*, but have learned to allow the Spirit of Christ in us to oppose our *flesh* so that we will not do that which we please (see Gal. 5:16-17 NASB).

If we continue our labor to "love Jesus back" by striving to stay more aware of our identity "in Christ," we can eventually respond to temptation by consistently *choosing* to "walk by the Spirit." Through the renewing of the mind that comes with our repentance following the conviction of the Spirit, we will begin to experience that the very temptation that formerly moved us toward disobedience will become a warning and trigger that will motivate us toward obedience. God has then effectively turned temptation around and stuffed it in Satan's face. We will have discovered that temptation can motivate us to make a conscious choice to honor Jesus over the desires of our *flesh* and the lures of the world. "Holiness, in all our behavior" can become our lifestyle (see 1 Pet. 1:15).

Two more faith principles that aren't quite as obvious must be recognized in these diagrams. First, overcoming temptation is a *process* that teaches us how to "walk by the Spirit." If we do not understand that it is a process, then we will become discouraged and water down our expectations for holiness in our walk. Learning how to walk (physically and spiritually) takes time and involves much failure, but each failure can be a step toward victory. Second, some areas of temptation will be overcome quickly. But others are powerful strongholds that require patience and persistence. That's why Paul exhorts us, "For the one who sows to his own flesh will from the flesh reap corruption, but the one who sows to the Spirit will from the Spirit reap eternal life. Let us not lose heart in doing good, for in due time we will reap if we do not grow weary" (Gal. 6:8-9 NASB).

When the Spirit Says "Go!"

Yet as great as overcoming temptation by the power of the Spirit is, "walking by the Spirit" has an even higher purpose. The Spirit leads us do the work God has specifically planned for us to be doing (see Eph. 2:10).

The Spirit does more than convict us to stop. He also convicts us to "go!" One evening, as a fairly new Christian, I was listening to a cassette-tape teaching when I had a distinct impression from God. I can't say I literally heard the impression with my ears, but I distinctly heard it, and I knew it was from God. I heard "This time next year you will be in seminary, a way will be provided, and Sally will be prepared." I knew it was of the Lord. I went home and shared with Sally what God had said to me. She blew up and angrily retorted, "God hasn't told me anything! He can speak to me too!" She was quite closed to the idea. I almost reacted back in anger, but I was checked with the thought, *If this is of God, then Sally will be prepared, just as He said*, so I let it rest. A few months later, Sally came to me. We had been at a missionary conference, and God had impressed upon her that we were indeed to sell our home and go to seminary. God still speaks!

Jesus, using the imagery of the good shepherd to refer to Himself, said, "The gatekeeper opens the gate for him, and the sheep recognize his voice and come to him. He calls his own sheep by name and leads them out. After he has gathered his own flock, he walks ahead of them, and they follow him because *they know his voice.* They won't follow a stranger; they will run from him because they don't know his voice . . . . I am the good shepherd; I know my own sheep, and they know me, just as my Father knows me and I know the Father. So I sacrifice my life for the sheep. I have other sheep, too, that are not in this sheepfold. I must bring them also. *They will listen to my voice,* and there will be one flock with one shepherd" (John 10:3-4, 14-16 NLT; emphasis mine). Paul, on the road to Damascus, heard the voice of the resurrected Christ speak a message that changed the whole course of his life and, eventually, the whole church of Christ (see Acts 9:2-20).

God does speak into our lives. Sometimes there is no clear voice, but rather impressions to pray, to make a visit, or to make a phone call. I am sure you have probably heard testimonies of such impressions that were acted on and left you, after listening to the testimony, believing that indeed the testifier had heard from the Lord. The Spirit is actively involved in our lives, and there are times we will experience His involvement—if we will make time for listening.

More often, the Spirit speaks to us through Scripture, His Spirit giving us understanding (see 1 Cor. 2:14) and a desire to be obedient (see Ezek. 36:26). He is at work in us: "For God is working in you, giving you the desire and the power to do what pleases him." (Phil. 2:13 NLT).

Sometimes the Spirit gives us discernment and knowledge. Paul writes, "We have not received the spirit of the world but the Spirit who is from God, that we may understand what God has freely given us. This is what we speak, not in words taught us by human wisdom but in words taught by the Spirit, expressing spiritual truths in spiritual words. The man without the Spirit does not accept the things that come from the Spirit of God, for they are foolishness to him, and he cannot understand them, because they are spiritually discerned" (1 Cor. 2:12-14 NIV).

Yet some messages from God are quite subjective. I have heard God, but I have misheard Him too. I have expected healings that didn't happen. There are cautions we must observe when we sense God speaking to us. What we perceive from God must never conflict with the clear teaching of Scripture. Furthermore, in the presence of many counselors, there is wisdom. Proverbs teaches, "Where there is no counsel, purposes are frustrated, but with many counselors they are accomplished" (Prov. 15:22 AMP). We need to share our hearts with others who we know are in fellowship with God. If there is no agreement from other believers that we are hearing God accurately, it is rare that we are truly hearing God accurately.

God is at work in our lives. He leads. He provides insight. He provides initiative. He gives discernment. He convicts. He corrects. He disciplines. He does this directly through His Spirit and His Word and He does this indirectly through other believers. We must be people of His Word, and we must listen for His voice. He still speaks! "Dear friends, you always followed my instructions when I was with you. And now that I am away, it is even more important. Work hard to show the results of your salvation, obeying God with deep reverence and fear. For God is working in you, giving you the desire and the power to do what pleases him" (Phil. 2:12-13 NLT).

You are greater than you know. God will speak to you if you will choose to listen. "Draw near to God and He will draw near to you" (James 4:8 NKJV).

Things You May Ponder and Discuss with Others

1. In the light of Jesus's agony on the cross to atone for our sin, how do you think our toying attitudes toward *acts of sin* leave God feeling? How do you think *your* attitude toward your *acts of sin* leaves God feeling?
2. Why did Paul pronounce himself a "wretched man" in Romans 7:24? Do you see "wretched man" as a proper description of yourself? Why, or why not?
3. Why can *flesh* appear righteous when it is actually corrupt?
4. Barclay describes sin in noun form as "a malignant, personal power which has man in its grasp" and suggests that it could be spelled with a capital "S". Read 2 Timothy 2:24-26 to see if Paul would agree with that. Does your own experience with sin verify Barclay's definition? If so, record some examples from your life that illustrate this.
5. Who is the Holy Spirit? Why has He come to earth?
6. In your opinion, why do Christians fail so often in walking in ways that imitate Christ?
7. Who did Paul describe as "foolish Galatians"? Do you qualify as one?
8. Should we begin every day asking the Holy Spirit to reign in us? Why or why not?
9. The Lord's Prayer, which is found in Matthew 6:9-13, does not mention the Holy Spirit. Yet what parts of this prayer require the work of the Holy Spirit in us if it is to be recorded as answered prayer?
10. What usually happens if we are not presently conscious of being "in Christ" when we are tempted? What activities and disciplines

do you consciously engage in to stay aware of your identity "in Christ"?
11. What do you think about the idea that God can use our temptations to sin to strengthen us in our battle to not sin?
13. Why must we see overcoming temptation as a process?
14. Why did Paul declare in 2 Corinthians 12:10, "When I am weak, then I am strong"?
15. In what ways have you watered down your expectations for your walk "in Christ" because of your failures?
16. What is the role of repentance in learning to "walk by the Spirit"?
17. How do we listen to God's voice? Why should we struggle to learn how to listen for His voice?

CHAPTER 7: "IN CHRIST," FORGIVENESS IS TO BE A LIFESTYLE

SPEAKING TO BELIEVERS, Paul writes, "As the elect of God, holy and beloved, put on tender mercies, kindness, humility, meekness, longsuffering [patience] bearing with one another, and forgiving one another, if anyone has a complaint against another; even as Christ forgave you, so you also *must* do" (Col. 3:12-13 NKJV; emphasis mine). In this verse, Paul has declared that we *must* forgive. Does that seem fair to you? Others do the wrong toward us, but we, the wronged, are required to forgive in return. This is not what we naturally want to do. We are much better at blowing up, revenge, stuffing, one-upmanship, or almost anything else than we are at forgiving. Forgiveness is just not the thing we want to do when we are wronged. Forgiveness, as it is popularly understood, just doesn't seem fair!

"Father, Forgive Me Just Like I Forgive Those Who Offend Me!"

Yet God's Word is quite adamant about this. In His model prayer, Jesus taught us to pray, "And forgive us our debts, as we forgive our debtors" (Matt. 6:12 KJV). I think that many of us, when we pray the Lord's Prayer, somehow see ourselves praying something other than what these words actually mean. They actually mean, "Father, forgive me just like I forgive others." The context of this verse makes this understanding quite clear. The very next verse following Jesus's teaching of these verses commonly known as the Lord's Prayer is, "For if ye forgive men their trespasses, your heavenly Father will also forgive you: But if ye forgive not men their trespasses, neither will your Father forgive your trespasses" (Matt. 6:14-15 KJV). Jesus wants His followers to be well aware that choosing not to forgive those who offend us is not an option for us.

Does this mean that if we harden our heart and refuse to forgive those who have offended us, then we will lose our salvation? I don't think so. But it does mean that if we refuse to forgive those who offend us, we will lose fellowship with Jesus, reward (see 2 Cor. 3:11-15), peace, and will become more vulnerable to Satan's deceit. It's a serious expectation from our Lord!

The apostle John had the following to say about this loss of fellowship:

> What we have seen and [ourselves] heard, we are also telling you, *so that you too may realize and enjoy fellowship as partners and partakers with us. And [this] fellowship that we have* [which is a distinguishing mark of Christians] *is with the Father and with His Son Jesus Christ* [the Messiah]. And we are now writing these things to you so that our joy [in seeing you included] may be full [and your joy may be complete]. And this is the message [the message of promise] which we have heard from Him and now are reporting to you: God is Light, and there is no darkness in Him at all [no, not in any way]. *[So] if we say we are partakers together and enjoy fellowship with Him when we live and move and are walking about in darkness, we are [both] speaking falsely and do not live and practice the Truth [which the Gospel presents]. But if we [really] are living and walking in the Light, as He [Himself] is in the Light, we have [true, unbroken] fellowship with one another, and the blood of Jesus Christ His Son cleanses [removes] us from all sin and guilt [keeps us cleansed from sin in all its forms and manifestations].* (1 John 1:3-7 AMP; emphasis mine)

We are not walking in light, but rather in darkness, when we are disobeying Jesus's clear teaching that we *must* forgive. We will not experience fellowship with Jesus when we are walking in darkness (see vv. 5-6 above). Even when the person we have wronged is unaware of our wrongdoing toward them, fellowship is lost. For example, if a man commits adultery against his wife and she does not know about it, her attitude toward him is not changed. But unless he is hardened by his continual deceitfulness in his marriage, the guilt that he bears because of his sin toward her will still mar the fellowship he experiences with her. Sin against those we are in relationship with brings harm to the relationship even if the one sinned against does not know about it. But it's more than this. Though Jesus's shed blood has covered our sin, Jesus is not ignorant of our sin. If He truly loves us, He cannot condone our sin with His continued fellowship. Sin brings harm not only to us, but also to others and to His kingdom, of which we are His ambassadors (see 2 Cor. 5:20). If there were no consequence to us for our sin, then God would not be loving us. A loving Heavenly Father cannot condone that which brings harm to the life and witness of His children. Instead, His love must confront the sin so that the offender can be made right (righteous). Love seeks another's highest good and confronts wrong. We cannot expect to experience fellowship with our loving Heavenly Father when we are defying His command to forgive.

If God allowed us to continue in our sin without confrontation, then our hearts and conscience would become hardened, and we would grow cold toward God as well as toward others. God, through the Holy Spirit, will always confront our sin. There will be consequences. Because He is love, God will not only confront our sin but will also call us to repentance. There will be ensuing loss of fellowship if we do not confess our sin to Him. Thus John continues,

> If we say we have no sin [refusing to admit that we are sinners], we delude and lead ourselves astray, and the Truth [which the Gospel presents] is not in us [does not dwell in our hearts]. If we [freely] admit that we have sinned and confess our sins, He is faithful and just [true to His own nature and promises] and will forgive our sins [dismiss our lawlessness] and [continuously] cleanse us from all unrighteousness [everything not in conformity to His will in purpose, thought, and action]. If we say [claim] we have not sinned, we contradict His Word and make Him out to be false and a liar, and His Word is not in us [the divine message of the Gospel is not in our hearts]. (1 John 1:8-10 AMP)

What does all of that have to do with forgiveness? Simply this: unforgiveness is sin and will result in loss of fellowship with God. God loves us too much to allow our unforgiveness to be without consequence. Let me share with you a parable to make this issue clearer.

There was a stay-at-home father of a dearly loved six-year-old daughter. Now the time came for her to begin school. The loved daughter was excited about the prospect. She eagerly climbed into the car with her dad, excited about getting to go to school for the very first time. She was now a big girl! When they arrived at the school, she excitedly hopped out of the car, smiled at her dad, and then skipped toward the school building. At the front door of the school, she paused, turned, and waved once more to her dad, again with a big smile, and then disappeared into the building. She was full of delight! Dad smiled and waved back. He was excited for her, but this was also a change, and he was going to miss her. That afternoon, he drove to school to pick her up, eager to hear of her day. But when she came out of the school building, her head was down, and she was shuffling her feet. He could tell that she had been crying. As soon as she climbed into the car, her dad asked with great concern, "Honey, what's wrong?" She told him of a little boy who had made her day miserable by the things he said to her and the way he treated her in general. Now what was this dad to do, for all the things he naturally wanted to do were illegal? *What would you do?*

What was the real problem? Dad had spent six years affirming his daughter's worth to her, extending to her a sense of being valued and important. Yet in just a few minutes, a young boy had mischievously undermined the sense of worth the father had instilled in her. How could this be? It was simply because his little girl was now *focused* on the way the little boy treated her rather than the way her dad treated her. As long as the little boy is her focus, or even comes to mind, the negative feelings of that focus will follow.

The "little boy" in this parable represents all of the hurtful things that are done against us that hurt us, that cause us to feel belittled and unimportant. Who is the little girl? She represents believers as seen through our Heavenly Father's eyes. He, in love, has transferred the worth of His Son to us, thereby wonderfully affirming and valuing us. Yet when we are primarily focused on, or even mindful of, the way the world has mistreated us rather than on the way our Heavenly Father has treated us, our focus makes us miserable. Furthermore, *God is displeased when we turn our focus from Him to others, for He is jealous for us.* He is described as "jealous" in Exodus 34:13-15: "You must worship no other gods, for the LORD, whose very name is Jealous, is a God who is jealous about his relationship with you" (Exod. 34:14 NLB).

Because of His loving jealousness for His children, God cannot condone our looking to substitutes for our identity. Thus, He demands that we forgive those who offend us. Through prayer, we are to release our grudge against our offender by giving our grudge to God (without attaching any conditions as to what He is to do with it). We are to pray something like this:

> Father, I give you the offense I feel toward _____(name)_____ for ____(tell God what your offender did and how you feel about it)_____. I choose to believe I am "in Christ" and place my trust in the work You have done to redefine me. I renounce my right for revenge, for vengeance belongs to you alone (see Rom. 12:19). You may do whatever You please with ___(name)___'s wrongdoing toward me, even if it is to totally exonerate them of their guilt—just like You forgave me for my sin and guilt. Because of Your love for and commitment to me, in obedience, and because it hurts me to hold on to their guilt toward me, I release their guilt and offer it to You. In so doing, I announce that their guilt now belongs to You alone, and I renounce my right to take that guilt back from You. I choose to seek "life" from You, alone. Forgive me for being so caught up in my hurt that I lost focus of your eternal love for me and temporarily made my hurt of greater significance to me than Jesus's hurt. In so doing, I allowed myself, my thoughts and actions to be defined by this temporary world and effectively ignored the benefits of the cross and Jesus's shed blood. Forgive me for my sin against You. Jesus suffered great humiliation in order to transfer His worth to me, and I have not fully received it. I forgive _____(name)_____ and gladly announce You as the source of my life. Thanks for delivering me from this hurtful focus on their sin against me. I choose You over their hurt! I choose Your comfort (2 Cor. 1:3-4). I choose to rejoice in You. Thank You for your great kindness and mercy toward me. In Jesus's name, Amen!

By so praying, we return our focus to God so that we are again conscious of the identity He has bestowed on us. If we do not choose to forgive, we have chosen to continue to give our offender the power to at least partially define us. To the extent that we have let our offender define us, we have also chosen to inhibit God's desire and plan to fully define us. Our focus must be on God alone so that we might know who we truly are. We belong to God, not the world, and only He should have the privilege of defining us.

The father in the parable above needs to teach his loved daughter to forgive. There will be many "little boys" in her life. The best solution for her is not to have her father discipline all the proverbial little boys in her life. Rather, she must learn how to forgive. Then, because of her change of focus, she will not continue to give the "little boys" in her life the power to define her in ways that make her miserable. *We will suffer great loss if we do not learn to forgive others, and we will also hinder our Heavenly Father in defining us in a far better way.*

We are that "little girl," and our focus is the key. Romans 8:5 clearly states that our focus is the key to walking after the Spirit: "For those who live according to the flesh set their minds on the things of the flesh, but those *who live* according to the Spirit, the things of the Spirit." Paul expresses this same concern when he writes, "For I am jealous for you with the jealousy of God himself. I promised you as a pure bride to one husband—Christ. But I fear that somehow your pure and undivided devotion to Christ will be corrupted, just as Eve was deceived by the cunning ways of the serpent" (2 Cor. 11:2-3 NLT). Let us all beware of compromising the identity we have been given "in Christ" with any false input from the world. *God is jealous for us. His name is Jealous* (see Exod. 34:14 NLB).

Even Jesus Was Not Exempt from the Father's Requirement to Forgive

Theology and the Word teach that Jesus was fully God and fully man (see Heb. 2:14-18). If that was the case—and it is—then Jesus would have the normal human emotions toward those who spit on Him, mocked Him, lied about Him, and absolutely rejected Him. Because of His normal human emotions, He could not have been the Savior of mankind if He failed to practice forgiving. Being fully man, He would have wanted revenge rather than to freely offer salvation to His rejecters. He had to forgive so that bitterness would not take root and draw Him away from His tasks as Savior and sympathizing High Priest. "For we do not have a high priest who cannot sympathize with our weaknesses, but One who has been tempted in all things as we are, yet without sin" (Heb. 4:15 NASV). *If Jesus were to be our Savior, then unforgiveness could not be an option for Him.*

Jesus needed to forgive if He were to be our Savior, and He had to do that for His sake. However, the fact that He forgave mankind did not change mankind; it only prepared the way for mankind to be saved. If mankind were saved by Jesus's forgiveness, then all mankind would be saved. There would be no need for repentance and profession of faith. But in order to be saved, we must all first see Jesus's offer of forgiveness, believe He is able to forgive our sins, know our need to be forgiven, repent of our sins, and ask Jesus for His free gift of salvation (see Rom. 6:23).

The Person Who Sinned Against Me Does Not Deserve Forgiveness!

We may choose not to forgive because we think our offender does not deserve forgiveness. That may be true, but neither did we, for our sins toward God were many; but that's not the issue. The issue is this: *forgiveness is not something we do for the other person but something we do for ourselves.* When we are focused on what someone did against us rather than on what Jesus did for us, we tend to become angry, bitter, and judgmental people. We give our offender the power to make us miserable!

Furthermore, our forgiveness of our offender does not change the offender or the offender's guilt before God. Though Jesus forgave all those participating in His crucifixion, only one is recorded in Scripture as saved. However, he was not saved because Jesus forgave Him, but rather because, in the light of Jesus's character, he saw himself as a sinner in need of being saved, and then asked Jesus for salvation. God's requirement for our forgiveness of others is because of *our* need, not for our transgressor's sake. *We need God to do a work in us so that we will not become corrupted by the wrong committed against us.*

Our Forgiveness of Others Does Not Require Forgetting

I like what Warren W. Wiersbe wrote concerning Hebrews 8:12 and 10:16-17 in his book, *Be Confident*. Commenting on a phrase common to both of these passages, "remembering our sins and iniquities no more," he writes,

> If God forgot anything He would cease to be God! The phrase "remember no more" means "hold against us no more." God recalls what we have done, but He does not hold it against us . . . . I have often heard people say, "Well, I can forgive—but I cannot forget!" Of course you can't forget. The more you try to put this thing out

of your mind, the more you will remember it. But that isn't what it means to forget. To forget means not to hold it against the person who has wronged us. We may remember what others have done, but we treat them as though they never did it. (p. 96)

We are not to forgive people because we think they will not offend us in that way again. Our forgiveness usually does not change the forgiven. Instead, our forgiveness of our offender keeps what they have done from changing us, from shaping our character and robbing us of fellowship with God. Forgiveness is not about our offender; it is about us! We are making a choice to treat our offenders better than they deserve because that is what God has done for us and because that is the way He wants us to treat others. It is our obedient response to Him and a choice we make for our own good.

We should not forget that Jesus knew our weaknesses and chose to forgive us anyway. God does not call us to have blind trust in people when He commands us to forgive. He wants us to make a choice based on who we are "in Christ." That choice should be made in full awareness of the character flaws of the one we are choosing to forgive—a choice made "in Christ" by love, not a choice made with self-focus and in ignorance. We are not to bear a grudge against them, but we are not to be blind to their flaws either. By forgiving, we are choosing to treat them better than they deserve to be treated—like the way God treats us.

Can Forgiveness Sometimes Change Others?

Forgiveness may give us an opportunity to help the other person to change. Certainly, knowing Jesus has forgiven us stimulates us to want to change. Forgiveness maintains friendships and keeps communication open. Forgiveness values the other person and may give them an ear to hear what we have to say. But even the forgiveness Jesus has made available to all has not brought about change for multitudes. Many still have not turned to Him and sought salvation.

Forgiveness may lead to an opportunity to help people change, but holding a grudge against someone does not stop them from doing anything. In fact, they can be completely unaffected while we seethe in anger and are crushed in spirit. Our anger does not give us power over others, but it does give us plenty of misery. *Forgiveness normally does not change others—just us!*

What about Trust?

Since forgiving someone does not necessarily change others, it does not then require that we should trust them. Why would they be different? Forgiving others does not mean that we should expect others to act differently. The change forgiveness brings about is the change in the forgiving believer; it does not usually change the forgiven. The forgiver has given up to God the grudge, the hurt, and the right to seek revenge. God mercifully receives from the forgiver all of those things that would cause the forgiver harm if they were held on to. But *the forgiver has not given up his mind and his common sense so that he must now trust those who have proven themselves untrustworthy.*

Our Forgiveness Is Not God's Forgiveness

Our forgiveness of others does not bring about God's forgiveness of them. When they sin against us, they sin against God too. Only God can forgive sins against Himself. *Our offender is not freed from the guilt of sin just because we forgive them.* The ones we have forgiven will have to go to God themselves in order to receive His forgiveness. John clearly states this: "If we confess our sins, He is faithful and just to forgive us *our* sins and to cleanse us from all unrighteousness" (1 John 1:9 NKJV; emphasis mine). If our offender has not confessed his sins against God, then he is not forgiven. Our forgiveness is not sufficient for their wrong.

What Is the Forgiveness God Demands We Extend Toward Others?

Forgiveness is a choice to obey God. It is a choice to value people, even when our *flesh* is repelled by them, because that is the way God wants us to treat others. It is a choice to honor our Lord by treating our offender as God has treated us rather than to represent our Lord badly by treating our offender only in terms of the way our offender has treated us. But forgiveness is not ignoring or forgetting their sin. It is releasing to God the grudge, the hurt, and the ramifications we feel we have the right to hold our offender responsible for. We are to do this fully aware that God might not require the punishment of our offender for their sin against us. God didn't require our own punishment for our sin against Him. Instead, He bore our sins on His shoulders on the cross (see 1 Pet. 2:24), so He certainly may do the same for our offenders. Forgiveness is the giving up of a felt offense and the right for revenge. Thankfully, it is also the giving up of a burden that weighs us down and can cause us harm. It is choosing to treat others better than we feel they deserve to be treated, to personally treat them in valuing ways even though they have devalued us by the way they treated us. *Forgiveness is God's gift to us so that we can stop focusing on our offender and, instead, refocus on Jesus to know who we are. It is peace where hurt reigned before.*

What If I Can Forgive Others But Not Myself?

If you cannot forgive yourself, you probably have a double problem: (1) you are not fully aware of your *flesh* problem, and (2) you are not sufficiently aware of sin as power that enslaves fallen man while shaping his *flesh*. *Flesh* wants to look good and never wants to look bad. Not being able to forgive yourself is a form of spiritual pride characterized by confidence in your ability to keep God's Law. You don't have that ability! Except for Jesus, every man is a failure in keeping God's Law. "All have sinned and fall short of the glory of God" (Rom. 3:23, NIV). It is as Jesus declared, "Without Me you can do nothing" (Rom. 15:7 NKJV). Paul stated quite plainly, "No one will be declared righteous in his sight by observing the law; rather, through the law we become conscious of sin" (Rom. 3:20 NIV). Seriously trying to keep God's Law clearly reveals our problem with the power of sin. Sin is an evil power that can only be overcome through our desperate dependence on God's Holy Spirit in us. We must be fully aware of two great truths: (1) our inability to overcome sin and (2) the Holy Spirit's ability to absolutely overcome sin. Do not waste your time beating yourself up for your inability to overcome sin. Instead, let your failure remind you that you must learn to depend on God's Holy Spirit in you rather than on yourself. *If you cannot forgive yourself, you have way too much confidence in your flesh and way too little respect for Satan's ability, in collaboration with the power of sin, to corrupt your flesh absolutely.* Why don't you just give your failures to God and let Him decide what He wants to do with them? Let God be Lord—you're not a very good god. Your higher-than-God's standards for yourself have only made you miserable.

My First Experience with True Forgiveness

My first experience with true forgiveness will always stick in my mind because of the uniqueness of it even though it is now been nearly twenty years since it happened. Sally (my wife) and I were in Phoenix, Arizona, with our two youngest children, Stephen and Michael. We were there for four months for the purpose of taking special training in counseling with Neus Leben (now VCL International or VCLi). While there, we stayed in the home of Gordon and Chris Donaldson, a wonderful couple who treated us magnificently. To this day, we are grateful for their hospitality.

Gordon and Chris were then about the age Sally and I are now (sixty-something years young), but at that time, in our youthful ignorance, we mistakenly thought of them as "old." We had great sympathy for these wonderful older folks who were putting up with a young family with boys five and seven-years-old. We knew they had to be somewhat stressed (though they never showed it or even hinted of it). So every weekend we would try to get our active little boys out of their house to give Gordon and Chris a little time for respite. On this particular Saturday, we decided that we would climb Squaw Peak, a very moderate mountain in the middle of the city. It was not steep (joggers kept running past us on our way up), but nevertheless, occasional protests of tiredness from our two boys marked the trek up the mountain. Yet when we started down, they became energized and exuberantly took off running. We were able to call to them a few times and hold them back, but eventually, they were around a curve and out of sight. However, we weren't worried, first because it was twenty years ago, and second, because many hikers coming up the mountain assured us they were playing beside the path and doing fine. Nevertheless, we hurried. Because of this, I experienced a little trembling in my calves, but otherwise, all was well.

My calves were a little sore the next morning, but by Monday morning, I was feeling great. As I was leaving, through a small glass window in the door I noticed Sally coming up the front walk. She had walked Stephen the one block to his school. Suddenly, I found myself in "little boy" mode; you know, the mode that immaturely pulls little girls' pigtails in order to flirt. I hid behind the door, and when she opened it, I surprised her with an enthusiastic, "Boo!" She jumped, and with her back against the wall, she angrily said, "You just like to laugh *at* people."

Now that's true of most of us who have *flesh* conditioned by laughing at the Three Stooges, but it was not the reaction I wanted from my wife, and that accusation did not sit well with me at the time. I was quite angered by her reaction. But since I was taking this special training in counseling, I simply walked out the door and slammed it angrily (tongue in cheek). It took me thirty minutes to drive to my training classes, and for the first twenty-five of those minutes, I angrily complained to the Lord, "How can I be expected to act loving toward, and be one with, someone who thinks I like to laugh *at* people!" I felt disrespected and hurt, and I complained exceedingly. I had continued to act like a little boy, though this time an angry one rather than a mischievous one.

Nevertheless, about five minutes before I arrived for counseling classes, the Spirit of God was able to break through my complaining. The Spirit placed this thought in my mind: "Johnny, where does your worth come from?" "Why, from you, Lord," I replied. "Jesus died to transfer His worth to me." "Oh," I experienced the Lord saying. "Then why are you trying to get your worth from Sally?"

The Spirit had socked it to me. I was stopped dead in my complaining tracks. I repented. "Lord, you're right. That is exactly what I was doing. I was mad because she didn't give me the worth I thought I deserved. I was wrong. Please forgive me. I have Your worth. The worth you passed on to me through your suffering on the cross is more than sufficient for this hurt and every hurt that I will ever experience. Thank you!" It was all over. I had come to my senses. I was ready to love Sally unconditionally again, the way Christ loved me. It was not to be a matter of whether or not I thought she deserved it. God deserved that I would do this, and I needed to do it for my sake and her sake too!

But that wasn't the end of the story. The Holy Spirit wasn't through with me. VCLi had taught me another scripture passage too. Jesus said, **"Therefore if you bring your gift to the altar, and there remember that your brother has something against you, leave your gift there before the altar, and go your way. First be reconciled to your brother, and then come and offer your gift"** (Matt. 5:23-24 NKJV). Through this verse, I knew Jesus was telling me that since I had offended Sally, it was also my responsibility to go to her and ask her to forgive me for my offense.

So *three* days later (this was much, much harder to do than forgiving her), I went to Sally and said, "Honey, do you remember the other day when you were coming in the door after walking Stephen to school and I 'booed' you? Well, I was wr-wr-wr-wrong. (It was hard to spit it out!) Will you forgive me?" She responded just the way she should have, saying, "I already have." (Why should we delay forgiving until the offender asks us to forgive when we're the ones who are miserable because of our unforgiveness?) She continued, "But let me tell you what was going on. Do you remember us climbing Squaw Peak with the boys last Saturday? When we came down the mountain so fast, my calves started trembling. They were sore Sunday, and really sore Monday. So after I walked Stephen to school, I walked two miles to try to stretch them, but they were cramping big time when I came up the walk." I could just reply, "Oh!" I understood. Cramps hurt badly, and why wouldn't she be out of sorts? It was really all over now. Forgiveness and the subsequent seeking of forgiveness from her for my wrongdoing back to her had changed everything.

The Five Essential Steps if There Is to Be Reconciliation Following Conflict

Five things had happened. First, the Holy Spirit convicted me of *my* sin, for my original focus had incorrectly been on how Sally had wronged me. Second, I chose to repent of my wrong. Third, I forgave Sally for the offense I felt as I heard her angry words. Fourth, I went to her and asked her to forgive me for offending her. Fifth, we talked it through.

Until this time, I had only stuffed my feelings when I was offended, and thus, we were never reconciled after there was offense. I just pretended everything was okay. But stuffing doesn't restore fellowship. In fact, it causes a little distance to form between the offended and the offender. The little offenses add up. Eventually, a lot of stuffing then ends up with explosions of anger over seemingly trifling events. But the explosion isn't about the trifle. The trifle is just the proverbial straw that breaks the camel's back. The explosion is about all of the things that have been stuffed that finally upchucked over a seemingly small offense. This upchucking causes confusion and reciprocal anger. When we experience this explosion over such a seemingly small matter, we are perplexed, thinking, "Why are they so upset over such a small thing?" We quite often then draw false conclusions. It doesn't make sense to us until we realize that it's about a whole lot of accumulated little grudges that pour forth in a big reaction, all because we haven't learned the art of forgiving each offense when it happens and then moving on to doing the work of reconciliation when it's needed.

What If Sally Had Not Chosen to Forgive Me When I Sought Her Forgiveness?

If Sally had not chosen to forgive me when I sought her forgiveness, we would not have been reconciled, for reconciliation takes two. But I would have been reconciled back to God. I would be able to listen to His Voice and thus be sensitive to the Holy Spirit's work in using my marriage to grow me toward spiritual maturity. My heart would not have been hardened (see Heb. 3:8, 15; 4:6-8) and the Holy Spirit would not have been quenched (see Eph. 5:19 NKJV). Furthermore, my obedience in forgiving and seeking forgiveness would have removed an obstacle to the Holy Spirit's conviction of Sally concerning her sin of unforgiveness. It is not my job to straighten Sally out. My job is to depend on the Holy Spirit so that I may love her the way Christ wants me to. When I fail and the Spirit convicts me, I am to forgive her and seek her forgiveness. I am to do things God's way and trust Him for the rest. I am Sally's husband—not her God.

Big Hurts Can Be the Accumulation of a Lot of Little Hurts

A few years ago, I counseled with a couple who had a literal fistfight the night before. When they told me what had caused the fight, it seemed absurd. It was such a little thing. Obviously, the little thing was not the cause of the fight. The cause was the accumulated aggression from many little hurtful episodes that went unresolved. Even small hurts can accumulate and become a big hurt when the little hurts are not dealt with. Looking at the precipitating event to discern the cause of the fight would have been an exercise in futility. The cause was accumulated unforgiveness. The accumulation of little hurts into one big hurt caused the violent reaction. We *must* learn to forgive!

Offending and being offended is not unique to marriage relationships. It happens in all relationships. It even happens between people who have no relationship. It is just more critical in marriage and relationships between best friends, family, and fellow church members *because* you can't just fuss, cuss, and walk away. The more important the person is to us, the more critical it becomes to resolve the hurt quickly through repentance, forgiveness, seeking forgiveness, and then talking about our differences in order to resolve them. But remember, *if the first three things do not precede the talking about the differences, the ensuing discussion can easily deteriorate back into conflict.*

Relationships Don't Dissolve Because People Are Offended!

Relationships don't dissolve just because people are offended. They dissolve because people don't know how to resolve the conflict and thus stay offended. And they dissolve because we stuff until the breach is so big that we no longer want to resolve the conflicts. Nevertheless, God's plan for Christians is that they resolve conflicts. I say "resolve" conflicts because even the most perfect man who ever lived, Jesus, experienced conflict. Paul taught, "Repay no one evil for evil. Have regard for good things in the sight of all men. If it is possible, as much as depends on you, live peaceably with all men. Beloved, do not avenge yourselves, but rather give place to wrath; for it is written, 'Vengeance is Mine, I will repay,' says the Lord" (Rom. 1:17-19 NKJV).

Paul recognized that it is not possible to be at peace with all men. That is because it takes two to have a good relationship, and we have control over only one of them, and sometimes even that seems limited. All of us can act like jerks, and sometimes persons can act like jerks toward us so often that a relationship is hardly possible. But Paul is pretty clear in Romans 1:18 in stating that the reason for the lack of peace is to be in the other person, not in us. We are not to respond in like kind with those who have rejected us.

Relationships between Christians are especially important. We must not forget Jesus's prayer for us. "I am praying not only for these disciples but also for all who will ever believe in me through their message. I pray that they will all be one, just as you and I are one—as you are in me, Father, and I am in you. And may they be in us so that the world will believe you sent me" (John 15:20-21 NKJV). Jesus is praying for our relationships, pulling for us who are believers to stay reconciled for the sake of our witness on earth, so that the world might believe following Jesus is credible.

A Bigger Picture

I want to try to draw a picture that will help you understand how vitally important it is that God's children would learn how to be reconciled when they have been hurt by others or have hurt others. We have already looked at Jesus's prayer for us in John 17. "That all of them may be one, Father, just as you are in me and I am in you. May they also be in us so that the world may believe that you have sent me" (John 17:21 NIV). Here, the issue for Jesus is our witness to others. But the issue is greater than just our witness. Our whole experience in this world is at stake. Consider this picture:

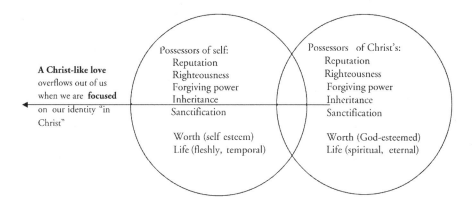

God has mercifully and graciously given believers a whole new identity. We have been placed in union with Christ. Believers are the esteemed of God, possessors of all that is in the circle on the right (and much more) only because we are "in Christ." But there is a problem. Every virtue that is ours because we are "in Christ" has a *flesh* duplicate. Not only do we have Christ's reputation based on the actions of Christ on our behalf, but we also have a self-reputation based on how *we* have acted in the world. Not only do we have Christ's righteousness, but we also have our own sense of righteousness based on our Christian activities. Not only do we have Christ's power to forgive; we have our own way of forgiving. Not only do we share in Christ's inheritance; we also have an inheritance that we think we deserve, which is based on what we have done. Not only are we set apart in Christ, but we also have our own way of being set apart to serve God. In other words, *we have worth based "in Christ" so that we are God-esteemed, but we also have worth based on our performance in the world, which we call self-esteem.* We are participators in and sharers of Christ's life, which is spiritual and eternal, but we also have self-life, which is of the world, i.e., based on the way the world has formed our *flesh* according to its temporal values.

God's plan for us is that we will be defined by being focused on what He has done for us through Christ so that we will feel loved, accepted, significant, secure, and so very grateful. Our gratitude comes from knowing that the worth God freely gives to us is far in excess of both the worth we think we deserve from the world and even the worth the world could grant to us if it chose to do so. When our identity in Christ is our focus, we are so overwhelmed with God's graciousness that Christlike love just naturally overflows out of us.

So if you were Satan, would you be accepting of a believer's focus on Christ for identity, or would you be at work to redirect the believer's focus back to the world? The answer is obvious, but for some reason we believers seem oblivious to Satan's technique. It is so simple. Until we learn how to forgive, all Satan has to do to get our minds off of who we are "in Christ" is to entice someone to hurt us. Then the flow of Christ's life through us is cut off, and we default back to *flesh*. Our overflow then looks like this:

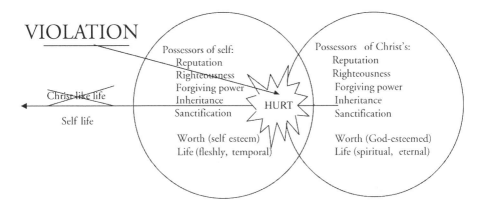

Our focus changes from the amazing grace offered to us "in Christ" back to this fallen world. When that happens, our actions default back to those of hurt *flesh*. The overflow of Christlike life is snuffed out, overcome by our focus on our hurt.

To see how this can happen, consider this possible scenario. In my work, I sometimes offer counsel to ladies behind closed doors, as successful counsel is not often done in a public place. Suppose one of the ladies I counseled would accuse me of sexual misconduct. People who know me would not likely believe the accusation, but some people would. Furthermore, some would take great delight in this accusation, gleeful of a supposed fall of any minister. Others would quickly spread the news.

My reputation would quickly go down the drain. It would not matter that I had done nothing wrong. Even if the lady later confessed that she had told a lie, some who had heard of her false accusation would not hear of her recant of the accusation. Others who want to think the worst of Christians would not believe the recant. My reputation would suffer irreparable harm.

No doubt my initial reaction would be an angry one. I would be badly hurt and also be hopeless in any attempt to totally undo the damage. What would I do? Since this has not happened, of course I do not know. My *fleshly* reaction would not be good, but my measured action would depend on how soon I was able to focus on my greatly undeserved worth "in Christ" rather than continuing to focus on the undeserved loss of worth that would come from this false accusation. But two things I do know. First, though my earthly reputation would be irreparably damaged, my eternal reputation "in Christ" would not be altered at all. For a season on earth, I would be hurt by this false accusation. But because I was providing godly counsel in Jesus's name when I was falsely accused, for all eternity I would live in the joy of God making right the world's wrong to His child. Jesus said it this way: "Blessed are you when people insult you, persecute you and falsely say all kinds of evil against you because of me. Rejoice and be glad, because great is your reward in heaven, for in the same way they persecuted the prophets who were before you" (Matt. 5:11-12 NIV).

The second thing I know is that even though I might not deserve some mistreatment that happens to me from the hands of others, I am not innocent. Three times in my life I have received tickets for traffic violations. All were questionable and somewhat undeserved. But in truth, I have no right to continue to be upset about any of the three tickets because there have been numerous times I could have quite justifiably received a ticket for a traffic violation and didn't, but only because there was no officer of the law present to witness it. The same is true of all of my conduct. I may not deserve some rejection that I receive, but I am not innocent. There have been numerous times I could be quite justifiably rejected by others were the whole truth evident, and especially if thought life is considered. I do not wish to have you know everything I have thought or done, for I am not an innocent person. I do not deserve the worth God has attached to me "in Christ," and I would do well to be more mindful of that when things happen to me that I don't like. What about you?

The Bottom Line

The bottom line is this: God has, at Jesus's expense, given believers everything we need to represent Him well even when others hurt us unjustifiably. We are overvalued "in Christ," but we have *flesh* problems that are rooted in self-love and pride that blind us to this truth and must be combated. We are often full of ourselves when we ought to be full of Christ. When we are squeezed, Christ should overflow, not "self." But this will never happen until (1) we learn to strive to focus on who we are "in Christ" more continually and (2) learn to respond "after the Spirit" when we are hurt. *We must learn to forgive when we are offended. Otherwise, we place ourselves in a position that allows our Christian walk to be continually mutilated by our fallen world.* We are not to be defined by the way this fallen world treats us, but rather to be "light" and "life" to our world. Nothing is as important to our testimony as our relationships. If we do not learn to "walk after the Spirit" and value other people, they will not be influenced by our testimony. Most people will not care about what we have to say until they first know we care about them. Rejection is going to happen to us. Sometimes it will be justified, and sometimes it will not be. We are going to be hurt, sometimes deservedly so, but many times our hurt will be undeserved. We must learn to walk out of rejection, and we must, as much as it is possible in us, seek to be reconciled with those who hurt us and those we have hurt (see Heb. 12:13-15).

How Do Offended Persons Become Reconciled?

1. *The most important key to being reconciled is to be clear on our identity "in Christ."* God has, "in Christ," passed on to us the worth that only Jesus deserves. God has given us this excessive, undeserved worth so that we can relate to others as ambassadors of Christ rather than out of neediness. Because of the exalted nature of God's gift of worth to us, we need to come face-to-face with others, knowing and aware that they cannot add to or diminish our true personal worth. We are in union with Christ. Out of our abundance in Him, we are to be givers in our relationships, expecting nothing in return. Remember, Jesus's worth cannot be added to. It is the ultimate! Our identity in Christ is a powerful position that, if believed, should put an end to our "fear of man."
2. Nevertheless, *offense is going to happen*! We must be aware that communication is a very subjective thing, and miscommunication that can be hurtful will sometimes take place. We also have a *flesh* problem that we must contend with, and sometimes we act beneath who we are "in Christ"—as do the persons we relate to. We are all capable of feeling hurt and of responding by trying to hurt back. That is especially true in close relationships.
3. *When offense occurs, the ball is always in our court. We are the ones who should initiate doing something to reconcile the offense even if the offense is initiated by the other person.* When we were a child, if we could convince Mom or Dad that the other person involved started it, we were home free. But once we become adults, there is no Mom or Dad to force the issue of reconciliation.

It no longer matters who started it. What matters is that we are estranged from our fellow believers. Furthermore, whenever there is offense, the offended often retaliates wrongly, and thus, they too are guilty of wrong. In God's eyes, another's offense does not justify our offense in retaliation. "**Repay no evil for evil.... Do not avenge yourself**" (Rom. 12:17, 19).

4. *Most often, when there is offense, it feels like the other person is more to blame.* But Jesus challenges those feelings, reprimanding us, "Why do you look at the speck in your brother's eye, but do not perceive the plank in your own eye? Or how can you say to your brother, 'Brother, let me remove the speck that *is* in your eye,' when you yourself do not see the plank that *is* in your own eye? Hypocrite! First remove the plank from your own eye, and then you will see clearly to remove the speck that is in your brother's eye" (Luke 6:41-42 NKJV). Because we clearly see our intentions but can only make assumptions concerning the intentions of our offender, we are often deceived, and sometimes blind, as to what is actually happening. When offended, it is a good practice to let the Spirit search our own heart to see how we might have contributed to the offense, even if our contribution feels ever so minor in our own eyes. If the Spirit shows us anything, *our first action is to repent*, to agree with God that we were not "walking by the Spirit" and to ask for God's forgiveness for our part. Then we are to *choose* to be willing to do our part in making things right with our fellow believer. One thing is sure: whenever two people are offended with one another, most likely, neither is "walking by the Spirit."

5. *If offended, we must first forgive before we do anything else.* To fail to forgive is to disobey God, Who gives commands for *our* well-being. He is totally *for* us. To fail to forgive is (a) to give our offender the power to separate us from fellowship with Christ, (b) to allow ourselves to be defined in lesser ways than Christ has defined us, and (c) to remove our perceived identity from God's hands and place it in the world's, simply because we are now *focused* on the offender rather than on Christ. This is displeasing and disrespectful to God. Forgiveness is also the action we are to take when offended by a stranger or a nonbeliever. Why should we seethe for a season when we can forgive? Why carry a grudge and be made miserable when we can (a) remember who we are in Christ, (b) focus on the

undeserved worth He has graciously extended to us, (c) give our grudge to Him, and (d) then rest in the peace of His love—His unconditional, undeserved acceptance of us?

6. If we have not reacted to being offended by being offensive in return, most of the time choosing to forgive our offender is all that needs to be done. *Extending forgiveness should be a daily choice of obedience for us, one that will leave us in a state of peace with God and, most often, with man. "In Christ," forgiveness is a lifestyle!*

7. *If we have acted offensively, or reacted offensively, and we recognize that the other is offended (or the Spirit has revealed this to us), then we should go to the offended and seek their forgiveness for our offensive behavior.* We are to do this even if we did not initiate the offense, for God calls us to be initiators of reconciliation. This is especially true when offense occurs in close relationships. *Having first forgiven the one we have offended for his perceived offense, we then go to him to admit what we have done wrong without calling attention to what he has done wrong.* The Holy Spirit is able to make the offender's wrong known to him without our help. To point out what the other did wrong is often no more than excuse making for our behavior and can disintegrate into another disagreement as our *flesh* enters into a self-justification mode (because we don't like to look bad). As persons "in Christ," we should not have to seek to be validated by others (even though that feels good), and we should always look for opportunities to validate others. "Christ in us" is our own sufficient validation.

8. *Once forgiving and seeking forgiveness has been done, we are made free to be able to talk (and to hear) and will often discover, as I did with Sally, that we have misperceptions that can easily be righted.* Why would any Christian in his right (righteous) mind, aware of whom he has been undeservedly made to be "in Christ," want to reject another? Anytime two people understand what it means to be "in Christ," reconciliation can and should happen.

A Tool for Reconciliation

The following diagram is a tool that has proven to be helpful in discussing offenses (or any important matter) in ways that should not accelerate into defensiveness and the resultant arguing. Even if they disagree, Christians should be able to respect one another, so *accuracy is the goal of good communication, not agreement.* When we do not make accurate exchanges of information, then assumptions creep in. We all probably know that *assume* can be viewed as *ass-u-me*. We are to communicate in ways that will keep assumptions from making an "*ass* of *U* and *me*." (If I have offended you with that statement, please forgive me. I am not trying to be offensive, but rather trying to emphasize a principle that is so vital to communication that I have chosen to take the risk of offense for the sake of emphasis.) Our communication can become offensive to others when it is so incomplete that assumptions must become part of it. When our communication requires assumptions, the behavior of the offended can deteriorate, and unnecessary arguments will ensue. No matter how well you know the other person, beware of assumptions! Instead, learn to communicate effectively. You might even want to copy the communication wheel below and stick it to your refrigerator as a reminder of how to communicate in important times.

The Communication Wheel

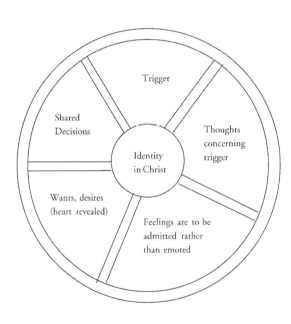

The hub of the "Communication Wheel," the central thing in keeping communication rolling, is our identity "in Christ". Knowing that our identity is "in Christ" frees us to listen without needing to protect ourselves and, as a result, become defensive. Our worth is never at stake because we belong to God and only God has the right to define us. If we are presently aware of that, we can listen without becoming defensive or attacking back when we feel attacked. Others can describe our behavior as bad, but they do not have the authority to declare us a bad person. Too often, we Christians do not listen well because our personal identity is fragile, and we feel we must protect ourselves.

Do not give others the power to define you. God alone has that right! Yet we are to listen well because we are "in Christ" and want to represent Him well. The critique others give us may help us see blind spots within ourselves. After listening, if a valid critique has been made, we can thank the person for caring enough to share with us, and we can then correct the wrong behavior that was pointed out to us. If an inaccurate critique is made, we can still thank the person for caring enough to share with us, and then let the critique roll off us like water off a duck's back. We can listen in this way when our identity is rooted "in Christ." *We are to share our hearts and to listen well, but we are not to give others the power to define us. We belong to God, and only He should have that privilege!*

Notice that there are five parts to the communication wheel diagram above. *The most effective communication will reference all five parts.*

1. *The trigger* in the wheel diagram is the event that stimulated this conversation: something you heard, saw, thought, etc. For example, "When I saw you roll your eyes . . . ," "When I heard the sharpness in your voice . . . ," "This thought crossed my mind . . . ," etc. So often it seems that something comes out of the blue. It doesn't. What was the trigger? It needs to be stated.

2. *Thoughts.* Not only does the trigger need to be stated but the thoughts that come to mind that are associated with the trigger also need to be stated. Two people can see the same thing and experience radically different thoughts concerning it. What did you think when you saw the eyes roll or when you heard the sharpness in the voice, etc.? After the first thought, what additional thoughts flooded your mind? If we do not state what we are thinking, then the other person will probably make assumptions, and we know where that goes: ass-u-me!

3. *Feelings also need to be reported.* Feelings tell you how important something is and how serious it is. Did those thoughts make you angry, sad, discouraged, fearful, hopeless, etc.? Share your feelings with words. Don't emote them—instead, report them. If you speak angrily, anger will likely be reciprocated. It is enough to just report feelings, saying something like, "When I saw you yawn while I was trying to share something of importance to me, I *thought, You don't even care about what is important to me,* and I *felt* angry and discouraged." Admitting our anger without expressing or venting it avoids the deterioration of a heated

exchange and keeps the issue discussable. When a conversation becomes heated, caring listening tends to stop. Labor to develop the discipline of reporting feelings rather than venting them.
4. *Wants and desires.* Also share your wants, your desires, your dreams. This is about the *heart*. It lets others know what is important to you. Why are you in this conversation? What is your hope? What do you really want?
5. *Shared decisions.* Finally, seek shared decisions. Let decisions flow after each has completely expressed himself. Try not to railroad decisions. People need to be valued, not run over, even if you are the one who has the authority to make the decision. The opinions of others are important and need to be listened to. Hear others out before decisions are made. You can hardly go wrong when you value people by listening to them. Furthermore, because of the importance of shared decisions, many times it is better to delay the decision until the other has had time to pray and reflect. The speaker has already thought about the agenda being discussed. It is good manners and considerate of others to offer the listener equal time to process the issue. *But be careful to not let the delaying of a decision become a tactic for avoiding the making of a shared decision.*

The Rules for the Speaker

The rules for the speaker are fairly simple:

1. *Attitude.* Set the tone by your attitude. Be polite. Don't just start talking. Ask for a time commitment from the listener. "Right then" may not be a good time for the other to talk, but if "now" is not a good time, be sure to agree on a later time. This lets the listener know this discussion is something important to you. Your consideration of them in knowing that this might not be a good time for them to talk values the other and gives them the opportunity to prepare so that they may listen well. Both of these are important.
2. *Thoroughness.* Try to cover all five areas of the communication wheel. Seek to be concise. *If you speak too long, confusion will result and listening will break down.*
3. *Personal Responsibility.* Use self-responsible "I" statements like "I think" and "I feel." Avoid *you*, *we*, and *everybody*. We do not

have the right to speak for the other person and even less right to speak for everybody. Furthermore, we do not always have the right perception of others even though we might think or feel otherwise. Seek to avoid terms like *always* and *never*. Those terms tend to focus attention on the few exceptions to the *always* and *never* claims and will cause the communication to digress. As a result, the discussion will be sabotaged rather than lead to joint understanding and a possible solution to the problem being discussed. When you are describing the other's thoughts, say "I think you think" or "I feel you think." You are not them, and you do not have the right to tell them what they are thinking or feeling. Saying *you* is like pointing your finger and making an accusation. It causes others to react, and it is not helpful. We are not the authority as to how someone else thinks. Don't assume you know what the other person is thinking and feeling! Check it out. *You* accusations are most often assumptions, and by now we know what happens when we *assume*.

4. *Prepare*. Think through how you are going to speak so that you may speak effectively. Plan to use all five parts of the communication wheel. It may be helpful for you to write down what you are going to say, especially when you are first learning to use the communication wheel. Writing will help you gain clarity and brevity, both of which are important. *Please remember that using this wheel to pattern your communication will feel clumsy at first because it is new. But with practice, it becomes much easier. If you will work at it, you will find the communication wheel to be an invaluable tool for communication, and those who are listening to you will be blessed.*

The Rules for the Listener

Listening well is more important than speaking well. James writes, "Understand [this], my beloved brethren. Let every man be quick to hear [a ready listener], slow to speak, slow to take offense and to get angry. For man's anger does not promote the righteousness God [wishes and requires]" (James 1:19-20 AMP).

Furthermore, the listener can literally draw out of the speaker what the speaker wants to communicate if he listens with skill. "Counsel in the heart of man is like water in a deep well, but a man of understanding draws it out" (Prov. 20:5 AMP). Additionally, when we have listened well, the speaker feels valued, for we have made what they wanted to say important to us. Finally, we will also be blessed in our relationships if we will help others to accurately express their thoughts as we will benefit by their counsel. "Fools have no interest in understanding; they only want to air their own opinions" (Prov.18:2 NLT). Here are the rules for listening:

1. *Thoroughly listen.* Listen for *all five parts* of the communication wheel. If a part is missing, ask questions to discern that part too.
2. *Identity.* Remember who you are "in Christ." This will help you to listen without being defensive.
3. *Hold your tongue. Be determined to finish listening* before *you start responding.* Too many discussions dissipate because the listener reacts and interrupts before the speaker has finished. "He who answers a matter before he hears *it,* It *is* folly and shame to him" (Prov. 18:13 NKJV; emphasis mine). This one point alone can change the whole nature of our communication. When both parties respect the other and want to understand what the other is saying, then a disagreement can become helpful communication rather than an argument.
4. *Check to be sure the speaker is finished before you start replying.* After the speaker has finished, summarize what has been said. Include all five parts of the communication wheel in your summary and then ask, "Did I hear you accurately?"

   a. If the answer is yes, you may then respond, also using the communication wheel. But you are now in the speaker's role, and the speaker is in the listener's role. It is now the former speaker's job to *finish listening* to you before they respond.
   b. If the answer is no, receive clarification, and then summarize the clarification. Then once again ask, "Did I hear you accurately?" If you are told that you have, you become the speaker. If not, gain further clarification. Continue this process until you have been told that you have heard accurately.

The Two Absolute Essentials of Communication

Two things are absolutely essential to good communication. First, you are to speak and listen, aware of your identity "in Christ" and in a way that values the other person. Second, you finish listening before speaking. Those two things outweigh all others.

Summary Admonitions

In an earlier chapter, the statement was made that *rejection happens*. If we are believers, it shouldn't, but it does. Our *flesh* is sin plagued and corrupted. Offense is often taken, and sometimes offense is taken when it was not intended. This offense must be dealt with. God has prepared us to overcome rejection by granting to us, for all eternity, the undeserved personal worth that only Christ deserves. God grants us worth far in excess of what we deserve so that we can join with Him in valuing others rather than seeking to be valued by them.

In order to continue to value others, we will often be required to forgive them for their perceived offenses. Remember, *forgiveness is to be a lifestyle.* Once we have forgiven, we will often need to seek forgiveness for the offense we have committed in retaliation. Then we can effectively talk things out. We are not to stuff, but rather to communicate! But if we do not forgive and seek forgiveness before we try to communicate, it is easy for our communication to disintegrate back into an angry exchange. Oneness is God's plan for believers. That oneness begins "in Christ" but is then to be extended to others. *Do not be content with separation.* That is living beneath what God has ordained for you. Furthermore, the ball is always in your court. Will you, "in Christ," take the initiative to seek reconciliation with those from whom you are estranged?

Life together should be a continuing dialogue. God cares about the relationships between His children. Valuing and being valued is His plan for us. It starts with Him. He communicates with us via the Word and the Holy Spirit. It is to continue with us. May God bless you in your upward look so that, being presently conscious of His love for you and His commitment to you, you may experience great power in living as He would have you to live – in blessed fellowship with others! *You are greater than you know. You are called to be a reconciler.*

> Therefore, if anyone *is* in Christ, *he is* a new creation; old things have passed away; behold, all things have become new. Now all things *are* of God, who has reconciled us to Himself through Jesus Christ, and has given us the ministry of reconciliation, that is, that God was in Christ reconciling

the world to Himself, not imputing their trespasses to them, and has committed to us the word of reconciliation. (2 Cor. 5:17 NKJV; emphasis mine)

Things You May Ponder and Discuss with Others

1. In your opinion, how can unforgiveness cause you to lose fellowship with Christ?
2. In your opinion, why does *love* discipline?
3. How are we deceived by the world into *not* living a lifestyle of forgiveness? List as many deceptions as you can that tend to keep believers from forgiving.
4. In what ways was unforgiveness modeled in your home?
5. Is there someone you are holding a grudge against and in need of forgiving? If so, (a) why does God want you to forgive and (b) why are you choosing not to forgive?
6. Why do we have a hard time forgiving ourselves, i.e., giving our failures to God and letting Him decide what He wants to do with them? Why do we want to be our own judge and dictate our own sentence?
7. Why do relationships dissolve when there is conflict?
8. The five steps we must take to be reconciled when we are estranged are (a) respond positively to the Holy Spirit's conviction concerning our sin in the estranging circumstance (even if it is a reaction to the wrong committed against us), (b) repent, (c) choose to forgive, (d) ask for forgiveness without blaming the other for our wrongdoing, and then (e) discuss what happened, hopefully with the aid of the communication wheel. Which of these steps do you have the hardest time doing? How will you overcome your difficulty?
9. Why is it so important to Jesus that His followers would learn how to forgive, and then practice forgiveness as a lifestyle? List as many reasons as you can.
10. When you are in verbal conflict with another person, do you tend to be more focused on understanding them, or on being understood? Which, according to God's Word, is more important? What do you need to do to learn to listen better?
11. Will you make a copy of the communication wheel and choose a learning partner to help you practice using it? You might

think of a conflict in your past, briefly describe the situation, and then playact the conflict with your learning partner. Place special emphasis on listening. (Hopefully, your discussions of old situations will turn out better for you this time.) *This is really important to do.* If you do not practice using the communication wheel when you are *not* under the pressure of an important exchange with a significant other, you surely will not use the communication wheel when you are under pressure.

CHAPTER 8: DELIVERANCE THROUGH FORGIVENESS

Finally, be strong in the Lord and in his mighty power. Put on the full armor of God so that you can take your stand against the devil's schemes. *For our struggle is not against flesh and blood, but against the rulers, against the authorities, against the powers of this dark world and against the spiritual forces of evil in the heavenly realms.* (Eph. 6:10-12 NIV; emphasis mine)

IN THE VERSES above, Paul has warned us that this talk of the devil's schemes and the powers of this dark world is more than the imaginations of an uninformed man. At one time, I naively bought into the thinking that the devil was only a figment of the imagination, but my experiences in counseling have clearly taught me otherwise. Jesus warns us that there is a devil who seeks to kill and steal and destroy (see John 10:10). Intellectually and emotionally, I would like to dismiss the concepts of Satan and hell. The problem is that *most of what we know of Satan and hell were taught by Jesus Himself, and His teaching cannot be dismissed. Yet though we should be aware of and concerned about Satan's schemes, because of God's Holy Spirit in us we should not be fearful. He is a mighty, more-than-sufficient Resource for fighting the schemes of the devil.* The apostle John assures us, "He Who lives in you is greater [mightier] than he who is in the world" (1 John 4:4b AMP). The Holy Spirit will fight for the believer in our spiritual warfare against the devil's schemes (see Eph. 6:11).

We have learned about our *flesh* problem, about how Satan and this fallen world can program our minds and emotions in ways that will make us susceptible to Satan's "strongholds." *Strongholds* are thought patterns with accompanying emotional confusion that make us vulnerable to the deceit of the forces of evil that seek to harm us and to keep us from knowing and trusting God. Paul, writing with God-given authority to the church at Corinth, warns us of strongholds. In Paul's second letter to the Corinthians, as recorded in the Amplified Bible, *strongholds* are defined as arguments and theories and reasoning and every proud and lofty thing that sets itself up against the (true) knowledge of God:

> For though we walk [live] in the flesh, we are not carrying on our warfare according to the flesh and using mere human weapons. For the weapons of our warfare are not physical [weapons of flesh and blood], but they are mighty before God for the overthrow and destruction of *strongholds,* [Inasmuch as we] refute *arguments and theories and reasonings and every proud and lofty thing that sets itself up against the [true] knowledge of God*; and we lead every thought and purpose away captive into the obedience of Christ [the Messiah, the Anointed One]. (2 Cor. 10:3-5 AMP; emphasis mine).

The New Living Bible translates the same verses in a way that emphasizes that strongholds refers to human reasoning:

> We are human, but we don't wage war as humans do. We use God's mighty weapons, not worldly weapons, to knock down the *strongholds of human reasoning* and to destroy false arguments. We destroy every proud obstacle that keeps people from knowing God. We capture their rebellious thoughts and teach them to obey Christ. (2 Cor. 10:3-5 NLT; emphasis mine)

I have quoted from two different versions of the Bible for the sake of clarity. What should be obvious as you read these two versions is that strongholds are to be overcome through God's spiritual provisions. My experience is that forgiveness is a powerful and basic provision from God for delivering believers from strongholds.

Deliverance through Forgiveness

Over the years, I have been amazed as I have watched God overcome strongholds of "stinking thinking." *Stinking thinking* and its emotional attachments are thought patterns that are most often rooted in childhood traumas, violations, fears, and misconceptions. God overcomes these debilitating thought patterns through the power of forgiveness—sometimes in a matter of minutes. However, *some strongholds are so powerful that they require persistent warfare over several months with a trusted discipleship counselor.* We often need help in identifying the lies and false perceptions that have caused us to live deceived. Furthermore, even righteous thinking "in Christ," forgiveness, and the resulting deliverance must be renewed from time to time or else we can experience drifting back into the old thought patterns. Satan and this world system are an ever-present nemesis, an adversary that persists in seeking to kill and destroy that which God has planted in us. We must be careful that we do not drift away from the truth and find ourselves once more under the control of sin that is embedded in old thought patterns (see Heb. 2:1).

Let me share a couple of stories that illustrate how strongholds develop. Jane (fictitious name) came to me experiencing depression and feelings of worthlessness. However, I could not discover an obvious basis for those feelings. She was a believer and a faithful, active member of her church. Her marriage was of significant length and of good quality. She was a responsible, respected worker in her job. She was an excellent mom.

Her problem was rooted back in her childhood. Jane was raised on a farm. Her father was sickly, and Jane was constantly reminded to keep quiet. Thus, her natural exuberance was inhibited rather than celebrated. Eventually, Jane's mother had to go into town to work and then do farm chores after she came home. Because her mother was so busy, Jane was constantly dismissed from her mother's presence in the kitchen so that her mother could get work done more quickly.

When Jane looked back at that time through her adult eyes, she saw her mom doing the best she could, as just trying to survive. Jane's look into her past saw her mother caring for her and loving her. But let's process this information through Jane's early childhood reasoning and emotions. Jane was constantly shushed and dismissed. Thus, she did not feel very important. She was isolated on a farm. She would naturally think, *What is wrong with me? Will anyone ever have time for me?* Her feelings of worthlessness as an adult were rooted in the basic thought patterns and feelings she developed while a little girl. Thoughts that "something is wrong with me" were basic to her understanding of her "self." She missed out on the comforting presence of her mother. These early thought patterns were very strong, so strong that they overrode all of her adult experiences that could have communicated to her a different view of her importance, but didn't. Because of the strongholds in her mind rooted in her childhood, she did not give them equal consideration.

Consider the case of the adult child of an alcoholic. Alcohol is the center of the home rather than the child. As a result, the basic sense of worth, security, and acceptance that a healthy mom and dad would give the child is missing. Thus, these children must look outside of the home if these basic needs are to be met. Some children of alcoholics compensate by becoming the class clown, "acting" lighthearted in order to cover the hurt on the inside. But it's all a façade. Some of the children may seek to overachieve. But their need to overachieve carries liabilities. They are hard on themselves. Achievement that would cause others to rejoice only causes the adult child of the alcoholic to feel "okay." They fear failure and its trademark branding, "unacceptable." They can become workaholics and driven overachievers. Because of their overcoming work ethic, they often suffer in interpersonal relationships. They expect the same perfection from others and, because of this, are often viewed as judgmental, insensitive, and arrogant. They can become insecure. On the outside, they look good. Their insides, however, are another matter. Their lives are not built on the security that comes from a loving parent's acceptance, but rather on a neediness to find acceptance.

I think of Claire (fictitious name). She was a beautiful young woman. There was no father in the picture. She felt she could never please her mom. She worked in an office as a receptionist. She desperately wanted someone to care about her. When men would compliment her, out of her desperate need to be important to someone, she would give them the use of her body. She desperately thought that if she did this for them, then surely they would value her, would love her back. But instead, they just used her and then deserted her. She wept as she shared. "Why? Why won't someone love me?"

From the illustrations above, we can see that *the rejection children experience can have a profound effect on the way they function as adults. We think of ourselves as rational beings, but often, our rationale and feelings are at the level of a child rather than that of an experienced adult.* Our minds are constantly assimilating information. Each concept we learn about ourselves or our world is added in with previous concepts and must be assimilated to link together with our previous concepts. Some concepts are more basic and will be foundational beliefs that are roots for assimilating new beliefs. Others are simply additions to the foundational concepts. It follows then that if a foundational thought is faulty, it can contaminate the thoughts associated with it since they are added onto that faulty foundation. (See pp. 80-89 of Neil T. Anderson's *Discipleship Counseling* for more detailed discussion of this subject.)

There are many things that wound people in our society and establish faulty mental foundations: sexual violations; divorce; drugs and alcohol addictions (of parents and of children); pornography; absent fathers and mothers; rejection by parents, peers, movies, and TV (even the commercials); misconceptions, legalism, prejudice, and misunderstandings—just to name a few. *This wounding carries with it the power to distort all of life, including our view of God.* These wounds cause deep scarring in our personalities, a scarring that comes from our interactions in a fallen world. This scarring is rooted in our past, but it has ramifications in our present and will influence our future too if it is not dealt with.

God wills to cleanse us from this scarring, from this distortion of His image in us, and from its distortion of our perception of Him. He desires to make us whole (holy). He has designed the process of forgiveness to accomplish this task.

The Process for Experiencing the Forgiveness that Brings Deliverance

Let us again listen to God speaking to us through Paul:

> For though we walk [live] in the flesh, we are not carrying on our warfare according to the flesh and using mere human weapons. For the weapons of our warfare are not physical [weapons of flesh and blood], but they are mighty before God for the overthrow and destruction of strongholds, [Inasmuch as we] refute arguments and theories and reasonings and every proud and lofty thing that sets itself up against the [true] knowledge of God; and we lead every thought and purpose away captive into the obedience of Christ [the Messiah, the Anointed One]. (2 Cor. 10:3-5 AMP)

God desires for us to be free from the worldly shaping that ensnares us and makes us a prisoner of Satan and his schemes that form *strongholds* in our minds. Paul's instruction to Timothy speaks of this loosing from the snare of the devil that takes us captive to do his will: "And a servant of the Lord must not quarrel but be gentle to all, able to teach, patient, in humility correcting those who are in opposition, if God perhaps will grant them repentance, so that they may know the truth, and *that* they may come to their senses *and escape* the snare of the devil, having been taken captive by him to *do* his will" (2 Tim. 2:24-26; emphasis mine). This loosing comes from two sources: (1) repentance, following the conviction of the Spirit through the study of the Word and (2) choosing to forgive our offenders.

The focus of this chapter is the deliverance that comes through forgiveness. Enslavement to sin is a by-product of stinking thinking, with its emotional entrapments, and failure to recognize and then renounce the deceptions. *The deceptions must not only be renounced, but also must be replaced by a declaration of the truth of who the believer now is "in Christ."* If Christians do not learn to do this, they will continue to walk in deception even though they have become believers. That is what happened to Claire and Jane, the ladies whose stories were told earlier in this chapter. They just wanted to be loved and accepted. But there were strongholds in their minds that perpetuated rejection. The same is true of the adult child of the alcoholic. They are driven to find acceptance, to fit in. But as children, they develop basic thought patterns that can cause them to experience rejection instead. Rejection is a powerful enemy. *Rejection by persons of importance to us creates thought patterns in us that perpetuate our experiences of rejection. The subsequent rejection then reinforces the thought patterns that perpetuate the rejection. It is a vicious cycle that must be broken.* We all need to experience God's deliverance, and that deliverance will come through our forgiveness of those who have failed us. *How do we gain the deliverance that is in forgiveness?*

Step 1 in Experiencing Deliverance through Forgiveness

Knowing the truth about who we are "in Christ" must challenge our old, distorted views of God and ourselves, for stinking thinking holds even believers captive through strongholds. Through ministering with VCLi's materials I discovered a technique that has been invaluable in leading others to experience God's deliverance through forgiveness. *The process begins with prayer.* We begin by asking God to show us persons and their words and acts toward us that have most shaped our thinking in ways that cause us to experience life negatively and painfully. It is important to seek God's wisdom in this because He can take us to the most important life-shaping events and people first. It is my experience that if we begin the forgiveness process by dealing with the foundational stinking thinking and hurts (strongholds), we will then discover that the hurts that have come later are also being demolished. When we undermine the foundation, the whole building may tumble down.

At this point, you might be asking, "Why not let a sleeping dog lie? Why do I want to dwell on the past?" The reason is that the dog is not asleep. Basic thought patterns that keep biting you are alive and well in your mind, and thus you are still being hurt even though the precipitating event may lie far in your past.

The events God will bring to your mind in response to your asking may be ones you seldom, if ever, think of anymore. Nevertheless, though they lie unseen in your past, they are still shaping your present, and if you do not deal with them, they will also shape your future. You are asking God to raise these events to the conscious level in order that you might finally forgive and, by so doing, might dismiss them, thus destroying their power to continue to make you miserable.

Turn a sheet of paper horizontally and divide it into four columns. At the top of the left column, write down the persons God impresses on your mind when you pray and ask Him who you should forgive first. Then write down their name and what they did. You will deal with others only after you have completely dealt with this first person. At the end of this chapter, you will find a sample "Deliverance through Forgiveness" worksheet as well as another one that has been filled out so as to be an illustration of this process we are beginning to work through. You might want to look at these two worksheets now, as they will likely help you understand where we are going and keep you from getting too bogged down in details at this point of learning.

You might benefit by having a partner to help you work through this, someone who has also read this book and has grasped their "identity in Christ." As the wisdom of Ecclesiastes says, "Two people are better off than one, for they can help each other succeed" (Eccles. 4:9 NLT). At first, this way of approaching forgiveness may be experienced as difficult, but once you have worked through forgiving one person, you will find that it gets easier and easier and that its effectiveness will have made the labor worthwhile.

Step 2 (Column 2) in Deliverance through Forgiveness

Now you are ready to fill in the second column. Write *Feelings* at the top of the column. Then ponder the shaping event you entered in column 1, and then in column 2, record the feelings you have experienced as a result of the hurt. It would probably be helpful at this point for you to go back to chapter 5, "Handling Rejection in Christ," in order to again become aware of the effects of rejection in your life. The forgiveness sheet that you are filling in now will become a healing instrument in the Holy Spirit's hand to undo the ways rejection has shaped your life. The deliverance forgiveness will bring to you can rightly be thought of as God's *redemptive work*. Below are a few examples of feelings you might find yourself recording. This is by no means an exhaustive list, but only a very limited list meant to help get you going.

- If a parent was condescending, i.e., always telling you how you could have done something better rather than encouraging you in what you had done, you may feel inadequate, dumb, angry, unacceptable, unimportant, bitter, belittled, displeasing, shamed, insecure, invisible, rebellious, determined, driven, etc.
- If a parent was especially harsh toward you, you may feel fearful of failure, fearful of displeasing anyone, shamed, unimportant, incapable of pleasing, unloved, bitter, anxious, angry, vengeful, guilty, etc.
- If you have been touched inappropriately sexually, you may feel dirty or trashed, unworthy of decent relationships, used, fearful, unprotected, hopeless, shy, distrustful, angry, bitter, depressed, helpless or powerless, etc.
- If your parents divorced, you may feel embarrassed, shamed, insecure, rejected, unimportant, fearful, anxious, unwanted, shy, guilty, responsible, etc.
- If either or both of your parents were alcoholics or addicts, you may feel bitter, resentful, unimportant, unprotected, vulnerable, unwanted, etc.
- If your parents were harsh and judgmental, you may feel inferior, angry, resentful, bitter, judgmental, cold, shamed, vulnerable, like a failure, etc.

- If you received rejection from your peers, you may feel vulnerable, shamed, inadequate, detached, unwanted, unimportant, unacceptable, etc.
- If you were disciplined severely or harshly, you may feel bitter, resentful, unacceptable, hostile, judgmental, etc.
- If those in authority over your life were harsh, critical, judgmental or unfair, you may feel stupid, inadequate, inferior, shamed, unmotivated, fearful, incompetent, etc.
- If your spiritual leaders (youth pastors, Sunday school teachers, pastors, choir directors) inappropriately used their authority (knowingly or unintentionally) to judge, humiliate, or manipulate you, you may feel distrust, confusion, deceived, shamed, unworthy of God's love, unspiritual, disloyal, etc.

Feelings naturally happen in us in response to the way we are treated by others. *Feelings start out as the result of our experiences with life, but they can then become so much a part of our thinking that they are given the power to dominate our behavior and thoughts. They are often even assimilated as a part of our identity.* For example, *trashed* is both a feeling and an identity. The same could be said of guilty, unwanted, inadequate, unacceptable, unimportant, invisible, shy, etc. The problem is that once we believe these things, we then act on them. Our behavior flows from events that initially triggered feelings that have now become identities. We need deliverance from these hurtful identities that were mostly formed in our younger years and are thus characterized by immature thinking in that area of our lives. Because they are perceived as truth (even though they might not be), these identities have the same power as truth in shaping our lives.

As you are considering how you felt when these negative events in your life took place, it is important that you keep age appropriate. You must think in terms of how you felt when the event took place, not about how you feel about the event now. Consider Jane, the depressed lady with the poor self-image I wrote about in the beginning of this chapter. Jane was not able to discern the effect her childhood had on her self-image because when she looked back, she saw the shaping events through her adult mind-set. Looking back, she saw her mom as doing the best she could and now sees herself as having been loved during that time. That is true, but that is not the way she saw and felt things when she was a little girl experiencing her momma's absence and shortness. *Her adult perceptions of the events clouded her understanding of the true effects of her childhood events on her psyche.*

Because we sometimes have trouble coming up with how we felt in a given situation, below you will find a vocabulary of feeling words to consider:

Abandoned	Empty	Manipulated	Stupid
Accepted	Exhausted	Mean	Surprised
Afraid	Flustered	Miserable	Suspicious
Ambivalent	Foolish	Misunderstood	Tempted
Angry	Frantic	Neglected	Tense
Anxious	Frustrated	Nervous	Terrible
Ashamed	Furious	Obsessed	Terrified
Awkward	Greedy	Offended	Threatened
Betrayed	Grieved	Outraged	Timid
Bewildered	Guilty	Overwhelmed	Tired
Bitter	Harassed	Panicked	Tormented
Bored	Helpless	Peeved	Torn
Burdened	Hopeless	Persecuted	Trapped
Cheated	Horrified	Pitiful	Troubled
Coerced	Humiliated	Pressured	Ugly
Concerned	Hurt	Puzzled	Unacceptable
Condemned	Hysterical	Quarrelsome	Unappreciated
Confused	Ignored	Rage	Uncomfortable
Controlled	Imposed upon	Rebellious	Unloved
Crushed	Inadequate	Rejected	Unorganized
Deceived	Infuriated	Resentful	Unsettled
Defeated	Insecure	Resigned	Unwanted upset
Defensive	Intimidated	Restless	Uptight
Depressed	Irritated	Ridiculed	Used
Desperate	Isolated	Sad	Vindictive
Destructive	Jealous	Screwed up	Violent
Devastated	Jumpy	Shocked	Vulnerable
Disappointed	Lazy	Shy	Weepy
Discouraged	Left out	Skeptical	Wicked
Disgraced	Lonely	Smothered	Worried
Disgusted	Lost	Sorry	Worthless
Dismayed	Low	Spiteful	
Distant	Lustful	Stunned	

Step 3 (Column 3) in Deliverance through Forgiveness

Since feelings can become identities, we must also record a third column if deliverance through forgiveness is to be effective. We need to see how we have been harmfully shaped in our *thinking* by our rejection, i.e., by the hurtful things that have stimulated and shaped our thought patterns and accompanying feelings. This column will basically be the ramifications of the hurt in our lives. The ramifications can lie in the stinking thinking that continues to affect our actions or be a resulting condition—things like bankruptcy, joblessness, divorce, poor self-image, isolation, bad temper, basic mistrust of people, fear of others, etc.

All of life lies in seven general areas. The first is the *psychological* area, the way we think, feel, and choose (the feelings recorded in column 2 are part of this). But the way we think, feel, and choose has ramifications in all of the other six areas of life also: (1) the *spiritual*, our relationship with God; (2) the *social*, our relationships with others; (3) the *financial*, our relationship with money; (4) the *physical*, the way we see and treat our temporary body; (5) the *marital*; and (6) the *parental*. You will want to examine each of these areas to see how you have been affected in each area by the hurt you listed in Column 1.

Examining the emotions you listed in Column 2 is the key to filling out Column 3. The feelings are clues as to how you will tend to think in each area. You might be helped in filling out column 3 through detaching yourself by asking how the emotions listed in column 2 would tend to shape another's thinking if they were the age you were when this event happened. Then see if they have shaped you in that way too. You might begin by circling the emotions that have become identities for you, i.e., those which have so shaped your thinking and actions that they are descriptions of your person or personality. Examples might be: fearful, dirty, insecure, angry, inferior, discouraged, anxious, unimportant, reject(ed), poor, used, bitter, rebellious, greedy, guilty, timid, shy, etc. All of these, and many more, have tremendous power to define our basic thinking about ourselves and, by so doing, also shape our actions. You might also look at the filled out "Deliverance through Forgiveness Worksheet" at the end of this chapter to facilitate filling out your worksheet.

1. The Spiritual Area of Life

If you contemplate the negative events in your life (those you recorded in column 1) and the resultant feelings they stimulated, you will be able to gain much insight as to how these hurtful events have shaped the way you think. But you must remember to be age appropriate. If you were six when this offense happened to you, ask yourself, "How would a six-year-old have perceived this offense? What kind of thoughts would he likely have?"

Start with the spiritual area. Write *spiritual* in column 3, and then ask God to show you how your thoughts concerning Him (especially at the feeling level) have been distorted. You will likely discover that the events in your life have so shaped your view of God that your view of Him does not completely agree with the way He is described in the Bible. If that is the case, you have allowed the world to shape your view of God rather than letting God (as He really is) shape your view of the world. For example, if your earthly father was distant and uncaring, you might very well be going through life feeling like your Heavenly Father is distant and uncaring. If your world experience is that you are not very important, then it is easy to feel (and even think) that your Heavenly Father also thinks that you are not important. The result is that you are not shaped in your spiritual thinking and feelings by your Heavenly Father as viewed accurately through the Word, but rather by your perception of Him as dictated by your experiences in the world. It is very important to be able to see these distortions and to deal with their inaccuracies.

2. The Social Area of Life

Next, write *social* in column 3. Then ask God to reveal to you how you have allowed your distorted thinking and feelings to affect the way you relate to others. Do you see yourself as one who has been lovingly adopted into God's family, loved and accepted for all eternity, or does your view of yourself flow from the rejection you have experienced through your world? Again, your feelings are a clue to self-discovery. How would these feelings affect the way anyone would relate socially to others? (Remember to consider your age level as you process the things that have happened to you. These feelings are rooted in your past, not in your present.) Fear of rejection can cause people to isolate themselves even in the midst of a crowd and thus experience loneliness even when surrounded by people. Seeing oneself as dirty rather than "cleansed by the blood of Jesus" can cause one to act in ways that draw unwanted sexual contact. Remember, past rejection stimulates ways of thinking and acting that perpetuate rejection. The wrongs committed against us can breed a spirit of anger or bitterness or an attitude of mistrust in us that repels others. *Things that happened in our past have ways of spoiling our present too.*

3. The Psychological Area of Life

Next, write *psychological* in column 3. Under this, write how this hurt you have described in column 1 and the feelings it generated in you has affected the way you see yourself, i.e., the way it has affected your thoughts, feelings, and choices. In a way, you dealt with that under "the social area of life." But this is deeper. Your behavior with others can be a facade. You may act the way you do so that others won't know the truth. You can act great on the outside and be miserable on the inside. You can make fun of yourself and be the life of the party and socially acceptable, but be dying on the inside, hiding feelings of inadequacy and low self-esteem. You may make fun of yourself so that others will laugh, but what they are laughing at is really no laughing matter to you. You may externally practice being very upbeat and positive, but it's not the truth. It's a show to cover up felt inadequacy, an acceptable way of hiding. You are only acting in order to fit in and to gain approval. But it's fake! For many, life is a deceiving performance. What is seen on the outside is a deceitful cover-up of the painful reality on the inside. When that is so, our insides need deliverance from the Author of Life, Jesus.

4. The Physical Area of Life

Next, write *physical* in column 3. How has the event that you stated in column 1 shaped the way you see your physical body and the way you care for your physical body?

God has given us a body to represent Him to our physical world. The body is important, and we should take good care of it. We should also ponder our amazing God when we see how wonderfully we are put together: the way the body heals itself, adapts to different conditions, and the ways it functions. Our bodies are amazing, adaptable creations and should cause us to ponder our even more amazing Creator. But our body is a temporary, fading wonder.

Our problem is that instead of seeing our body as the tabernacle of God, we may see it as a means of obtaining worth from the world. We can dress it in ways that please the world, but that displease God. We can use it in ways that discredit God. We can overfeed it; we can drug it as a means of temporarily feeling good with disregard for the negative long-term consequences. How has the hurt that you recorded in column 1 and the feelings it generated in you effected the way you see and use your body? Remember to stay age appropriate when examining your feelings and thoughts about your body. You may not believe something in your adult mind but nevertheless find yourself acting contrary to the way you think you believe. Your feeling will be a real clue as to how you really think. Remember that much of what we do is *reaction* to stimuli. We are not in "thinking" mode, and thus we act/react in accordance with the old thought patterns. From these, we need God's deliverance.

5. The Financial Area of Life

God owns everything. We who are believers are only to manage that which He has temporarily entrusted to us, and we are to manage in ways that are pleasing to the One who actually owns it. But many of us see the money God has entrusted to us as our own, to be used to gain pleasure from and acceptance in the world. We honor ourselves rather than God in the way we dispense money. We compromise God in the way we obtain money. We use money in a vain attempt to find "life." How has the hurt you have recorded in column 1 and the feelings it generated in you influenced your use of and attitudes toward money? Are you in financial difficulty because of the way you failed to use money wisely in order to try to feel better about yourself? *Ask God* to show you how the wrongs you recorded in column 1 have affected you in the financial area of life.

6. The Marital Area of Life

This is a complicated area of life, and many books have been written about it. But here we are asking, "How has this wrong that you recorded in column 1 and the feelings it generated in you influenced your attitude and actions toward your spouse?" Ask God to reveal to you the things you need to record. We are not present-moment people, but whole-life people. Our present response to others, including our spouse, may be a reaction rooted in something that happened a long time ago.

I remember a young man whose father was condescending toward him. The son, in turn, found himself acting in condescending ways toward his wives. The ramification of his father's attitude toward the son was thought patterns in the son that perpetuated his father's sin, even though he found his father's condescending attitude exceedingly distasteful. The son's own condescending attitudes toward his wives significantly contributed to his marriage failures. When the son saw this, he repented, forgave his father, and God delivered him. Today he is happily married.

7. The Parental Area of Life

Here, we are also dealing with the subject of many books. Ask God how this hurt you recorded in column 1 and the feelings it generated in you has affected the way you parent. Too often, we parent the way we have been parented without checking the Word of God to know how God wants us to parent. Thus, the sins of the fathers are passed on to the children's children. If something was done against us by a parent that is extremely hurtful, we may find ourselves doing the same or maybe doing the opposite extreme. Abused children can become abusive parents. Harsh discipline by our parents can stimulate a neglectful, permissive parenting style by us. None of this is of God. Whether we are passing on the same or its opposite, our parenting and attitudes are still being shaped by our parents rather than by God's Word.

Step 4 (Column 4)

God is concerned about the way we are treated, but He is also concerned about the way we respond to the way we were treated. The fruits of the Holy Spirit (love, joy, peace, patience, kindness, goodness, gentleness, and self-control) can all be thought of as representative ways of acting toward others. Jesus teaches hard words in Luke 6:28-30: "**Bless those who curse you. Pray for those who hurt you. If someone slaps you on one cheek, offer the other cheek also. If someone demands your coat, offer your shirt also. Give to anyone who asks; and when things are taken away from you, don't try to get them back**" (NIV). Thus, this step in forgiveness must move us beyond what was done to us and focus us on what we have done wrong as a result.

We may have sinned back toward the one who hurt us or have sinned toward others because of the hurt and stinking thinking that still dwells in us because of the sin committed against us. Either way, our devaluing has led us to act in devaluing ways toward others. We need to become accountable to God for our sin, stop blaming our actions on what others have done to us, repent, and forgive. We must remember that God requires forgiveness for our sakes, not for the sakes of the ones who have wronged us. The reason God demands that we forgive is so that we will be defined by Christ (the One Who has treated us better than we deserve) rather than defined by those who mistreat us. We belong to Christ, and only He has the right to determine our worth. When we do not forgive, we have chosen to give others the power to define us and to influence us to act beneath who we are "in Christ." Through forgiving, we lay aside the hindrances in our *flesh* that inhibit the flow of Christ's love through us (see Heb. 12:1). Forgiveness is also the way we stop the cycle of passing the sins of the fathers to successive generations (see Exod. 20:4-6, Num. 14:18). I believe that most often children suffer for their father's sins because they tend to adopt their father's *flesh* patterns as their own. Forgiveness frees us from those bondages that are established in our *flesh* because of our reactions to those who sin against us. It is truly deliverance.

Therefore, in column 4, we are to record the wrong things we have done back to our offender or toward others because of the offense against us. Again, *ask God* to reveal to you the wrong things you have done in response to the acts committed against you by your offender. This is a most important step. It will bring us God's purifying cleansing from the wrong behaviors we exhibited toward others because of the ramifications of the offenses committed against us. Through choosing to forgive, we can break the cycle of continually passing the hurt we have received on to others.

Now we are ready to seek God's deliverance, remembering that Jesus came to redeem us from the curse of sin. Jesus "gave Himself on our behalf that He might redeem us [purchase our freedom] from all iniquity and purify for Himself a people [to be peculiarly His own, people who are] eager and enthusiastic about [living a life that is good and filled with] beneficial deeds" (Titus 2:14 AMP).

The Prayer that Brings Deliverance

Once you have filled out the four columns, you are ready to offer to God the prayer that brings deliverance, praying through one column at a time.

1. Praying through Column 1

We must forgive our offender in the sense that was discussed in the last chapter. We must give God *their* offense, *our* hurt, and *our* grudge. Hanging on to the offense only brings us misery. *Unforgiveness is like hitting yourself, hoping the other person feels your pain. It doesn't make sense.* Pray,

> Father, I give you _____(name)_____'s sin against me when he/she _____(tell God what they did)_____. I choose to renounce my right to hold this grudge and to hang on to this hurt. Because I have given their sin against me to You, I also declare to You that their sin against me is now sin against You alone. I ask you to loose me from the bondage toward wrong acting that is rooted in what he/she did. Please loose Your Holy Spirit to empower me to focus on You alone to know who I am. Remind me often of Whose I am—Yours. Please loose me from my *fleshly* desire for revenge, which usurps your rights. Only You have the right of revenge [see Rom. 12:17-21 below]. Please empower me to overcome this perceived evil with good, to do what is right in Your eyes. If for some reason I take up this grudge again, remind me that the offense does not belong to me anymore but to You only, and then empower me to let go again. Only that is right! I choose to trust You to handle this offense without my help, even if you totally forgive them of their sin, just the way You have forgiven me of my sins. I choose to place my focus on You. I may not have deserved what ___(name)___ did toward me, but I deserve what You have done *for* me even less. I choose to honor You by striving to do what is right in Your eyes. Their offense against me is now Yours alone. Have Your own way, O Lord. In Jesus's name, Amen!

Paul established this pattern for prayer in his letter to the church at Rome, writing, "Do not repay anyone evil for evil. Be careful to do what is right in the eyes of everybody. If it is possible, as far as it depends on you, live at peace with everyone. Do not take revenge, my friends, but leave room for God's wrath, for it is written: 'It is mine to avenge; I will repay,' says the Lord. On the contrary: 'If your enemy is hungry, feed him; if he is thirsty, give him something to drink. In doing this, you will heap burning coals on his head.' Do not be overcome by evil, but overcome evil with good" (Rom. 12:17-21 NIV). *The Message* adds clarity to this Roman passage, paraphrasing it in this way: "Don't hit back; discover beauty in everyone. If you've got it in you, get along with everybody. Don't insist on getting even; that's not for you to do. 'I'll do the judging,' says God. 'I'll take care of it.' Our Scriptures tell us that if you see your enemy hungry, go buy that person lunch, or if he's thirsty, get him a drink. Your generosity will surprise him with goodness. Don't let evil get the best of you; get the best of evil by doing good (Rom. 12:17-21 MSG)." Peter takes this even further than Paul, promising a blessing to those who do not repay evil with evil: "Don't repay evil for evil. Don't retaliate with insults when people insult you. Instead, pay them back with a blessing. That is what God has called you to do, and he will bless you for it" (1 Pet. 3:9 NLT).

2. Praying through Column 2

You are now ready to deal with the feelings you listed in column 2. Please remember that they originated a long time ago but have likely now become a part of your identity. Even though the feelings recorded in column 2 may have been appropriate for you when the "identity-shaping event" happened, in the light of what Christ has done *for* you, these old feelings are no longer appropriate for you. They need to be renounced and thus dismissed. As a believer, you are now a "new creation in Christ" (see 2 Cor. 5:17).

To "renounce" simply means to "unannounce." Romans 10:9-10 states, "If you confess with your mouth that Jesus is Lord and believe in your heart that God raised him from the dead, you will be saved. For it is by believing in your heart that you are made right with God, and it is by confessing with your mouth that you are saved" (NLT). There are two extremely important concepts in this passage that we must understand: "saved" and "confessing with your mouth."

Salvation is a word that is far more comprehensive than most of us have realized. *Saved* is the Greek word *soteria*. William Barclay, the brilliant expositor of the Greek New Testament, writes of *soteria*:

> If we are to get the full value and the full meaning out of this word, we must ask the question: What is a man saved from? What is the deliverance which *soteria* promises? Before we begin to examine the

NT for this purpose we must note one thing. The verb *sozein* means both to save a man in the eternal sense, and to heal a man in the physical sense. Salvation in the NT is "total salvation." It saves a man, body and soul.

a. *Soteria* is salvation from "physical illness" (Mt. 9:21; Luke 8:36, in both of which cases the verb is *sozein*). Jesus was concerned with men's bodies as well as with men's souls.
b. *Soteria* is salvation from danger. When the disciples were in peril they cried out to be "saved" (Mt. 8:25, 14:30). This does not mean protection from all peril and from all harm, but it does mean that the man who knows that he is within the *soteria* of God knows, as Rupert Brooke had it, that he is "safe when all safety's lost." It is the conviction that nothing in life or in death can separate him from the love of God.
c. *Soteria* is salvation from "life's infection." A man is saved from a crooked and perverse generation (Acts 2:40). The man who knows the *soteria* of God has within him and upon him a prophylactic quality, a divine antiseptic which enables him to walk in the world and yet to keep his garments unspotted from the world.
d. *Soteria* is salvation from "lostness." It was to seek and to save the lost that Jesus came (Mt. 18:11; Luke 19:10) . . . . It was to turn him from the way that led to the most deadly kind of death to the way that led to the most vital kind of life.
e. *Soteria* is salvation from "sin." Jesus was called Jesus because he was to save his people from their sins (Mt. 1:21). By himself man is the slave of sin. He cannot liberate himself from it. He can diagnose his situation easily enough, but he cannot cure his disease. The saving power of Christ alone can do that. "He breaks the power of canceled sin. He sets sin's prisoner free."
f. *Soteria* is salvation from "wrath" (Rom. 5:9). The NT cannot be emptied of the conception of judgment. That conception is fundamental to it. Jesus Christ did something, God did something, which freed men from the wrath of injured holiness and transgressed justice. In Jesus Christ something happened which put a man into a new relationship with God.

g. *Soteria* is eschatological. That is to say, we can begin to enjoy it here and now, but its full impact and its full wonder will only come to us in the day when Jesus Christ is enthroned King of all the world (Rom 13:11; I Cor. 5:5; II Tim. 4:18; Heb. 9:28; I Pet. 1:5; Rev. 12:10).

Soteria is that which saves a man from all that would ruin his soul in this life and in the life to come. (Barclay 1974. *New Testament Words*. 274-276)

Jesus came to redeem the world. All that Satan has done to contaminate the world will one day be cleansed by God. The world will be fully restored, as Jesus is also our redeemer. He wants to save us not only from our "lostness" but also from "sin" and "life's infection" (see point C above). God desires to redeem our hurt, to make the wounded whole (see Isa. 51:9-16). God desires full salvation for his people, our redemption.

The second concept in Romans 10:10 that is vitally important to making the wounded whole is the "confessing with our mouths" that brings our salvation (*soteria*). Sin likes to operate in the dark. Confession brings it into the light where God heals. James instructs Christians to **"confess your sins to each other and pray for each other so that you may be healed. The earnest prayer of a righteous person has great power and produces wonderful results"** (James 5:16 NLT). Healing and confession are linked. That is another reason why you might want a partner to help you in extending forgiveness to the person(s) who has/have wounded you. But whether it is in privacy that you confess your sin of unforgiveness and then forgive or it is with a trusted, mature believer helping you, the "confession with our mouth" (which implies "out loud") is essential to healing.

I see two obvious reasons for speaking our verbal confessions out loud. First, if we do not speak aloud, we do not take authority over Satan. Satan is not omnipresent and omniscient as is God. Satan can observe our actions (as can any other being) and, by so doing, surmise our thoughts and thus appear to be reading our thoughts. But he cannot hear our thoughts. Thus, thoughts do not take authority over Satan. Second, when we speak aloud, we most likely have considered our thoughts so that we can speak clearly. Just as we learn a subject best when we have to teach it, so is it that our clarity of understanding improves when we ponder our thoughts so that we might more accurately verbalize them. Verbalizing thoughts helps to make hurtful flesh patterns more obvious to us.

Less obvious reasons for "confessing with our mouth" are found in the teaching of James 3:

> ²If anyone does not offend in speech [never says the wrong things], he is a fully developed character and a perfect man, able to control his whole body and to curb his entire nature. ³If we set bits in the horses' mouths to make them obey us, we can turn their whole bodies about. ⁴Likewise, look at the ships: though they are so great and are driven by rough winds, they are steered by a very small rudder wherever the impulse of the helmsman determines. ⁵Even so the tongue is a little member, and it can boast of great things. See how much wood or how great a forest a tiny spark can set ablaze! ⁶And the tongue is a fire. [The tongue is a] world of wickedness set among our members, contaminating and depraving the whole body and setting on fire the wheel of birth [the cycle of man's nature], being itself ignited by hell [Gehenna]. ⁷For every kind of beast and bird, of reptile and sea animal, can be tamed and has been tamed by human genius [nature]. ⁸But the human tongue can be tamed by no man. It is a restless [undisciplined, irreconcilable] evil, full of deadly poison. ⁹With it we bless the Lord and Father, and with it we curse men who were made in God's likeness! ¹⁰Out of the same mouth come forth blessing and cursing. These things, my brethren, ought not to be so. (James 3:2-10 AMP)

We may draw the following conclusions concerning the "confessions we make with our mouths" from the verses we have just read:

a. Everyone has problems with the confessions (use) of their tongues (v. 2).
b. Learning to control our tongues is a sign of maturity (v. 2).
c. He who controls the tongue controls the whole body (v. 3).
d. The tongue is like a rudder, a powerful influence on the direction in which a body moves (v. 4).
e. The wrong use of the tongue burns (harms) oneself as well as others (v. 5).

    f.   Satan gains control of us by influencing the way we use our tongues (v. 6).

    g.   We cannot tame our tongues; we must choose to submit them to the control of the Holy Spirit so that they will be a blessing to God and others (vv. 7-8, see also Gal. 5:16-17).

    h.   When we are not choosing to walk after the Spirit in the way we use our tongues, we can default back to being a curse to ourselves and to others (v. 9).

    i.   But our tongues don't have to be a curse and ought not to be (v. 10).

There is an old saying that says, "Sticks and stones may break my bones, but words can never hurt me." Though there is wisdom in that statement when properly understood, the more common experience is "Sticks and stones may break bones, but words can break even hearts." Our tongue can be a rudder that steers our lives in the direction God is directing. But it can also be a destructive spark that painfully sets a whole forest ablaze. The things we declare with our mouths are extremely important in our Christian walk. We must keep submitting our tongues to God for His use and His glory.

Points C, D, E, and F above are to be our focus in order to experience deliverance from the "strongholds" in our *flesh*. We are to use our tongues to align ourselves with God's plan for our personal redemption. We are to verbally choose to agree with God and to "renounce" as inappropriate those feelings that have accompanied our acceptance of an identity that is rooted in the world rather than "in Christ."

James clearly teaches that we are not to put up with being defined by our world any longer. He is quite upset with believers who take their identity from this fallen world, and he doesn't mince any words in his declaration:

> You [are like] unfaithful wives [having illicit love affairs with the world and breaking your marriage vow to God]! Do you not know that being the world's friend is being God's enemy? So whoever chooses to be a friend of the world takes his stand as an enemy of God. Or do you suppose that the Scripture is speaking to no purpose that says, 'The Spirit Whom He has caused to dwell in us yearns over us and He yearns for the Spirit [to be welcome] with a jealous love'? But He gives us more and more grace [power of the Holy Spirit, to meet this

evil tendency and all others fully]. That is why He says, 'God sets Himself against the proud and haughty, but gives grace [continually] to the lowly [those who are humble enough to receive it]'. So be subject to God. Resist the devil [stand firm against him], and he will flee from you. Come close to God and He will come close to you. [Recognize that you are] sinners, get your soiled hands clean; [realize that you have been disloyal] wavering individuals with divided interests, and purify your hearts [of your spiritual adultery]. [As you draw near to God] be deeply penitent and grieve, even weep [over your disloyalty]. Let your laughter be turned to grief and your mirth to dejection and heartfelt shame [for your sins]. Humble yourselves [feeling very insignificant] in the presence of the Lord, and He will exalt you [He will lift you up and make your lives significant]. (James 4:4-10 AMP)

We are to be redeemed, delivered from all that would keep us acting beneath who we are "in Christ." A key to this deliverance is the use of our tongue. Proverbs 18:21 describes the importance of the way we use our tongue in this way: "**Death and life are in the power of the tongue, and they who indulge in it shall eat the fruit of it [for death or life]**" (AMP). Death is separation from God. We are to use our tongues to draw near to Him. "**Draw near to God and He will draw near to you**" (James 4:8 NKJV).

Dealing with column 2 is pretty simple for believers when we realize we are (1) "in Christ," (2) a new creation, and (3) undeservedly so. We are to renounce (unannounce) the old feelings because, though they were valid at the time, they are no longer accurate or appropriate for our status as "new creatures in Christ" (see 2 Cor. 5:17). We are then to follow up the renouncing by announcing the truths that should create appropriate new feelings. Then we ask the Holy Spirit to keep reminding us of the truth we have just confessed, to convict us when we use our tongue inappropriately, and to lead us to repentance and the proper use of our tongue.

Here are a few examples to help you get started toward your deliverance:
- Father, in response to what ___(name)___ has done, I have developed feelings of being unacceptable. *I renounce unacceptable* because it is not a proper feeling for who I am now "in Christ."

The truth is that you have made me acceptable by covering my failures with the blood of Jesus. You have chosen me and made me a member of your family. You, the King of Kings and Lord of Lords, have loved me and found me acceptable. *I renounce unacceptable* as a proper feeling for who I am now *and announce* that *I am* acceptable. Thank you, Lord.

- My Heavenly Father, in response to what __(name)__ has done, I have become bitter. That is an inappropriate feeling for me, for I am Your child and "in Christ." You have gifted me with the righteousness of Christ. You have made me an heir with Him. You have given me glorious new worth "in Christ," worth far beyond anything the world could give me. Because of who I have been made to be "in Christ," *I renounce bitterness.* It is no longer a proper feeling for me. The truth is that *I am* blessed. *I announce* that *I am* loved and accepted, an undeserving possessor of all that Jesus has earned. Jesus suffered greatly in order to give a new life to me. I receive it and *announce* joy and gratefulness. *I am* greatly blessed. Thank You, Father.

- Father, in response to what __(name)__ has done, I have felt insecure. *I renounce insecurity* because it is not an appropriate feeling for one who has You, the Lord of Lords and King of Kings, standing for me and Your Holy Spirit living in me. I have focused on how the world has treated me and have often been unmindful of how committed You are to me. *I renounce insecurity* and declare it to be an inappropriate feeling for me now. *I announce* that *I am* "eternally secure in Christ." Thank You, Father.

- Father, in response to what __(name)__ has done, I have acquired a spirit of anger within me. That spirit has caused me great pain. *I renounce the spirit of anger.* It is no longer appropriate for me, as *I am* one who now has the Holy Spirit fighting for me and my Lord Jesus committed to me. *I announce that I am* chosen, loved, and accepted. Thank You, Father.

- Father, in response to what __(name)__ has done, I have felt trashed (soiled, dirty). That was so. But now, that is under Your blood which has washed me as white as snow. *I am* in union with Christ, made holy, blameless, and beyond reproach. *I renounce* feelings of being soiled, dirty, and trashed because they are inappropriate feelings for me now. *I announce* that *I am* holy, blameless, and beyond reproach. Thank you, Father.

Summary: *The pattern is always the same.* You begin by looking at the list of feelings you have recorded in column 2. They were appropriate for you to feel at that time. But as God's chosen, as a "new creature in Christ" (see 2 Cor. 5:17), they are no longer appropriate. They need to be renounced. With the renouncing, you are to state the reasons "in Christ" as to why they are now inappropriate and then announce feelings that are congruent with truth as recorded in God's Word. Notice how *I am* is highlighted in the announcements. These are "new identity" statements. You are a "new creature in Christ" (see 2 Cor. 5:17). Use your tongue to declare that truth. This is your declaration of independence from labels that have been stuck on you by Satan and the fallen world, securely glued to you by your *flesh*. Let the Holy Spirit pull them off and wash you clean as you renounce the labels and then replace them by declaring truth from God's Word (your word of testimony – see Rev. 12:11). Remember that Satan can't read your thoughts. To take authority over him you must declare truth out loud with your tongue. He is to be resisted, not catered to. The Holy Spirit uses these declarations to begin tearing down the "strongholds" of stinking thinking, inappropriate feelings, and bad habits that Satan has established in our minds.

When you have finished your declarations, conclude with prayer, asking the Holy Spirit to convict you quickly when you misuse your tongue. God desires to help us choose to act according to His good purposes (see Phil. 2:13). The Holy Spirit is willing to convict you when you misuse your tongue. When the Holy Spirit convicts you of the misuse of your tongue, repent quickly. Agree with the Holy Spirit that you have misused your tongue and spoken a lie. Then speak the truth out loud. You should say something like this: "I just used my tongue to declare __(state the untruth you declared)__. I renounce that confession and call it a lie." Then state, "The truth is __(state the truth)__." This is exactly what you did when you prayed the deliverance prayers above. Finally, ask God to forgive the misuse of your tongue, and thank Him for his cleansing (see 1 John 1:9). This is cleanup work that is necessary for learning new patterns for the use of our tongues.

We must not continue to use our tongues to state untruths and thus demean Christ's costly work on our behalf. He deserves better than that from those of us whom He has saved from death and is saving (redeeming) from the destructive work of sin in our lives! *Our tongues should constantly be used to glorify His saving work and to give Him thanks. If we would walk in ways pleasing to our Lord, soliciting the Holy Spirit's help in guarding the way we use our tongues is one of the most important things we can do.*

3. **Praying through Column 3**

Column 3 is dealt with in a way very similar to column 2. The difference is that you are now renouncing false beliefs for a "new creature in Christ" rather than renouncing inappropriate feelings. Once again, state the false belief, renounce it, call it a deceiving lie from Satan and the fallen world, announce the truth, and thank God for His convicting, loosing work through the power of the Spirit.

Here are a few examples of how to pray and take authority over the lies of Satan and this fallen world. As you are reading through these examples, if the Spirit convicts you that this is something you need to pray now, then pray now—out loud! Don't wait until you finish the book. Actually, you would probably be blessed if, after reading these prayers so that you will know what they say, you would then read them prayerfully.

- Father, I have believed that you didn't care about me. *I renounce* that belief and call it a lie, a clever deception delivered through this fallen world to separate me from You. The truth is that You do love me. Jesus died for my sins and would have done so if I were the only sinner on earth. The parables of the lost sheep and the lost coins clearly tell me this (see Luke 15:1-10). You brought me to Jesus so that He might give me eternal life (see John 6:44, 17:2). You love me as much as you loved Jesus, for Jesus prayed for those of us who become believers: "May they experience such perfect unity that the world will know that you sent me and that you love them as much as you love me." (John 17:24 NLT). The truth is that *I am* loved by You, my Creator, and special in Your eyes. Thank You, Father.
- Father, I have believed that I am worthless, that I have nothing of value to contribute to your kingdom or to anyone else. I *renounce* that belief and call it a lie. *I am* fearfully and wonderfully made (see Ps. 139:14). You have saved me for good works, works that you have set aside and planned long ago for me to do (see Eph. 2:10 NLB). *I am* a part of the body of Christ on earth (the church), and *I am* gifted by the Spirit to make a positive difference (see 1 Cor. 12:7-11). *I am* "in Christ." I can do all things through Christ who strengthens me (see Phil. 4:13). Thank You, Father.
- Father, I have believed that I am dirty and soiled and that no decent person would be interested in marrying me. That means

that I have believed Jesus's blood is insufficient to cover my sins and make me clean. I *renounce* that belief and call it a lie. *I am* clean. Your promise is that if I confess my sins, you are faithful and will purify me from all unrighteousness (see 1 John 1:9 NIV). You are not a liar. I have confessed, and thus You have purified me. Father, I receive your purification of me as truth. *I am* pure, made pure by Jesus's blood. I am not to partner with an unbeliever (see 2 Cor. 6:14). Please guard my lips and protect me from stinking thinking (unbelieving).

- Father, because of the way I have been mistreated, I have felt that I need to be in control. The truth is that only You have the power to be in control, and my need to control has only brought me many problems. I *renounce* my controlling behavior and the thinking behind it *and announce* that you are my Lord. You have placed your Holy Spirit in me and will lead me into all truth (see John 16:13). Your plans for me are good (see Jer. 29:11). Your will is good, pleasing, and perfect for me (see Rom. 12:2). *I am* Your child, and I will trust you to lead (see Isa. 58:11). Thank you, Father.
- Father, I have sought life by accumulating things and money (see Eccles. 5:10). I have thought in terms of "my" money and "my" things rather than in terms of being a steward of "Your" money and "Your" things (see Hag. 2:8). Your Word declares that "**the love of money is the root of all kinds of evil**" and that "**people who want to get rich fall into temptation and a trap and into many foolish and harmful desires that plunge men into ruin and destruction**" (1 Tim. 6:9-10 NIV). I *renounce* ownership of my life and the things in my life. *I announce* that all things belong to You, and my job is to be a good steward of that which You have allocated to me to manage. Forgive me for turning to your creation to find life (from things and people) instead of to You, the Creator of all. You are life (see John 14:6). I will seek life through You alone. Thank You for giving me eyes to see and faith to believe the truth found in Your Word concerning money and possessions.
- Father, I have sought to find love and acceptance through pleasing people. It has been more important to me to please them than to live to please You. I have been wrong to do that. *I renounce* "people pleasing" as a means of finding worth. *I announce* that I have only one to please, and that person is You. I am to treat

everyone else right, the way you would have me to treat them, but I am not to get my identity from them. My identity does not come from people. You created me, and only You have the right to pronounce my worth. No one else knows me as well as you do, and thus, no one else is as able to accurately judge me. Yet You, the only one Who truly has the right and the ability to judge me, have chosen not to condemn me for my sins. Instead, You have covered my sins with the blood of Jesus. You have placed me in union with Christ and given me His worth. You have loved me as You loved Him (see John 17:24 NLT). You have made me a joint heir with Him (see Rom. 8:17 NKJV). I do not deserve any of this, but it is nevertheless true. You have adopted me into Your family (see Eph. 1:5). Thank you, Father. Forgive me for looking to others instead of to You to know who I am. *I am* Your child, redeemed from the work of Satan and the fallen world, a citizen of heaven, and defined "in Christ." Thank You!

I do not know what you will experience as you *renounce* your false beliefs and then *announce* the truth, for the Spirit works in each of us as He chooses. But I do believe you will like what He does. Rejoice in the freedom He gives you, but also remember that your unbelieving "stinking thinking" is a part of your *flesh*.

You will need to reaffirm these truths all of your days, but this is especially important in the next few days. Flesh is not eradicated. You must be wary of Satan's schemes and trust the Holy Spirit to set Himself against your flesh so that you will stay free. As the author of Hebrews warns, "So we must listen very carefully to the truth we have heard, or we may drift away from it" (Heb. 2:1 NLT). *The goal is not to perfect your flesh so that you will not have to constantly depend on the power of the Holy Spirit. Instead, you are to perfect your dependence on God's Holy Spirit in you so that you can walk in His strength (see Zech. 4:6, Rom. 8:4).*

Peter is quite clear that we must maintain our deliverance by our continued dependence on the Spirit, writing, "Prepare your minds for action, keep sober in spirit, fix your hope completely on the grace to be brought to you at the revelation of Jesus Christ. As obedient children, do not be conformed to the former lusts which were yours in your ignorance, but like the Holy One who called you, be holy yourselves also in all your behavior; because it is written, 'You shall be holy for I am holy'" (1 Pet. 1:13-16 NASB).

These verses make it very obvious that *we must strive to be conscious of who we are "in Christ" so that we will not drift back into conformity to the lusts of the flesh that formerly dominated us.* If that were not so, Peter would not have warned us to fix our hope completely on Jesus. (Paul warned us of the same in Romans 8:5-7 when he told us we must set our minds on the Spirit.) So we should not be surprised if we occasionally fail in our "walk after the Spirit," for Satan is the cleverest of all deceivers. But likewise, do not waste your time beating yourself up for having such sorry *flesh*. Everyone's *flesh* is crummy. *Flesh* cannot be perfected (see Rom. 8:7). Instead, repent, focus your attention back to Jesus, and start "walking by the Spirit" again.

The Holy Spirit *convicts* when we fail to honor Jesus with our walk so that we might be cleansed from our sin. Satan, on the other hand, *condemns* us in the hope that we will be discouraged and fail to get up and start walking after the Spirit again. That is probably why Paul reminds us of what God can do for those who love Him, even though we have failed and no matter how often we have failed (see 1 Cor. 1:26-31). In the verses immediately following his admonition to set our minds on the Spirit so that we might please God, he adds, "And **we know that God causes all things to work together for good to those who love God, to those who are called according to His purpose. For those whom He foreknew, He also predestined to become conformed to the image of His Son, so that He would be the firstborn among many brethren**" (Rom. 8:28-29 NASB)." Strive for holiness. Fight for it. But when you fail, repent and get up. Set your eyes back on the Spirit and start walking again. *God can work good even out of the failures of those who love Him and who are called to honor His purposes for their lives—that's His promise to us!*

4. Praying through Column 4

Forgiveness is all about staying in a right relationship with God. Because God always seeks what is best for us, He holds us accountable for the sins we commit against those who have first mistreated us as well as for the sins we then commit against others because of our messed up *flesh*. It is not His will that we would be shaped in any way by the wrongs done against us. Instead, He would have us shaped in every way by His righteousness toward us. Thus, so that we might be purified, the final step in securing the forgiveness that brings God's deliverance to us is asking God to forgive us for our wrongdoing toward those who first wronged us and for our wrongdoing toward others that is rooted in the way we were mistreated.

God's command is straightforward: "**If we confess our sins, he is faithful and just and will forgive us our sins and purify us from all unrighteousness**" (1 John 1:9 NIV). God is not like us. If someone sins against us, we want to distance ourselves from them. But when we sin against our Holy God, He approaches us, offering His forgiveness so that we might be cleansed from our wrongdoing *and* reconciled to Him. We tend to hold the sins of others toward us against them, but unlike us, God desires to absolutely cleanse us from our sins against Him. He wants to make us pure, so (1) He must tirelessly pick us up, dust us off, and set us on our feet again; (2) He must break us from the habit of blaming others or our circumstances for our shortcomings (which keeps us in bondage); and (3) He must work diligently to help us choose to "walk by the Spirit."

God does this cleansing in those of us who respond to the conviction of His Holy Spirit when we choose to (1) agree with Him that we have sinned, (2) take personal responsibility for our wrong actions (rather than blaming our offender for our actions), and (3) offer heartfelt confession to God for our wrongdoing, saying, "I was wrong when I ____(statement of what we did wrong)____. Will you forgive me?" Following our confession, we should acknowledge His forgiveness by saying something like "Thank you, Father, for forgiving me and cleansing me of my sin." This acknowledgment is nothing more than trusting He will forgive just like He promises He will (see 1 John 1:9). It is our act of faith in His promises that will bring pleasure to Him and cleansing for us.

Forgiveness, Alone, May Not be All that God Wants You to Do

Asking God to forgive you and the person who has hurt you may not be all that God requires of you, however. We saw in the last chapter that sometimes the Spirit may lead you to go to the person you have wronged (or even wronged back) in order to bring about reconciliation. The Spirit may also draw you to go to your offender in order to do a deeper work of deliverance in you, a work that would not be possible were you not to choose to obey.

As a young pastor I taught a group of older men. One Sunday one of the men came to me and told me something that I experienced as hurtful.

The men usually went and had coffee in the kitchen after Sunday School. There, one of the men who had been in my class was badmouthing me for something I had done while teaching. The first letter in the Greek word for Christ is chi, a letter very similar to the English letter "X." During the lesson I had written the Greek letter Chi on the blackboard followed by "mas" as an abbreviation for Christmas. This had been very offensive to this man and he was complaining about what I had done, judgmentally accusing me of crossing (X-ing) Christ out of Christmas. I, in turn, was offended that he would think that of me, and doubly offended because he had demeaned me in front of the other men. I had already perceived him as being somewhat judgmental and critical, so I already did not feel close to him. Thus having a good attitude toward him at this time was extremely hard for me. You see, in my *flesh* I am a people pleaser who doesn't handle criticism well, and I wanted to just let the offense go. That is the way my *flesh* has been programmed to automatically react. But the hound of Heaven, the Holy Spirit, was heavy on me to go see him. I very reluctantly obeyed the Spirit's prompting and God did a marvelous work. We bonded. Not only were we reconciled, but everything about our relationship was bettered. None of that would have happened if I had not followed the leading of the Spirit. I am grateful to this day for having done what I really did not want to do, and made better for it – we both were! God started tearing down a *stronghold* in my *flesh* that day.

Sometimes the Spirit requires us to go to another in order to break unhealthy soul ties. This is particularly true of violations of God's Word in the sexual area where the two become "one flesh." I'm thinking of a young man who came to me because of problems in his relationship with his girlfriend. He was a sincere new Christian, a quick learner, and devoted to doing what was right. I explained soul ties to him and was led by the Spirit to request of Him that he call a young lady he had been sexually involved with in the past and ask her to forgive him for his wrong actions and attitude toward her. He reported back that making that call was the hardest thing he had ever done in his life, but God had gloriously blessed it. He explained to her that he had become a Christian, was convicted for having sexually violated her, and asked for her forgiveness. Two people experienced God's cleansing through his act of obedience. He found out that she, too, had become a Christian, and the conversation was very positive and uplifting to both of them. But something else happens. When we have to become responsible for the violations we have committed toward others, we are fortified against repeating that behavior, determined that we will not go through that pain again. God did a deep work toward tearing down a stronghold in that young man's *flesh*, a work that would not have happened had he not chosen to obey the Spirit and seek the forgiveness of the young lady he had offended.

When God impresses you to go to your offender (or to one you have offended), at least two things are happening. First, God is loving you enough to redeem the hurt. Second, He wants you to be restored to a right relationship with your brother "in Christ." Pretending there is no hurt does not accomplish that. The breach must be dealt with in order to restore the relationship. But even better, when the Spirit leads you to seek to be reconciled, through your obedience you might find yourself in an even stronger relationship than before. A transparent relationship that deals with hurt is a deeper relationship than one that neglects hurt.

The Holy Spirit will not always lead you to go to the one who has offended you. Sometimes this is because, even though you have forgiven, nothing is different with the offender. No restoration would take place by going to them, but only deeper estrangement. When this is the case, you are to be content in knowing that there is nothing in you that is keeping you from treating the other person right and seeking their best. You must also realize that often, when someone is choosing to withhold their friendship from you, the problem is in them. When that happens, be content to pray for your offender and watch your tongue. But pray privately—don't call a prayer meeting. Making public the way you have been wronged by requesting prayer for your offender can look spiritual but may, in reality, be only a veiled seeking of revenge. This public sharing can even become leaven that corrupts the whole church if it stimulates sinful gossip.

Sometimes God may lead you to share with others that you have forgiven them. You would certainly do that if they asked you to forgive them. You have probably read some testimonies where going to one who has offended you in order to share with them that you have forgiven them is redemptive for the person. Sometimes this does have great benefit. But let the Holy Spirit prompt you to do that, for that is not the norm. Often your announcement would only cause pride to surface in the one to whom you made the announcement. If that is the case, you will not like their retort, and will just have to forgive them for something more. Remember, forgiveness is first something we do in obedience to God for our sakes -- so that we can refocus on God to know who we are. God normally requires our forgiveness of others in order to bless us. Going to others is normally for the purpose of asking them to forgive us for the way we have offended them, and done without mention of what they may have done to offend us. It is a way we stay clean before God by becoming responsible for our offensive behavior. If we hear another is offended and the Spirit prompts us to go to another, even though in our eyes we have done nothing wrong, think of this as offering grace to your brother or sister in Christ. We should not let our own pride resist the Spirit's work of reconciliation through us. God's heart desires reconciliation for His children, and our hearts should too. That's why Paul taught, "If possible, so far as it depends on you, be at peace with all men" (Rom. 12:18 NASB).

"You meant evil against me; but God meant it for good" (Gen. 50:20 NKJV)

The words of this paragraph heading were spoken by Joseph to his brothers who were kneeling before him, cowering and fearing for their lives. Previously, when Joseph was a young boy, with murder in their hearts the brothers had sold Joseph into slavery. Joseph went through great suffering because of their dastardly act (see Gen. 50). But Joseph had a bigger picture of life than himself—a picture that delivered him from the perils of a "self" focused life. He knew how big his God was and that only a "God" focus in life made sense. He knew that, humanly and worldly speaking, his brothers deserved the wrath they feared that he could and would inflict on them. Yet Joseph knew God was bigger than their evil and that He would use their evil for the greater good.

We must never lose sight of the fact that we live in a fallen world that is an enemy of God (see James 4:4). Satan wishes to "kill and steal and destroy" (John 10:10). Peter warns us:

> Casting the whole of your care [all your anxieties, all your worries, all your concerns, once and for all] on Him, for He cares for you affectionately and cares about you watchfully. Be well balanced [temperate, sober of mind], be vigilant and cautious at all times; for that enemy of yours, the devil, roams around like a lion roaring [in fierce hunger], seeking someone to seize upon and devour. Withstand him; be firm in faith

[against his onset—rooted, established, strong, immovable, and determined], knowing that the same [identical] sufferings are appointed to your brotherhood [the whole body of Christians] throughout the world. (1 Pet. 5:7-9 AMP)

Jesus came to redeem us from this fallen world—to undo its harmful effects in our lives. The evil one is in the world, and many have been taken captive by the devil to do his will (see 2 Tim. 2:24-26). *Our fight is not against those who have hurt us, but against the one who ensnares them and leads them in doing harm to us (see Eph. 6:12).* We have been delivered from this world, made citizens of heaven. God has bestowed on us worth far in excess of the best this world could ever offer to us. We are to join with Joseph in recognizing that God is willing to work good of that which was intended as evil against us and even to use the work of Satan for good. That is what God did when He let the world, under the influence of Satan, place Jesus on the cross. Just as with Jesus and Joseph, God can also work the evil done to us for good if we will respond to it righteously.

We should not be surprised when others try to harm us. But we are not to return their harm in like kind. We represent Christ to a fallen world, a lost mankind. Not only will God redeem us from the harm others would cause, but He is even able to use the harm meant for us to bring greater good to mankind. Joseph's life pictured that for us. Perhaps this is what Paul meant when he talked about sharing in Jesus's sufferings as being a good thing, writing,

> Now if we are children, then we are heirs—heirs of God and co-heirs with Christ, if indeed we share in his sufferings in order that we may also share in his glory. (Rom. 8:17 NIV)
>
> What is more, I consider everything a loss compared to the surpassing greatness of knowing Christ Jesus my Lord, for whose sake I have lost all things. I consider them rubbish, that I may gain Christ and be found in him, not having a righteousness of my own that comes from the law, but that which is through faith in Christ—the righteousness that comes from God and is by faith. I want to know Christ and the power of his resurrection and the fellowship of sharing in his sufferings, becoming like him in his death, and so, somehow, to attain to the resurrection from the dead. (Phil. 3:8-10 NIV)

Believers will share in His glory and will be fully redeemed. We must not waste our time being angry with God for allowing bad things to happen to us. Instead we must open our eyes and look for His eternal purpose for our lives. Forgive those who have hurt you, even those who have hurt you severely, so that you may know and experience His deliverance and the fullness of His life poured out for you. *You can do this because the Holy Spirit within you can turn defeat into victory "in Jesus's Name." You are greater than you know!*

Things You May Ponder and Discuss with Others

This chapter is where the rubber meets the road. The time has arrived for you to begin to deal with and walk away from past hurt. I pray that you will try to apply this chapter to your life. You have nothing to lose and, perhaps, a lot of freedom to gain.

1. Are you aware of persons who have hurt you so much that you can still feel the pain of their hurt even to this day? List those names now.
2. Can you identify "strongholds" in your life, areas in which it is particularly difficult for you to walk in Christlike ways? Can you remember hurt(s) that could be linked to the difficulty you are experiencing in these areas? If so, write down the name of the person(s) who caused the hurt.
3. Refer back to questions 5-8 at the end of the chapter on rejection, chapter 5. Did you find yourself relating to either of the two bullet lists of attitudes and thought patterns that are characteristic of rejection? If so, try to remember persons and incidences that would have evoked those thought patterns and attitudes, and then record what you have remembered.
4. Go to the section in this chapter titled "Step 1 in Experiencing Deliverance through Forgiveness." Read this section again, and then ask God to reveal to you anyone that you need to forgive. Record the name(s), no matter how long ago the event took place.
5. If you have listed more than one person in questions 1-4 above, *ask God which one you need to deal with first.* Normally, the oldest offense should be dealt with first, but this might not be the case for you. Anything and anyone you listed in the first

four questions will also need to be dealt with, though that may not be the starting point for you.

6. Prepare a forgiveness worksheet like the one that follows at the end of this chapter. Then, in column 1, write down the name of the offender God revealed to you in question 5 as well as *what that person did (or didn't do) that hurt you.*

7. After you have written down the name God has placed in your mind along with what that person did to hurt or reject you, go to the section in this chapter titled "Step 2 (Column 2) in Deliverance through Forgiveness" and do the work that section leads you through. As you think about what you recorded in column 1, try to recognize how that hurt affected you *at that moment* (i.e., be age appropriate). For example, if it happened when you were three, try to process the event like a three-year-old would process it.

8. When you finish with column 2 of your worksheet, go to the section titled "Step 3 (Column 3) in Deliverance through Forgiveness" and do the work that section leads you through. Again, do not analyze the event through your adult mind-set. Instead, think in terms of how the event would have affected you back then.

9. When you feel you are ready, move on to the section titled "Step 4 (Column 4)" and do the work that this section lays out for you to do. Remember, *it might be very helpful to have a trusted, mature friend help you to fill out these columns. Sometimes we are so emotionally involved in past events that we have difficulty in processing their effect on our lives accurately.*

10. You are now ready to experience God's wonderful, freeing deliverance. Please do the work laid out in the rest of this chapter, one column at a time, either by yourself or with the help of a friend. I am excited for you. I believe you will feel cleansed and loosed from the hurt when you are finished. But know that afterwards you will probably have to keep reminding yourself of what you have done and take authority over your thoughts and feelings in Jesus's name. When the old feelings and thinking resurface, retell yourself the truth and renounce the lies again, for victory is God's plan for you. Do not lose heart! Be persistent, as this work in deliverance is often a process. If the hurt is particularly deep, you may find yourself peeling

hurt off in layers, one at a time. Being loosed from one level of hurt may free you to look at deeper layers of hurt that you have not even been conscious of, for they were absorbed into later hurts. You can be loosed from the deeper hurt too. If, because of the deepness of the hurt, you do not begin walking in victory, know that there are Christian counselors who understand the struggle who will walk with you out of the hurt. Please keep in mind always that Christ has come to redeem us from the harm that sin, the world, and the devil have worked into our lives. Do not give yourself permission to continue to live in the pain of rejections past. Instead, choose to walk in victory through forgiveness.

11. When you finish working through the first rejection that God placed on your mind, ask Him to reveal the next hurt you need to deal with and then deal with it, just like the first hurt.
12. Keep at this process until you know God has finished cleansing you of your hurts. This process could take a while, but it will be worth the effort. Then, if we are to consistently walk in victory, *forgiveness must become a lifestyle.* You will find that forgiving will come easier and easier as you practice—and will be so freeing!

Deliverance through Forgiveness Worksheet

Purpose: (1) That we may come to our senses and escape from the snare of the devil, having been held captive by him to do his will (2 Tim. 2:26 NASB), and (2) that we may pull down strongholds, cast down arguments and every high things that exalt itself against the knowledge of God, and bring every thought into captivity to the obedience of Christ (2 Cor. 10:4-5 NKJV).

(1) The Offense: Who? and What?	(2) Our Emotional Reactions	(3) Effects on Our Thinking and Acting	(4) Our Wrong Responses and Offenses in Return
		Psychological Effects: Emotions (see column 2) Choices (see column 4) Stinking thinking concerning ourselves Spiritual - effects on our relationship with God Social - effects on our relationship with others Physical - effects on the way we view and use our bodies Financial - effects on the way we view and use money Marital - effects on the way we view our marriage Parenting - effects on the way we parent	

Deliverance through Forgiveness Worksheet

The Offense	Feelings	Effects on Thinking and Acting	Wrong Responses and Offenses
Mom: About my fourth grade, we (my family) were sitting at the table eating fried chicken. I was carrying on excessively about how I was the one who had discovered the gland in the top of the chicken back, being generally full of myself. Mom must have been either pretty tired of my carrying on about what I had discovered or out of sorts for some other reason, for she sharply said to me, "Johnny, do you think that in all of the hundreds of years that people have been eating chicken that you are the first one to discover that gland!" I shut up—in more ways than one. Note: This may seem like a trifling event, and it is, but it is remembered to this day and has had an impact on my person. Thus it has to be dealt with, for it is not in the past. This was not deliberate, malicious, or premeditated, but words are powerful.	Hurt Crushed Shamed Put down Insecure Bewildered Foolish Stunned Condemned Discouraged Fearful of Rejection	Psychological - Emotionally reserved, guarded against making mistakes, somewhat insecure. Natural introvert. Hard on myself, but not others. Will work hard to succeed. Spiritual - It is easy for me to be insecure with God, to condemn myself, and to fear disappointing Him. It is particularly hard to feel that He approves of me and takes joy in me. Social - I am socially shy with a modest fear of looking foolish; I withhold information that might be useful to others because I fear being put down and don't want to look bad; I am reluctant to take chances; I am not outgoing, but private—often quiet and withdrawn. Hard worker. Trustworthy. Sincerely thankful; easily gracious. Physical - Disciplined, but self-critical. Work hard at performing well. Financial - Conservative. Responsible. Generous. Marital - Fear rejection. Needy of acceptance and approval. Reserved. Insecure. Guarded. Private. Find self-condemning to be easy. Parenting - Withhold direction. Careful not to put down. Encouraging. Expect best, and sometimes not realistic. Trusting, and sometimes blind. NOTE: Some effects of rejection are positive, but they have baggage.	Tend to be an introvert and private, and thus do not share my life enough. Will respond when others come to me, but do not reach out sufficiently. Withhold information and insights that could be helpful to others if I would risk sharing it. Withhold myself. Social shyness keeps me from having many good relationships. Self-protective; do not risk being rejected. Thus, I do not help others in accordance with my gifting. Not emotionally free to be a better encourager. NOTE: Normally specific offenses would be listed here. I took no offense against my mom, but I was too reserved and not often vulnerable with her. She's dead now. I wish I had these insights while she was still alive.

CHAPTER 9: WHAT EVERY CHURCH MEMBER NEEDS TO KNOW

A. "It's Not About You!"

"It's not about you" is the opening sentence of Pastor Rick Warren's best-selling book, *The Purpose Driven Life*. That sentence can be troublesome and surprising to the many who feel important. But it would be neither troublesome nor surprising to most women in Africa who are, at best, considered as a child or a piece of property. Nor, if they had a voice, would it be surprising to the millions of aborted babies in the world. Nor would it be surprising in any way to the abused and the used of the world. It would not create a dilemma in thought for the billions of very poor working people all over the world or the starving or homeless. For most, it is just a statement of life as they experience it. If you are surprised or troubled by this declaration, it is because you are part of the blessed minority.

The Declaration of Independence of the United States of America declares,

> We hold these truths to be self-evident, that all men are created equal, that they are endowed by their Creator with certain inalienable rights that among these are life, liberty, and the pursuit of happiness.
>
> That to secure these rights, governments are instituted among men, deriving their just powers from the consent of the governed.

America can make the declaration that all men are created equal and believe it, but that does not mean that all will be treated as equals, even in America. Worth must be given to us by those who have the power to declare it to us. These "inalienable rights" (equality, life, liberty, and the pursuit of happiness) must be secured by persons of power and "governments instituted among men," or they will be denied for most of mankind. For most of mankind, it is not about us, even though as persons of *flesh* we would desire that it would be about us.

B. Yet, It Is About You!

Pastor Warren was right when he said, "It's not about us." It is about God. He is our Creator and Sustainer. It's about His kingdom on earth, about His will being done, and about His glory being made manifest. He is the One we are accountable to and the One who will judge our lives at death. "And just as each person is destined to die once and after that comes judgment, so also Christ died once for all time as a sacrifice to take away the sins of many people. He will come again, not to deal with our sins, but to bring salvation to all who are eagerly waiting for him" (Heb. 9:27-28 NLT). When our time for judgment comes, it will not matter how important we think we are or how important the world thought we were. Only God's judgment will matter, the judgment that only He, as our Creator and Sustainer, has the right to make.

But this One with all power Who will judge us and declare our eternal destiny has not sat back in a judgmental mode to see if we will hang ourselves. *He has been actively involved in redeeming us.* Jesus died to take away our sins and will come again to bring full salvation to all who are eagerly waiting for Him (see Heb. 9:28 above). This One who deserves all praise—the One Who is the Almighty, the One to Whom every knee will bow (see Rom. 14:11), this One Who is of ultimate significance—has declared us significant. Very significant. He has shared the worth of Jesus with those who have become believers. It is not about us. Our worth is not in ourselves, based on our accomplishments. It is not independent of God, but fully dependent on God. It is not intrinsic, but bestowed by Him. *Mankind, in the light of eternity, is but insignificant fading vapors, lost and soon to be gone. But the One Who is eternal and of supreme significance has imparted eternal life to us. He has granted us forgiveness, cleansing, significance, and dignity. It is all about Him, but He, as the totally unselfish One, has made it all about us as well.*

The Psalmist had it right when he declared, "When I view and consider Your heavens, the work of Your fingers, the moon and the stars, which You have ordained and established, What is man that

You are mindful of him, and the son of [earthborn] man that You care for him? Yet You have made him but a little lower than God [or heavenly beings], and You have crowned him with glory and honor. You made him to have dominion over the works of Your hands; You have put all things under his feet" (Ps. 8:3-6 AMP). *He has made it about us too!* We were created in His image. We horribly fell, and His image in man was woefully marred. But He is in the redeeming business too. In the end, Satan will not prevail!

C. It's About Community—He Has Made Us Greater Than Ourselves

God in Christ has granted us personal worth. It is all about Him, but He has made it about us as well. But it is about us "together," not just about us "individually." Our greatest significance lies within a redeemed community—the church, the body of Christ. We are to be more than redeemed persons; we are to be part of a redeemed society. We, individually, are part of a greater whole whose glory we share in. We are a part of something far greater than our individual selves. It is only when we grasp this truth that we discover our true eternal selves. I think this reality is what Jesus was referring to when He said, "For whoever wants to save his life will lose it, but whoever loses his life for me will find it" (Matt. 16:25 NIV; see also Mark 8:35, Luke 9:24).

Paul is certainly clear concerning this greater glory that is ours together when he speaks to the Corinthians concerning God's plan for the church, Christ's body, writing,

> Now to each one the manifestation of the Spirit is given for the common good. To one there is given through the Spirit the message of wisdom, to another the message of knowledge by means of the same Spirit, to another faith by the same Spirit, to another gifts of healing by that one Spirit, to another miraculous powers, to another prophecy, to another distinguishing between spirits, to another speaking in different kinds of tongues, and to still another the interpretation of tongues. All these are the work of one and the same Spirit, and he gives them to each one, just as he determines. The body is a unit, though it is made up of many parts; and though all its parts are many, they form one body. So it is with Christ. For we were all baptized

by one Spirit into one body—whether Jews or Greeks, slave or free—and we were all given the one Spirit to drink. Now the body is not made up of one part but of many. If the foot should say, "Because I am not a hand, I do not belong to the body," it would not for that reason cease to be part of the body. And if the ear should say, "Because I am not an eye, I do not belong to the body," it would not for that reason cease to be part of the body. If the whole body were an eye, where would the sense of hearing be? If the whole body were an ear, where would the sense of smell be? But in fact God has arranged the parts in the body, every one of them, just as he wanted them to be. If they were all one part, where would the body be? As it is, there are many parts, but one body. The eye cannot say to the hand, "I don't need you!" And the head cannot say to the feet, "I don't need you!" On the contrary, those parts of the body that seem to be weaker are indispensable, and the parts that we think are less honorable we treat with special honor. And the parts that are unpresentable are treated with special modesty, while our presentable parts need no special treatment. But God has combined the members of the body and has given greater honor to the parts that lacked it, so that there should be no division in the body, but that its parts should have equal concern for each other. If one part suffers, every part suffers with it; if one part is honored, every part rejoices with it. (1 Cor. 12:7-26 NIV)

Paul is clear in the Corinthian passage above that we are part of a greater whole and we have been granted a significant role to play in the whole. We are linked together with other believers. We are called to function as one. When one part suffers, every part suffers, and when one part is honored, all rejoice in the honor. All are one "in Christ" and one for Christ. It is not about us; it is about Him. But He is for us and makes it about us too. So it is about us after all, but us in community as a part of His church. Together we share in His glory (see John 17:20-26)!

Sally and I have just returned from a four-week period of ministry in some of the villages in Malawi, Africa. Since returning, I have been asked several times if I had fun. I am glad I went and would quickly go again. I have been deeply touched, but having "fun" or even a "good time" are not descriptions I can identify with. I loved the people, but I saw deep poverty. I saw beautiful young women who aged quickly because of the hardness and harshness of the life that was expected of them. I saw women working the fields with large hoes, with babies strapped to their backs. I saw women and children carry heavy burdens on their heads, necessities like large buckets of water and wood to build fires by which they might cook. These burdens were not being carried short distances either. I saw dirty children in worn-out, often-torn, clothing. Because of the extreme problem of AIDS, I saw many orphans and widows in the villages. Because life is hard and money is scarce, I saw mostly very thin people. I saw miles of fields prepared for planting, all by hand. I saw no tractors or conveniences—just a lot of very hardworking people who walked everywhere and were survivors. I saw disease that could easily be prevented were it not for the poverty.

But that's not all I saw. I saw caring—lots of it, both from local and international sources. I saw those in the villages caring for one another. I saw Christians coming from outside the villages to minister to and feed the many orphans and widows in the villages. It's not that the tribes would not take care of the orphans and widows—they would. But they just didn't have anything extra to share. I saw children carrying younger children on their backs, looking out for them. I saw sharing. I saw a people who loved to sing and to dance and to worship God. I saw grateful people, committed people, and joyous people. I saw integrity and deep respect for elders and tradition.

I read about some things that I did not see because I was not where it was happening. I read about a deeper poverty than what I was seeing in the villages. I read about those who had migrated into the cities looking for an easier, better life. But there aren't enough jobs in the cities. Furthermore, in the city they lose their tribal protection and relationships. There is no one to care for and share with them. There is loneliness. There are more conveniences, but not enough food or legitimate money by which to buy it. So there is crime, rape, homelessness, isolation, and fear. I heard it said that in the cities one-third of the people hire one-third of the people to protect them from the other one-third. That's not a fully accurate statement, but it accurately conveys the idea of what is happening in the cities. Some things are a lot worse than a harsh, hard life in a village that has a sense of community.

I came to understand something about God while I was in Malawi. It sunk in to me that our Western culture—with its extreme emphasis on the individual, the securing of the individual's freedom to act however one wants to act (as long as it's not against the law), and to think however one wants to think—is not a Christian idea. God's idea is community, sharing with and caring for others, respect for authority, and fearing to elevate oneself above the community and do wrong. I saw clearly that God is a God of community, not individual freedom. God did not place individual rights over the community. There are some things that are so important to community that they must be absolutely forbidden for the sake of the community.

God is for His people and acts in the best interests of the community. He doesn't place the welfare of individuals over the community. Some things were so important for God's people that the community was required to discipline those acts severely even to the point of death. Sexual sins among God's people were dealt with severely. Are our communities better off because of our modern sexual freedoms? Sexually transmitted disease is rampant! Diseases such as AIDS make orphans and widows of many and increase the burden of care for communities. Many have suffered greatly because they are victims of incest, rape, and improper touching.

We cannot begin to understand some things in the Bible if we have no knowledge of how much God cares about His people and the witness of His people. God's Word does not protect the reputations of individuals. The sins of biblical heroes are not hidden. Corrupted leaders like Saul were removed from leadership. Even David, a revered king described as a man after God's own heart, was punished severely for his sins. Ananias and Sapphira (see Acts 5:1-10) and Achan with his whole family (see Joshua 7) were made examples by death to the people of God. God has not continued to punish immediately, for He has now spoken and demonstrated His will for His people (although 1 Cor. 11:27-31 is the cause for our serious reflection). But our works will be judged and with absolute fairness (see Heb. 9:27, 2 Cor. 5:19). The message is clear. God is for His people over individuals. We are first the "people" of God. We are loved, chosen, and highly favored, but we are chosen to be a responsible member of God's community with an "other" focus, not a selfish one. We must understand that we are a part of God's *community* of faith.

D. It's About Faith

> One of the Pharisees asked Jesus to have dinner with him, so Jesus went to his home and sat down to eat. When a certain immoral woman from that city heard he was eating there, she brought a beautiful alabaster jar filled with expensive perfume. Then she knelt behind him at his feet, weeping. Her tears fell

on his feet, and she wiped them off with her hair. Then she kept kissing his feet and putting perfume on them. When the Pharisee who had invited him saw this, he said to himself, "If this man were a prophet, he would know what kind of woman is touching him. She's a sinner!" Then Jesus answered his thoughts. "Simon," he said to the Pharisee, "I have something to say to you." "Go ahead, Teacher," Simon replied. Then Jesus told him this story: "A man loaned money to two people—500 pieces of silver to one and 50 pieces to the other. But neither of them could repay him, so he kindly forgave them both, canceling their debts. Who do you suppose loved him more after that?" Simon answered, "I suppose the one for whom he canceled the larger debt." "That's right," Jesus said. Then he turned to the woman and said to Simon, "Look at this woman kneeling here. When I entered your home, you didn't offer me water to wash the dust from my feet, but she has washed them with her tears and wiped them with her hair. You didn't greet me with a kiss, but from the time I first came in, she has not stopped kissing my feet. You neglected the courtesy of olive oil to anoint my head, but she has anointed my feet with rare perfume. I tell you, her sins—and they are many—have been forgiven, so she has shown me much love. But a person who is forgiven little shows only little love." Then Jesus said to the woman, "Your sins are forgiven." The men at the table said among themselves, "Who is this man, that he goes around forgiving sins?" And Jesus said to the woman, "Your faith has saved you; go in peace." (Luke 7:36-50 NKJV)

This is a most intriguing story. Here is a contrast between a Pharisee, a self-righteous, publically declared "good" man, and a woman who is a publicly known sinner. Yet the Pharisee is condemned while the woman is not only not condemned, but even commended for her faith. Both put great stock in not sinning against God by keeping the Law. One was good at keeping the Law, both in his own eyes and in the eyes of his community; the other was a miserable failure at keeping the Law, both in her own eyes and in the eyes of her community. Nevertheless, Jesus declared saving faith only to the woman who was publically seen as a miserable failure with no perceived personal goodness, but spoke words of condemnation to the Pharisee who was perceived as "good."

1. It's Not About Personal Goodness

It is interesting to me that every religion of the world except Christianity trusts in *personal goodness* for salvation. Christianity, however, through the mouth of Jesus Himself, declares, "No one is good except God alone" (Luke 18:19).

Paul too strikes out at fallen man's deceived declaration of personal goodness. In Romans 3:20, he warns those who trust in personal goodness that the Law itself does not declare us good, but instead shows us how sinful we are. He writes, "Obviously, the law applies to those to whom it was given, for its purpose is to keep people from having excuses, and to show that the entire world is guilty before God. For no one can ever be made right with God by doing what the law commands. The law simply shows us how sinful we are" (Rom. 3:19-20 NLV).

We might deceive ourselves by comparing ourselves favorably to those we perceive as wicked, but all of us who dare to compare ourselves to Jesus will fall way short of personal goodness. Innate personal goodness for fallen man is a deception that thrives through man's *fleshly* perversion of the idea of goodness. We choose to look at ourselves relative to others rather than to look at ourselves absolutely in terms of Jesus's goodness. In so doing, we may derive relative goodness, but never absolute goodness, because our standard for goodness is perverted. *When I "honestly" look at myself in terms of innate goodness, I am not pleased, but rather appalled, by my temptation toward selfishness and corruption. And there is absolutely no justification for this, for I was raised very well.*

The blindness of perceived personal goodness was Simon the Pharisee's problem, and it had horrible ramifications. First, he refused to recognize the Savior of fallen mankind. Secondly, because of his pride, which was rooted in his inaccurate sense of personal goodness, he looked down his nose at a very needy woman and declared her as unworthy of association with him. In contrast, Jesus, in His pure goodness, reached down to her to lift her up so that she might stand with Him for all eternity.

a. We Are "in Christ" but Totally Undeserving of That State

We who are participators in the grace of God must stand with Him to know who we have been declared to be "in Christ"—possessors of His shared glory (see John 17:22). It is our awareness of this undeserved significance that enables us to say "no" to the world's exaltation of us. The world's acclaim of us can never measure up to the significance we have "in Christ" and must not be seen as a replacement for it in *any* sense. Knowing that we are "in Christ," sharers in His glory, can prevent us from being lured into settling for the temporary, fading significance that comes through the fallen world's acclaim. *We are already in a more glorious state than that of the greatest glory the world can offer. But we must not forget that this significance does not come through personal merit. It comes only through God's merciful, gracious forgiveness—forgiveness made necessary because of our lack of personal merit.*

Only as we hold tight to both of these truths (Jesus's shared glory and our own state as undeserving participators in it) will we stand with Jesus, freely offering the good news of this grace to others. *All believers received this needed grace because we were fallen and in dire need of receiving Jesus as life. But it is only when we perceive that we are absolutely undeserving of this glory that we will stand with the needy (as Jesus did) rather than above them (as did Simon the Pharisee) and offer them life "in Christ." Our attitude when we make this offer of life in Christ should be that of one beggar telling another beggar where we have found bread.*

It is when we stand with the needy rather than above them that we become a trusted bridge to Christ. Without that attitude, we often appear to the needy as arrogant and insensitive, and thus our offer to them of life in Jesus will likely be seen as a reproach. Then it is likely that our offer to them of "life in Jesus's name" will be rejected because of the *fleshly* pride of both the needy and we who are blessed "in Christ." We must approach the needy as did Jesus, who though He had every right to judge this woman, chose to value her instead. *We who are "in Christ" have much to be grateful for, but* watch out! Pride can easily become the fleshly companion of Christ's blessing. *There should be no place in the Christian's life for pride rooted in personal goodness. In truth, our personal goodness has the aroma of stench.*

b. We Are Not to Judge People, Only Deeds—and Those Only by Word

Our Lord Jesus admonished us to refrain from judging others. He said,

> Judge not, and you shall not be judged. Condemn not, and you shall not be condemned. Forgive, and you will be forgiven.

> Give, and it will be given to you: good measure, pressed down, shaken together, and running over will be put into your bosom. For with the same measure that you use, it will be measured back to you. And He spoke a parable to them: "Can the blind lead the blind? Will they not both fall into the ditch? A disciple is not above his teacher, but everyone who is perfectly trained will be like his teacher. And why do you look at the speck in your brother's eye, but do not perceive the plank in your own eye? Or how can you say to your brother, 'Brother, let me remove the speck that is in your eye,' when you yourself do not see the plank that is in your own eye? Hypocrite! First remove the plank from your own eye, and then you will see clearly to remove the speck that is in your brother's eye." (Luke 6:37-42 NKJV)

The judging that takes place in this passage in Luke 6 is the judging that goes beyond judging actions as wrong, going all the way to declaring others as persons of lesser value. This judging, in effect, forgets our own continued need for grace. Our *fleshly* pride can cause us to fail to recognize that we too could be in the same position of those we judge were it not for the grace of God. In truth, there are probably some who appear so despicable to us that we can easily judge them as "unworthy of grace and forgiveness." But that is not the Spirit of Jesus. This kind of judgment comes from our *flesh* (the desire to look and be better than others), not from the Spirit of Christ living in us. Knowing this will enable believers to offer unbelievers Christ's love with sensitive, honoring compassion. It is not that we are condoning sin, but rather that we are valuing people. It is no problem to declare (judge) an action as wrong, whether it is our deed or the deed of another. Yet we must be careful that our judgment of "wrong action" will be based on the declaration of God's Word, not on the basis of the valued opinions of others we want to fit in with.

Jesus did not condone sin, but He did value sinners. Consider the story of Jesus we find in John 8.

> The teachers of the law and the Pharisees brought in a woman caught in adultery. They made her stand before the group and said to Jesus, "Teacher, this woman was caught in the act of adultery. In the Law Moses commanded us to stone such women. Now what do you say?" They were using this question

as a trap, in order to have a basis for accusing him. But Jesus bent down and started to write on the ground with his finger. When they kept on questioning him, he straightened up and said to them, "If any one of you is without sin, let him be the first to throw a stone at her." Again he stooped down and wrote on the ground. At this, those who heard began to go away one at a time, the older ones first, until only Jesus was left, with the woman still standing there. Jesus straightened up and asked her, "Woman, where are they? Has no one condemned you?" "No one, sir," she said. "Then neither do I condemn you," Jesus declared. "Go now and leave your life of sin." (John 8:3-12 NIV)

The attitude of the Pharisees was that Jesus must be stopped, His influence quenched, and that the shaming of a woman such as this didn't matter. So they publicly humiliated her in a most condemning way, branding her as one who was not and could never be worthy of their friendship. Jesus, in contrast, stood with her. While not condoning her sin (she was told to "go and leave your life of sin" [verse 12]), He nevertheless gave her forgiveness, dignity, hope, and a new start. Should we not also have the attitude Jesus had toward those who are living obviously sinful lives?

c. The "Hypocrisy Factor" in Churches

There is another important thing in Jesus's encounter with the Pharisees that we must not miss. The *older* ones were the first to have their consciences convicted, drop their stones, and walk away (see John 8:8). As we age, we become even more aware of our shortcomings. But we do not necessarily share about those shortcomings with others. We are more likely to hide them instead. The young must then assume that as they age, they will outgrow their sinfulness. This obviously is not true, but the silence of the older generation about their own personal struggles sends a veiled message to those struggling with sin and thus becomes a source of hypocrisy in most churches. Through our silence about our own struggles with sin, we, in effect, post a Sinners Not Welcome sign at the church door. Because we do not speak about our struggles, when people get in trouble, they no longer tend to feel comfortable in a church full of people who appear not to struggle with sin. They no longer see themselves as fitting in with such a pious group. How unfortunate, for *all who have gained spiritual maturity have gained it only through much repentance and much struggle to escape the power of sin. Struggle is a fact of life in our quest for holiness.*

I believe this is what is pictured in John 8. The older, supposedly more pious, scribes and Pharisees were confronted with the truth of their own hidden sin when Jesus declared, "If any one of you is without sin, let him be the first to throw a stone at her" (v. 7). When the older men left, the younger, seeing the hidden sin of their elders revealed, also left. The older Pharisees pretense of piousness no longer empowered the hopeful, yet naive, young Pharisees to act in like fashion.

Flesh is something we will always strive against. It is this fallen world's programming of our brains, programming rooted in our fallen nature that desires to gain significance from the world (fallen creation) rather than to cling to Christ (our Creator) for significance. We will struggle against *flesh* until the day we die. We want to look good to the world and fear looking bad. Unchallenged *flesh* can make judgmental, critical Pharisees out of all of us. The truth, however, is that *we are only forgiven and undeserving members of the family of God who have needed and will need much grace. Our attitude needs to be that of one beggar telling another beggar where we have found bread. Then our faith will be contagious.*

d. Why Doesn't God Eradicate *Flesh* from the Believer?

So, why doesn't God eradicate our *flesh* from us so that we will not have to struggle so? A part of our basic fallen nature is a desire to become independent, self-sufficient persons. If we had the choice, I believe that most of us would choose to approach God as self-sufficient persons who naturally make righteous choices and never look bad—as persons worthy of fellowship with Him. We naturally prefer to make God proud of us through our accomplishments rather than to depend on Him to help us. Thus we naturally want to achieve significance our way, independent of God's help. We have learned this from our interaction with our fallen world. We desire that the world would designate us as "significant," which it does on its terms. Thus we are easily deceived, for the worth we seek to achieve independently of God is of this world, which is an enemy of God. James admonishes us, saying, "You adulterers! Don't you realize that friendship with the world makes you an enemy of God? I say it again: If you want to be a friend of the world, you make yourself an enemy of God" (James 4:4 NLT).

But it's other than that too! I see several undesirable ramifications of seeking worth through self-effort and our accomplishments rather than through a dependant relationship with God:

1. *Our work for God would then be confined to our natural abilities, which are limited and ineffective in spiritual matters.* How limited and ineffective would our work for God be? Look around. Working limited to our own natural abilities is the way most Christians work for the Lord now. How are we Christians doing by walking after the Lord in our own strength? How is it working for you? God has a reason for letting us be naturally ineffective. When seen correctly, the limitations of our *flesh* force us to learn how to "walk by the Spirit" so that we may know His power in accomplishing His work and thus be able to accomplish far more. Jesus completely depended on the Father. He said of Himself, "**The very works that I do by the power of My Father and in My Father's name bear witness concerning Me [they are My credentials and evidence in support of Me]**" (John 10:25 AMP). As Jesus completely depended on the Father, we must completely depend on the Spirit. If Jesus, as perfect man, turned to a source beyond Himself, we as imperfect men must even more fervently seek help from a source greater than ourselves, the indwelling Holy Spirit. If we are to accomplish the work of Jesus, we must learn how to depend on the Holy Spirit for power and direction.
2. *If we did accomplish God-sized work in our own strength, we would become proud and even more independent.* We might say, "Daddy, look what I did," but then our accomplishments would not grow us closer to Him, but would make us even more independent of Him, as we would have gained sufficiency by our own strength.
3. *We would not grow in our intimacy with God and in our faith.* God's call draws us beyond ourselves and our *fleshly* limitations. As we learn to depend on His strength and experience His faithfulness, we lean into His bosom like a child who finds security in his father's strength. Thus we grow in our intimacy with Him and in faith (i.e., confidence that we can "in Christ" do that which He calls us to do).

Summary: We do not achieve maturity through our own strength, but by learning to walk in the power of the Spirit. We must allow the Holy

Spirit to set Himself against our *flesh* so that we might not do those things that we naturally please to do (see Gal. 5:16-17). Our *fleshy* desires for self-sufficiency and personal goodness can be harmful to us at the spiritual level, for these two desires tend to create independence from God rather than dependence on Him. Jesus was totally dependent on the Father. *We must be too. We must face the fact of our personal inadequacy to walk out the faith in our own strength, quit pretending we can be good apart from God's help, and desperately depend on the Holy Spirit to do through us what we cannot accomplish by ourselves.*

If God did not require our dependence on the Holy Spirit, He would, in effect, limit our accomplishments to those things we are able to do in our own strength. The result is that we would take pride in our accomplishments and would tend to seek self-glory through our accomplishments rather than being sold out to seeking His glory alone. Furthermore, without the Spirit's strength, our accomplishments would be far less, and His kingdom would not be effectively extended. Independent of Him, we can do nothing of eternal significance (see John 15:5). Yet, when dependent on Him, "we can do all things through Christ who strengthens us" (Phil. 4:13 NKJV). In contrast to that, walking successfully, independently of Him, causes our pride and self-sufficiency to grow rather than our faith, our dependence on Him, or our intimacy with Him.

God chooses not to eradicate our *flesh* because the weaknesses of our *flesh* make us aware of our desperate need to walk in the power of the Spirit. Walking "after the Spirit" necessitates our learning to depend on Him and, in so doing, to experience Him as faithful. Learning to trust Him as we walk after the Spirit and, as a result, experience His faithfulness to us fosters intimacy with Him. The final result is that we will walk humbly with our Lord and will delight in doing the things that are important to Him. Furthermore, we will be grateful to Him for choosing to do His work through us so that we may share in His joy. Our own personal inadequacy causes us to draw near to God, and when we do, He will draw near to us (see James 4:7-8).

2. Faith Is the Starting Point, the Middle, and the End of Our Walk "in Christ"

In the story of the Pharisee (Simon) and the woman of sin that we have just considered at the beginning of this chapter (see Luke 7:36-50),

Jesus condemned the self-righteous Simon and then declared to the woman who knew her sin condition, "Your faith has saved you; go in peace" (Luke 7:50 NIV). Faith is the starting point in our walk in Christ, the focus of our walk, and the victory of our walk. Just what is faith? Faith for this woman was dedicating the rest of her life to returning love to the One who was her only hope for eternal life. It was rooted in love for Jesus and was a response to the gracious love she first saw in Him. The same should be true for all believers.

Faith must have an object, and this object is centered in the life and work of Jesus. This woman had faith in (i.e., belief in) Jesus's ability to save her despite her life of sin. Paul makes the case for saving faith in Romans.

> Against all hope, Abraham in hope believed and so became the father of many nations, just as it had been said to him, "So shall your offspring be." Without weakening in his faith, he faced the fact that his body was as good as dead—since he was about a hundred years old—and that Sarah's womb was also dead. Yet he did not waver through unbelief regarding the promise of God, but was strengthened in his faith and gave glory to God, being fully persuaded that God had power to do what he had promised. This is why "it was credited to him as righteousness." The words "it was credited to him" were written not for him alone, but also for us, to whom God will credit righteousness—for us who believe in him who raised Jesus our Lord from the dead. He was delivered over to death for our sins and was raised to life for our justification. (Rom. 4:18-25 NIV)

Thus, Paul presents faith as trust in God to accomplish what man is hopeless to do by himself, i.e., an unwavering belief in the power of God to keep His promises to man. Faith believes God will empower us to do whatever He has called us to do. The author of Hebrews explained faith this way: "Now faith is being sure of what we hope for and certain of what we do not see" (Heb. 11:1 NIV).

Furthermore, this trust (faith) that God will do what He declares He will do is credited as righteousness, i.e., as making the one who believes "right" with God. It also satisfies God's justice. Man's sin debt is fully paid through the shed blood of Jesus unto death, a death God substitutes for the Law's requirement of death for sinners (see Rom. 6:23). My death would not have benefit for you, for my death is required for my own sin. However, man's sin is fully paid for through the death of God's sinless Son. Why? Unlike all of us, Jesus had no sin to demand His own death. Furthermore, as the second Person of the Trinity, He is of infinite worth. This means that His death is a more-than-sufficient substitute death for the sins of *all* who believe. Thus, justice is served.

So, first of all, faith is belief in a body of truth centered around the work and person of Jesus on earth. Basically, it is a trust in Jesus to do for the believer what he cannot do for himself, i.e., save himself from the righteous death penalty that is his due because of his sins. It is God's good pleasure to offer the gift of salvation to all who believe. As the author of Hebrews declares, "And without faith it is impossible to please God, because anyone who comes to him must believe that he exists and that he rewards those who earnestly seek him" (Heb. 11:6 NIV). Our God of incomparable grace has chosen to reward those who earnestly seek Him and who will believe in the work of Jesus on their behalf.

But faith is about more than salvation from the death penalty God's Law requires of all who sin (see Rom. 6:23). In Galatians, faith is presented as the prerequisite of spiritual growth. Here, a seemingly exasperated Paul chastises, "Are you so foolish? After beginning with the Spirit, are you now trying to attain your goal by human effort? Have you suffered so much for nothing—if it really was for nothing? Does God give you his Spirit and work miracles among you because you observe the law, or because you believe what you heard?" (Gal. 3:3-5 NIV). Paul has here equated faith with belief that the Holy Spirit *will* work miracles through those who believe—that God *will* do work through them that is beyond their own best human effort. Faith is the belief that God will indeed act through the believer to accomplish His own will, something the believer is not capable of in his own strength alone. Faith stretches us to believe God for the impossible, to have so much trust in His desire to work through us that we will actually attempt that which we know we cannot do in our own strength. We try because we believe He is leading and will do His work through us if we will just step out in faith.

Faith does not spring from taking personal inventory, but rather from looking into the heart of God and making ourselves available for His service. Faith incorporates a boldness to try the seemingly impossible if we believe God is in it. It involves dying to self-sufficiency and trusting in God-sufficiency. It moves us beyond self-protection. It acknowledges that our lives are not our own but God's.

John the Revelator declares, "They *overcame him* [the devil] by the blood of the Lamb and by the word of their testimony; they did not love their lives so much as to shrink from death" (Rev. 12:11 NIV; emphasis mine). Men and women of faith have long been so certain of the reality of God that they were willing to forfeit their earthly lives in order to honor Him. They could do this because they believed in the intrinsic goodness of a trustworthy God who has made Himself known to man through Jesus Christ. As Paul said it in his letter to the Romans,

> And we know that God causes everything to work together for the good of those who love God and are called according to his purpose for them. For God knew his people in advance, and he chose them to become like his Son, so that his Son would be the firstborn among many brothers and sisters. And having chosen them, he called them to come to him. And having called them, he gave them right standing with himself. And having given them right standing, he gave them his glory.

Nothing Can Separate Us from God's Love

What shall we say about such wonderful things as these? If God is for us, who can ever be against us? Since he did not spare even his own Son but gave him up for us all, won't he also give us everything else? Who dares accuse us whom God has chosen for his own? No one—for God himself has given us right standing with himself. Who then will condemn us? No one—for Christ Jesus died for us and was raised to life for us, and he is sitting in the place of honor at God's right hand, pleading for us. Can anything ever separate us from Christ's love? Does it mean he no longer loves us if we have trouble or calamity, or are persecuted, or hungry, or destitute, or in danger, or threatened with death? [As the Scriptures say, "For your sake we are killed every day; we are being slaughtered like sheep."] No, despite all these things, overwhelming victory is ours through Christ, who loved us. And I am convinced that nothing can ever separate us from God's love. Neither death nor life, neither angels nor demons, neither our fears for today nor our worries about tomorrow—not even the powers of hell can separate us from God's love. (Romans 8:28-38 NLT)

Satan wills to see us destroyed and programs our minds for destruction. We must overcome him in the same way that it is declared in Revelation 12:11. We must put our hope in Christ alone (which is faith). We must then replace the stinking thinking that is in our head with right thinking that comes through believing what God's Word teaches (see Rom. 12:2).

We must believe Christ and testify of the sufficiency of His blood to cover our sin. We must believe Christ and trust in the presence of the Holy Spirit to empower our walk. We must believe that **"God is at work in us to will and to act according to His good purpose"** (Phil. 2:13). He has not left us as orphans. We must become increasingly more conscious of His presence in us so that we will choose to walk after the Spirit. We must recognize the role of our *flesh* in combating faith. We must see how Satan would use our *flesh* to confuse and defeat us. We must also trust God to set His Holy Spirit against our *flesh* so that our *flesh* will not accomplish what it pleases. But more importantly, we must experience the renewing of the mind that comes as we set our mind on the things of Christ and walk in the power of the Spirit.

We can walk in victory. I like the way Peter said it in Titus:

> Once we, too, were foolish and disobedient. We were misled and became slaves to many lusts and pleasures. Our lives were full of evil and envy, and we hated each other. But—"When God our Savior revealed his kindness and love, he saved us, not because of the righteous things we had done, but because of his mercy. He washed away our sins, giving us a new birth and new life through the Holy Spirit He generously poured out the Spirit upon us through Jesus Christ our Savior. Because of his grace he declared us righteous and gave us confidence that we will inherit eternal life." This is a trustworthy saying, and I want you to insist on these teachings so that all who trust in God will devote themselves to doing good. These teachings are good and beneficial for everyone. (Titus 3:3-8 NLT)

As the author of Hebrews teaches, "We must pay more careful attention, therefore, to what we have heard, so that we do not drift away. For if the message spoken by angels was binding, and every violation and disobedience received its just punishment, how shall we escape if we ignore such a great salvation?" (Heb. 2:1-3 NIV). It is so easy to forget who we have been declared to be "in Christ" and to slowly drift back to a world-based identity so that we react after our flesh. It is so easy to place our faith in what the world teaches us rather than in what God teaches us. We must be diligent to walk as persons of faith, look to God to know who we are, and then choose to "walk by the Spirit." Our goal is to represent Christ well by returning His love during the rest of our residence on earth. It takes effort to stay focused on Christ. Wouldn't it be nice if we let the hurts and disappointments we experience in the world prick us back to a focus on Christ? We can, if we work at it! He will lead if we will choose to work, and to keep on working, at following.

3. The Help and Hindrance of "Feelings" in Matters of Faith

Feelings can be one of the great hindrances to walking by faith. This is because we often misunderstand the role God intended for feelings. Feelings are to be seen as an instrument panel. When a warning light comes on in an instrument panel, the attendant is warned to first pay attention to that area the "warning" is reporting on and only then (after close examination) make a decision about what he will do as a response to the warning. Likewise, feelings are a warning light that God has placed in us so that we might check out an area of irritation and then make a decision as to how we will respond. Unfortunately, many of us are hot-wired to our feelings. We give our feelings so much authority that they control us. As a result, our feelings stimulate us to give in to our old habit patterns (*flesh*). Could we not begin to examine the source of our feelings so that we can make a proper decision based on who we are "in Christ" instead? *Feelings can be like a ring in our nose that anyone or anything can insert a finger into and then, from that power position, lead us in the direction they desire us to go in—even if that direction is not the one we really want to go in. Such is the power of flesh.*

On the positive side, feelings can expose our stinking thinking if we examine their source rather than blindly follow the feelings. But unexamined feelings naturally cause us to default back to our old habit patterns of behavior. Feelings are wonderful things that add spice to life. But they should inform us, not enslave us. We are to be a people of faith, fully aware of our feelings and considerate of the feelings of others. Some of us need to work at being more aware of the role of feelings so that they might inform us of our stinking thinking. Others of us need to work at not being so snared by our feelings.

A well-know diagram used by Dr. Bill Bright, the founder of Campus Crusade for Christ, pictures an old coal-fueled train with a caboose labeled Feelings. The engine is labeled the Word of God, and the coal car is labeled Faith. The idea is that feelings are to follow decisions made by faith in God's Word. Feelings are the caboose in the train of life. They should follow and inform us, not lead us. If you get the picture, then you understand that if feelings are leading a train, then the train is either going downhill and is out of control or is in reverse and is being pushed by the engine. In either case, the caboose is not controlling the engine. That's the way it ought to be. Feelings should tag along and make us more alert in any given situation, but they are not be our sole guide or our *soul* guide.

Consider this diagram I picked up in a seminar taught by Dr. Frank Minirth.

Circumstances + (Thinking and Actions) ⟶ Feelings

Feelings are the by-product of our circumstances and the way we think and act in our circumstances. While we are not at liberty to just feel different, if we change any of the three factors that cause the feelings, we can change the feelings. As an example, consider Mary, who has no date for the prom and is feeling miserable and unlovely. But then she receives a phone call from the captain of the football team asking her to attend the prom as his date. With the invitation, her feelings instantly change! When her *circumstances* changed, her feelings changed. But we can also accomplish a change in feelings if we couch our circumstances in different thinking. Suppose that though Mary has no date to the prom, she has an exciting alternative to going to the prom. If her mind is engaged in embracing this alternative activity, would that not also change her feelings, even though her circumstance of not being asked to go to the prom has not changed? Changing the way we *think* about a circumstance also changes the way we feel about a circumstance.

We can also change feelings through our *actions*. Suppose that you wake up depressed over something and just stay in bed. Then the depression would likely intensify. But suppose you are able to make yourself get out of bed and go to the gym and work out. Would that not have a positive effect on your feelings? Actions can also change feelings.

When persons come to me for counsel, often they are in a circumstance that they cannot change. However, if one can alter the way they think or act in their circumstance, they can alter the miserable feelings that accompany the circumstance. Therefore, with a different attitude and plan of action, though they are still in the same circumstance, they have altered the circumstance's power to make them miserable.

Do you know what the Bible calls right thinking followed by right acting? Faith! Faith empowers the Christian to live in the same circumstance without being overwhelmed by the circumstance. However, if one does not choose to look at his circumstances with eyes of faith, the circumstance can overwhelm him even though he is a Christian. Faith always has the power to change a circumstance's effect on the believer and, many times, also has the power to change the circumstance. This is especially true in the area of relationships. A change in one party of a relationship often initiates reciprocal change in the other party. To put it simply, since a relationship involves interaction between two people, if one changes, then the nature of the relationship changes.

There is a dangerous consequence when we fail to view our circumstances with eyes of faith. Our circumstances lie in our fallen world that is stamped with the influence of Satan. The world also greatly influences our thinking and our actions in response to our circumstances. Thus, our feelings have largely been shaped by the world. The result is that when feelings determine our actions, we have effectively chosen to allow Satan and his fallen world to control us. Satan is the master of deception, and our feelings can make us putty in his hands.

If we are Christians who have not understood our identity "in Christ" and then applied this truth in the way we process this temporary fallen world's impact on us, then feelings can pull us back into our old ways of thinking and acting even though we are new persons in Christ (see 2 Cor. 5:13). *But there is a good side too.* When we realize that feelings are to be seen as an instrument panel, then feelings can spur us to examine our thinking and actions for their appropriateness to our identity "in Christ." We can ask questions like, Why am I feeling the way I do? Am I acting beneath who I am "in Christ"? Am I approaching my circumstance with stinking thinking rather that godly thinking? Has God allowed this circumstance as a means of maturing me into the likeness of Christ? Furthermore, *choosing to examine our feelings so that they inform us rather than control us will, in time, even alter our feelings. Our feelings will begin to align with the truth and become appropriate to our identity "in Christ."*

Many Christians feel inferior because of past circumstances. This feeling of inferiority then dominates their thinking and determines the way they approach life. Why should they not examine this feeling of inferiority in the light of who they are "in Christ," recognize that it is invalid, and renounce it? The same could be said about feeling insignificant, unacceptable or unaccepted, worthless, and hopeless. The list of feelings could go on and on. All of these feelings enslave millions of Christians, and all are inappropriate. But *if we do not challenge the way we feel with the truth of who we are "in Christ," then our lives will continue to be affected by that stinking thinking. A lie believed to be truth tends to have as much power as truth in shaping us.*

Properly addressed, our feelings can become a great ally. The fruit of the Spirit-led life listed in Galatians 5:23 (love, joy, peace, patience, kindness, goodness, faithfulness, gentleness, and self-control) is a "feel good" state of mind. Though these fruit are technically not feelings, they do represent a "mood set" that should be common to our lives as Christians. When this mood is not present, its absence points to the probability that we are not "walking by the Spirit." If that is the case, we are most likely walking after the *flesh. Our emotions are great indicators of the nature of our walk. Why not let them make you aware of whether you are focused on Christ, or on the world, at the present moment? Feelings are meant by God to be a blessing, not a curse.*

E. It's About Our Church "Family"

Families that function as God intended are a great blessing and are special. They provide a safe haven where we can be nurtured and loved, encouraged and enabled to go out into a world that can be harsh. Then at the end of the day, we are fortified by coming back out of the world and into the home that God has designed to nourish and restore us.

All believers have been adopted into the family of God. God has chosen believers to be His special family. Our churches are to be safe places of nourishment, encouragement, and training that equip us to go out into our sinful world. We are then to regularly return to our church homes to be encouraged and fortified. Our churches should be a place where we can be real and still be loved and valued.

Sally and I recently twice experienced the fellowship of the *church universal* while we were in South Africa. First, when we were sitting down for breakfast at a bed-and-breakfast in Johannesburg, I noticed there was only one other person present. I invited him to join us. As we talked, he realized we were Christians. Before breakfast was over, we knew a lot about him and were able to share in his life's problems. We had prayer with him; he was encouraged, and we were all blessed.

After breakfast, we rented a car and drove to the dam area of Blyde River Canyon. As Sally was beginning to take a picture of me, with our beautiful surroundings as a backdrop, a gentleman asked Sally if she would like him to take the picture so that both of us could be in it. She was delighted and quickly accepted. As we talked with this special couple, Alan and Rosemary, we soon discovered they were Christians. We had a time of wonderful sharing and fellowship and found out that they were from Phalaborwa, the small community in which we would be staying the next three nights in order to tour the Kruger game reserve. I told them that we would like to take them out to dinner while we were there, and they accepted. We got their phone number.

Our sightseeing the next day in this mountainous area was shortened by low clouds that made seeing impossible, so we drove on to Phalaborwa much earlier than anticipated, arriving at 2:00 PM. I gave Alan and Rosemary a call, but they didn't want us to take them out; they wanted to bless us instead. Alan picked us up and gave us a tour of Phalaborwa—it didn't take long—and then we went to his home. He had grilled steak, sausage, and lamb chops. It was a feast for us, especially after existing the previous four weeks in Malawi with peanut butter as our staple food. But the most special thing was spending five hours in true Christ-exalting Christian fellowship with a couple we had met less than twenty-four hours before, and that through a seemingly chance meeting (though I believe it was God-ordained) at a dam many kilometers away from Phalaborwa. Alan and Rosemary were the highlight of our trip, even though Blyde River Canyon was gorgeous, and two days driving through the Kruger game reserve was also very special. We will remember their kindness and our fellowship together forever. Memories of Blyde River Canyon and Kruger game reserve will fade rather quickly.

Through Alan and Rosemary's opening of their home to us and our intimate sharing with them (all because of our common fellowship in Christ), they became like family to us in a land thousands of miles away. That's what God wants for His chosen people. We found that fellowship in South Africa, but how do we find it in our local churches? How does the local church become the family to us that God has intended for His children?

How should we, as members of the family of God, treat one another? What does "walking after the Spirit" look like in the church environment?

I want to share with you a few biblical evidences of "walking after the Spirit" in our relationships within our churches. But *before you read through these, please receive this prayer of protection and blessing:*

> I pray that you will walk in the Spirit as you consider these evidences. May you be protected from finding fault in others as you read these evidences and thus stay free from a critical, complaining spirit. May you not condemn yourself in areas where the Spirit convicts you of failure in your walk. May you not get caught up in self-condemnation by remembering that *flesh* cannot be perfected and that only with the Spirit's help can we prevail over *flesh* (see Gal. 5:16-17). If the Spirit convicts you as you read, may you choose to repent of walking after the *flesh* and then choose to walk after the Spirit. May you choose to believe God's plan for relationships in His Church, strive to walk in His ways even when others are not and, by so doing, become a role model for others to follow. May you know the joy of obedience and the victory of faith in the way you walk in your church relationships. In Jesus's mighty name, Amen!

As you read the material that follows, please do not become judgmental toward your church. Churches are made up of people like us who fail, make mistakes, and need encouragement, but also of those who carry within ourselves the love of God. We as individuals can make our churches better. But in order to do this, we must first examine ourselves. We must ask ourselves if we are "walking by the Spirit" in the way we interact with others in our churches. Are we being salt and light to her through our actions? Since we are the church, we can make our church better simply by walking after the Spirit so that we are part of the solution rather than part of the problem. We can rarely do that by sitting back or criticizing our church and her leaders. We *can* "walk by the Spirit." We are "in Christ"—thoroughly loved, accepted, and encouraged so that we might be loving and accepting encouragers of others. Because the Spirit of Christ is in us, we can, through our actions and by the use of our tongues, become a spark that encourages purifying fire to burn in our churches.

The following bullets are some things each of us can examine to evaluate whether or not we are fulfilling our responsibility to God to help make our church more like the nourishing, living organism He would have her to be. *If we are "walking by the Spirit" in our church, then our walk will look somewhat like this:*

Evidences of "Walking by the Spirit" in Our Churches

- We will be faithful in gathering with other believers to encourage others in their walk "in Christ." This will be even more important to us when things are not going well for us or for our church.

    The author of the letter to the Hebrews was concerned that persons would drift away from the church and devotion to their faith because of the difficulties they were experiencing (see Heb. 2:1). He warns them to not neglect to meet together, as some have already started doing, but rather to meet and encourage one another (Heb. 10:25).

- We will be coming to worship, looking to experience God's presence in others and in ourselves.

    The Spirit of Christ is present in all believers (see Rom. 8:9). We should be seeking to honor His name, asking God to make us aware of how we might be a blessing to others as He makes us sensitive to their needs and aware that others carry His life within themselves. We will experience life differently when we are aware of His presence. Likewise, we change the atmosphere in the church when we acknowledge His presence and look for the manifestations of His love. We should enter our church buildings in expectant awareness of the presence of the Holy Spirit, ready to contribute and eager to listen (see 1 Cor. 14:26).

- We will be seeking to stimulate one another to love and do good deeds.

    The world is constantly at work to stimulate us to be like it. God warns us that we are to stimulate one another to act like Jesus. We can, because the Spirit of Christ is in us. But when we are focused on (or being stimulated by) the world and its ways, we don't. The author of Hebrews implies that this is one of the main reasons for meeting together, saying, "**Let us consider how to stimulate one another to love and good deeds, not forsaking our own assembling together**" (Heb. 10:24-25 NASB). Notice from this verse that *stimulating others is something we have taken the time to consider how to do; it is something we are to think about.*

We need to be stimulated by other believers, and other believers need to be stimulated by us in order to combat the fallen world's constant pull on us to be like it. We can begin to do this by reminding others that they are "in Christ," sharers of His divine nature (see 2 Pet. 1:14). The *gifts* of the Spirit are *listed in order of importance* in 1 Corinthians 12:28. In that list, you will notice that *the second most important gift is that of "prophet."* Verse 31 then admonishes believers to seek the most important gifts. The gift of prophecy is defined by Paul as one who helps others grow in the Lord, strengthening, encouraging, and comforting them (1 Cor. 14:3 NLT). *Prophesy is a gift we all need to have expressed to us, and a gift that God, through Paul, admonishes us to earnestly seek for our ministry to others.* We should get the message. God wants us to seek the gift of prophesy so that we might strengthen, encourage, and comfort others. We all have a great need to both experience it *and* express it.

- We will be sharing in one another's sufferings and sorrows (see 1 Cor. 12:26).

Compassion is of God. Jesus says of His Father in the sermon on the Mount, "God blesses those who mourn, for they will be comforted" (Matt. 5:4 NLT). When we are "walking after the Spirit," we are compassionate with one another. Paul sees our own compassionate nature as coming through our own experience in receiving God's compassion, writing, "Praise be to the God and Father of our Lord Jesus Christ, the Father of compassion and the God of all comfort, who comforts us in all our troubles, *so that* we can comfort those in any trouble with the comfort we ourselves have received from God" (2 Cor. 1:3-4 NIV; emphasis mine).

- We will be rejoicing in one another's victories. (See 1 Cor. 12:26).

We are to see ourselves as "one" with fellow believers, coparticipants in the body of Christ. If they are honored, we share in the honor and should rejoice with and for them. There is to be no jealousy or envy among the members of the body of Christ. Those are characteristics of "walking after the flesh" (see James 3:14, Titus 3:3, 1 Pet. 2:1). We are to learn to be content with the things God allocates to us (see Phil. 4:11) and to rejoice with fellow members of the body of Christ who are blessed in any way.

- When a fellow believer is overcome by some sin, we will be going to him in order to gently and humbly help our brother back onto the right path.

    But when we go, we are to be aware that we could fall into that same temptation ourselves; we are not above the temptation or above the one who has succumbed to temptation. By going in that awareness, we can share in each other's troubles and problems with the humble attitude that Christ would want us to express as we share (see Gal. 6:1-3).
- We will be happily sharing our resources with fellow believers in need.

    We must remember that what we have is not our own. God owns it all and entrusts portions to us as He wills. We are to be good stewards of all that He has given us. Even if we are only lending to others, we should be willing to get nothing back (see Luke 6:34-36). Proverbs reminds us that when we help the poor, we are lending to the Lord, and that He, the Lord, will repay the debt (see Prov. 19:17). Bond servants of God do not own anything. It all belongs to the Master. Yet we are to be working hard and giving generously to others in need (see Eph. 4:28).
- We will be leading a life worthy of our calling by (1) being humble and gentle; (2) being patient, making allowance for each other's faults because of our love; and (3) making every effort to keep ourselves united in the Spirit, binding ourselves together in peace (see Eph. 4:1-3).
- We will be shunning lying and, instead, speaking truthfully and in love (see Eph. 4:25).
- We will be working to avoid being controlled by anger, as that gives the devil a foothold in our lives (see Eph. 4:26-27).
- We will be laboring to abstain from foul or abusive language and will be striving to always use our mouth for encouragement instead (see Eph. 4:29).
- We will be laboring to get rid of all bitterness, rage, anger, harsh words, slander, and evil behavior. We will be actively involved in replacing those things with kindness, tenderheartedness, and forgiveness, thus living as Christ lived (see Eph. 4:31-21).
- We will be seeking to follow Christ's example of love (see Eph. 5:2).
- We will be seeking to abstain from even any hint of immorality in our fellowship, from any kind of impurity or greed. We will

not be engaging in any obscenity, foolish talk, or coarse joking. These are out of place for God's holy people. Furthermore, thanksgiving will flow easily from our tongues (Eph. 5:3-4).
- We will be reverencing the Word of God, eager to hear it, to study it, and to apply it in our daily lives (see Ps. 119:9, 130; Acts 17:11; Rom. 15:4; Matt. 22:29; 1 Pet. 1:22).

The bottom line to all of these characteristics of "walking after the Spirit" in our churches is found in Philippians 2:1-7:

> If you have any encouragement from being united with Christ, if any comfort from his love, if any fellowship with the Spirit, if any tenderness and compassion, then make my joy complete by being like-minded, having the same love, being one in spirit and purpose. Do nothing out of selfish ambition or vain conceit, but *in humility consider others better than yourselves.* Each of you should look not only to your own interests, but also to the interests of others. Your attitude should be the same as that of Christ Jesus: Who, being in very nature God, did not consider equality with God something to be grasped, but made himself nothing, taking the very nature of a servant. (NIV; emphasis mine)

In this passage of Scripture, Paul, as did Jesus in His prayer recorded in John 15, is pleading for the church to recognize who she is so that she may adequately represent the love of God to the world. We are to "in humility consider other better [or more important] than ourselves" (Phil. 2:3). But there is only one way that we can pull that off. We must first realize that because we are "in Christ," others aren't actually better or more important than ourselves, but just *considered* that way. This attitude must flow from knowing deep within ourselves that we have been revalued by God, and, furthermore, given a value far above anything we deserve—far above the greatest valuing that could come to us through the things of the world. We can have this attitude when we (1) accept and treasure God's valuing of us and know that the world cannot add to it, (2) know that this valuing of us is *100 percent a gift* from His heart and that we are *100 percent undeserving of this gift*, (3) know that God has given to us in abundance so that we have more than we need for ourselves and thus enough to share, and (4) know that His heart's desire for us (for our sakes as well as for the sake of others) is to freely serve, expecting nothing in return. This attitude must flow out of knowing our abundance "in Christ" and the knowing of our position as *members* of the family of God who are to represent Him well. Our *flesh* sometimes makes this attitude difficult for us to achieve, but God is willing to set His Spirit against our *flesh* so that we do not have to yield to the desires of our *flesh* (Gal. 5:16-17). Because the Spirit of Christ is in us, we can represent Him well, with humility consider others better than ourselves, and become as a servant.

Notice how all of these characteristics of "walking after the Spirit" in our churches involve our attitudes and the use of our tongues. If we would just (1) work at keeping our minds focused on what Christ has accomplished for us, (2) realize that we haven't come close to deserving what He has done for us, (3) believe that God has freely given to us so that we can freely give to others, (4) be determined to use our tongues as a rudder to steer our ship of life parallel to the life Jesus lived on earth, and (5) out of our abundance in Christ choose to use our bodies to serve others, then our churches and lives would be gloriously different.

We are the key to our churches being better. Our prayer, our actions, the way we use our tongues and exercise our gifts, our enthusiasm, and the way we love people brings light into even the greatest darkness. Your light can make a difference. Light always overwhelms darkness. Darkness cannot overwhelm light. Light wins over darkness every time there is conflict between the two.

F. We Are Greater Than We Know!

A beautiful prayer of Paul for the church is recorded in his letter to the church at Ephesus. May this prayer be effective in your life!

> I pray that from his glorious, unlimited resources he will empower you with inner strength through his Spirit. Then Christ will make his home in your hearts as you trust in him. Your roots will grow down into God's love and keep you strong. And may you have the power to understand, as all God's people should, how wide, how long, how high, and how deep his love is. May you experience the love of Christ, though it is too great to understand fully. Then you will be made complete with all the fullness of life and power that comes from God. Now all glory to God, who is able, through his mighty power at work within us, to accomplish infinitely

more than we might ask or think. Glory to him in the church and in Christ Jesus through all generations forever and ever! Amen. (Eph. 3:16-21 NLT)

We are saved to be life givers. God has placed His life in us through His indwelling Holy Spirit so that we may share His life with others. God gives to us in abundance so that we can in turn have plenty to give to others (not necessarily possessions, but most certainly things like joy, encouragement, and valuing). We must not let feelings of personal inadequacy overwhelm us. We are "in Christ," and "Christ is in us." We are His ambassadors in our world and in our churches. We represent Him wherever we go and carry His power within us so that we are able to represent Him well.

Summary: It's not about me. It's about God and His kingdom. But God, by virtue of His very nature, makes it about me—and about you. If we would know who we are, we must first know Who He, our Creator, is. We are greater than we know; we are possessors of His life and meant to be sharers of His life, the life which He has placed within us. Because we share His life, life is about others for us too, just as it is for Christ. We who would find our lives must lose them "in Christ," but all who lose their lives for Christ's sake will find them. We live in a very imperfect vessel. We are possessors of corrupted flesh with a distorted vision of what life is truly about. We have been victimized by Satan and this fallen world. Both would kill and steal from us, seeking to destroy us. Others have hurt us too. But Satan is our real enemy, not others. The good news is that **"greater is He who is in us than he who is in the world"** (see 1 John 4:4). Christ has come to redeem us from all the corruption that has come to us in this world. But more than that, He would have us to be His helpers in cleaning up the mess! His eternal blessing is already ours, and our reward is coming (see 1 Pet. 1:4-5)!

Luke the Physician records words from the mouth of Jesus that (if believed and acted upon) will bring healing to our total being:

> And there was handed to Him [the roll of] the book of the prophet Isaiah. He opened [unrolled] the book and found the place where it was written, "The Spirit of the Lord [is] upon Me, because He has anointed Me [the Anointed One, the Messiah] to preach the good news [the Gospel] to the poor; He has sent Me to announce release to the captives and

recovery of sight to the blind, to send forth as delivered those who are oppressed [who are downtrodden, bruised, crushed, and broken down by calamity], To proclaim the accepted and acceptable year of the Lord [the day when salvation and the free favors of God profusely abound." (Luke 4:17-19 AMP)

This proclamation that Jesus made was a quote from Isaiah 61:1-2. Jesus quoted it to announce Who He was and to establish His purpose on earth. As His followers (disciples), His purpose for living should become our purpose also. The Isaiah passage goes on to say, "But you shall be called the priests of the Lord; people will speak of you as the ministers of our God" (Isa. 61:6 AMP). These former captives—the oppressed, downtrodden, bruised, crushed—who were broken down from calamity were prophesized to be the priests of the Lord. *That's us!* We are greater than we know! We have been deceived by Satan and this fallen world through our *flesh*. We need to renew our minds. We have an eternal destiny. We are participators in the glorious redemption that Christ brings.

> Through Christ you have come to trust in God. And you have placed your faith and hope in God because he raised Christ from the dead and gave him great glory. You were cleansed from your sins when you obeyed the truth, so now you must show sincere love to each other as brothers and sisters. Love each other deeply with all your heart. For you have been born again, but not to a life that will quickly end. Your new life will last forever because it comes from the eternal, living word of God. (1 Pet. 1:21-23 NLT)

We, as believers redeemed in Christ, have an eternal purpose together. We have been loved and are being equipped for love. We are "in Christ," blessed so that we might be a blessing. We are called and empowered to be encouragers and difference makers. We are bound together with other believers to represent Christ, to be His living body still at work in this world. Jesus has charged us, commissioned us, instructed us, and equipped us, saying, "I have been given all authority in heaven and on earth. Therefore, go and make disciples of all the nations, baptizing them in the name of the Father and the Son and the Holy Spirit. Teach these new disciples to obey all the commands I have given you. And be sure of this: I am with you always, even to the end of the age" (Matt. 28:18-20 NLT).

God has done everything needed to make believers a vital part of this great commission. *The question each believer must ask himself/herself is,* "Will I believe God and choose to 'walk by the Spirit,' or am I going to continue to walk after my *flesh*, deceived, defined, and paralyzed into inactivity by God's enemies, Satan and this fallen world?" *You are greater than you know! Will you believe?*

Things You May Ponder and Discuss with Others

1. How can life be both "about you" and "not about you"?
2. Why is community more important than our individual selves?
3. Why is valuing ourselves important to valuing our community?
4. How can a focus on "personal goodness" be harmful?
5. Why is it extremely important to know that our state of being "in Christ" is 100 percent undeserved?
6. Why is it extremely important to know that our state of being "in Christ" is 100 percent true?
7. Why doesn't God eradicate our *flesh* condition when He saves us?
8. What is the role of faith in our growing up to full maturity?
9. How can your "feelings" help you to grow in faith?
10. Examine the section of this chapter titled "Evidences of 'Walking by the Spirit' in Our Churches."

    a. Ask God which ones you personally need to focus on, and then record them.
    b. What do you need to do in order to grow in the evidences you just selected in part "a"? Record your answers.
    c. Be careful to not let the conviction of the Spirit in the areas He wants you to work on become condemnation. Condemnation is not of God.
    d. In considering these evidences of "walking by the Spirit" in our churches, why is it more important to examine yourself than others?
    e. What are the dangers for you in evaluating the spiritual walk of others?

11. In what ways have you discovered that you are greater than you knew by reading this book?
12. Will you believe?

REFERENCES

Anderson, Neil. 2003. *Discipleship Counseling.* Ventura, CA: Regal Books.

Barclay, William. 1974. *New Testament Words.* Philadelphia: The Westminster Press.

Gunter, Sylvia. 1991. Prayer Portions. Birmingham, AL: Alpha Graphics.

Solomon, Charles R. 1991. *The Ins and Outs of Rejection.* Denver, CO: Charles R. Solomon.

VCLi staff. 1999. Victorious Christian Living Conference Workbook. Phoenix, AZ: Victorious Christian Living, Int'l.

Wiersbe, Warren W. 1982. *Be Confident.* Colorado Springs, CO: David C. Cook.

Edwards Brothers Malloy
Oxnard, CA USA
July 29, 2014